VISUAL
ENCYCLOPEDIA OF
dinosaurs

CONSULTANT
DOUGAL DIXON

VISUAL
ENCYCLOPEDIA OF
dinosaurs

CONSULTANT
DOUGAL DIXON

 DK

LONDON, NEW YORK, MELBOURNE,
MUNICH & DELHI

DK London
Project Editor Rosie O'Neill
Senior Editor David John
Editor Sarah Phillips
Managing Editor Andrew Macintyre
Managing Art Editor Jane Thomas
DTP Designers Natasha Lu, Siu Yin Ho
Production Controller Rochelle Talary
Picture Researcher Rob Nunn
Picture Librarian Sarah Mills

With thanks to the original teams

DK Delhi
Project Editor Sheema Mookherjee
Editor Chumki Sen
Designers Mugdha Sethi, Kavita Dutta
DTP Designer Balwant Singh
Manager Aparna Sharma

Consultant Dougal Dixon

First published in Great Britain
in 2005 by Dorling Kindersley Limited,
80 Strand, London WC2R 0RL
A Penguin Company 2 4 6 8 10 9 7 5 3 1
Copyright © 2005 Dorling Kindersley Limited

Material in this edition has appeared previously in the
following books:
Encyclopedia of Dinosaurs and Prehistoric Life
© 2001 Dorling Kindersley Limited
Dinosaurs and Prehistoric Life
© 2003 Dorling Kindersley Limited
Backpack Books – 1,001 Facts about Dinosaurs
© 2002 Dorling Kindersley Limited

A CIP catalogue record for this book is
available from the British Library.

ISBN 1-4053-08389

Reproduced by Colourscan, Singapore
Printed and bound in Singapore by Star Standard

See our complete catalogue at
www.dk.com

Contents

HOW TO USE THIS BOOK

THIS BOOK STARTS with the
evolution of life. It is followed
by four sections on fishes and
invertebrates, amphibians and
reptiles, dinosaurs and birds,
and mammals. A final section
tells you about the study of
dinosaurs, and the people
who studied them.

*Animal size compared
with that of an adult man*

THEMED PAGES
These pages dwell on
general themes related
to prehistoric animals
and dinosaurs, such as
feeding habits, shown
below. They also describe
main groups, such as
theropods or
ankylosaurids.

DINOSAURS AND BIRDS

PROTOCERATOPS

PROTOCERATOPS ("before the horned faces") was an
early horned dinosaur with a relatively small horn.
It had a broad neck frill at the back of its skull,
which was larger and taller in males.
Its small nasal horn was between
the eyes and it had two pairs
of teeth in the upper jaw.
Tall spines on the top
of its tail made it
appear humped.

SHEEP OF THE GOBI
Protoceratops is very well-
known from the many
specimens discovered buried
under the sand in Mongolia. Its
fossils are so abundant in the Gobi
Desert that it has been called

*Nasal horn
between
the eyes*

PROTOCERATOPS
• Group: Ceratopsia
• Family: Ceratopsidae
• Time: Cretaceous period (135–65 MYA)
• Size: 1.8 m (6 ft) long
• Diet: Plants
• Habitat: Scrubland and desert

274

*Protoceratops
was a four-
footed animal*

*The main picture recreates the
animal's looks based on fossil evidence*

PROTOCERATOPS
• Group: Ceratopsia
• Family: Ceratopsidae
• Time: Cretaceous
  period (135–65 MYA)
• Size: 1.8 m (6 ft) long
• Diet: Plants
• Habitat: Scrubland
  and desert

FACT BOX
Quick reference facts provide data on
the animal's group, family, time
period, size, diet, and habitat.

*Annotations highlight
characteristic features
about the animal*

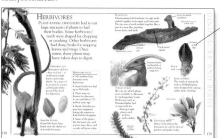

HERBIVORES
PLANT-EATING DINOSAURS had to eat
large amounts of plants to fuel
their bodies. Some herbivores'
teeth were shaped for chopping
or crushing. Other herbivores
had sharp beaks for stripping
leaves and twigs. Once
eaten, these plants may
have taken days to digest.

158   159

ABBREVIATIONS USED IN THE BOOK	
MYA million years ago	
METRIC	IMPERIAL
m metres	ft feet
cm centimetres	in inches

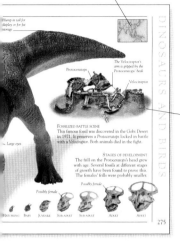

Red dots on the map show the main fossil finds

Additional pictures highlight interesting facts about the animal

CLADOGRAM PAGES
Each cladogram shows the chain of evolution for a particular animal group.

ANIMAL PAGES
The main sections consist mostly of animal pages, which focus on individual prehistoric animals. In the page shown left, you are told about *Protoceratops* – its looks, lifestyle, and interesting habits.

Each strip depicts the animals and plants of a certain timeline

FOSSIL TIMELINE
A fossil timeline feature at the beginning of the book provides a period-by-period look at prehistoric life. It traces the evolution of plants and animals, both on the land and in the water. A map shows what Earth was like during each period.

REFERENCE PAGES
This section tells you about famous dinosaur hunters and their finds. It also explains how fossils are found and preserved. Finally, it gives you a list of meanings, or glossary, of the difficult words.

FINDING OUT ABOUT THE PAST

ONCE IT WAS REALIZED that fossils are the remains of once-living things, people have strived to interpret these clues to the past. Palaeontology, the study of ancient life, involves reconstructing the former appearance, lifestyle, behaviour and evolution of once-living organisms. It shows how modern organisms arose, and how they relate to each other.

EARLY FINDS AND THEORIES
Palaeontology as we recognise it today, arose in the late 18th century. The discovery of fossil mastodons (relatives of elephants) and of *Mosasaurus*, a Cretaceous marine reptile, firmly established that species became extinct.

PALAEONTOLOGISTS AT WORK IN MONGOLIA

FOSSILS AND THEIR SURROUNDINGS
Most fossils are found when they appear on the surface at places where there is continual erosion of rock by the wind and water. Excavators need to study the sedimentary layer in which a fossil is found to learn about its history.

THE STUDY OF DEATH
Taphonomy is the study of how animals died and what happened to their bodies between death and discovery. It reveals much about ancient environments.

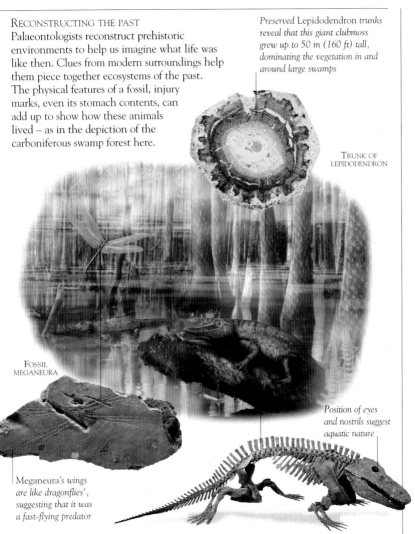

RECONSTRUCTING THE PAST

Palaeontologists reconstruct prehistoric environments to help us imagine what life was like then. Clues from modern surroundings help them piece together ecosystems of the past. The physical features of a fossil, injury marks, even its stomach contents, can add up to show how these animals lived – as in the depiction of the carboniferous swamp forest here.

Preserved Lepidodendron trunks reveal that this giant clubmoss grew up to 50 m (160 ft) tall, dominating the vegetation in and around large swamps

TRUNK OF
LEPIDODENDRON

FOSSIL
MEGANEURA

Position of eyes and nostrils suggest aquatic nature

Meganeura's wings are like dragonflies', suggesting that it was a fast-flying predator

11

FOSSILS

NATURALLY PRESERVED
remains of once-living
organisms, or the traces
they made, are called
fossils. They are first
entombed in sediment
and later mineralized.
There are fossils of
microscopic organisms,
plants, and animals.

*Animal dies and
decomposes in a riverbed*

*A skeleton buried
by sediment is
protected from
scavengers*

*Rocks are condensed
layers of sediments
such as sand or mud*

*This armour plate
comes from a
sauropod*

FOSSILIZED
SALTASAURUS
SKIN

*Tracks
formed on
soft mud*

*Three-toed
tracks were
made by
predatory
dinosaurs*

THEROPOD
TRACKWAY

TYPES OF FOSSIL
The remains of plants and
animals (shells, teeth, bones,
or leaves) are called body fossils.
Traces left behind by organisms
(footprints, nests, droppings)
are called trace fossils.

HOW FOSSILS FORM

Fossilization occurs when an organism, or something produced by it, is buried in sediment. These then become mineralized. Some fossils, however, are formed when the original object has been destroyed by acidic groundwater, and minerals have later formed a natural replica of the object.

FOSSILIZED
HEDGEHOG PHOLIDOCERCUS

EXCEPTIONAL FOSSILS

Soft parts of organisms are usually lost before fossilization. However, rapid burial in soft sediment sometimes ensures that soft parts are fossilized.

The skeleton may be partially decomposed underground

More sediments may bury the fossil deeper

Erosion at the surface of the Earth reveals fossils

Minerals may change the fossil's composition

Moving continental plates may carry sediments far from their original location

Many exposed fossils are destroyed by wind and water

RESULTS OF FOSSILIZATION

Some fossils change colour due to the replacement minerals. This ammonite fossil is gold because it is composed of iron pyrite, also called "fool's gold".

EVOLVING LIFE

THE FOSSIL RECORD preserves the history of life from the earliest single-celled organisms to the complex multi-cellular creatures – including plants, fungi, and animals – of more recent times. It traces the the history of life from 3,800 million years ago to a few centuries past.

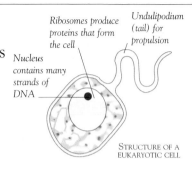

Ribosomes produce proteins that form the cell

Undulipodium (tail) for propulsion

Nucleus contains many strands of DNA

STRUCTURE OF A EUKARYOTIC CELL

ORIGIN OF EUKARYOTES
More complex single-celled organisms, called Eukaryotic cells, evolved as a result of cooperative functioning. Fossil records of these appear 2,000 million years ago.

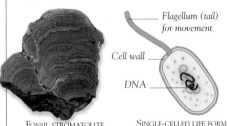

Flagellum (tail) for movement

Cell wall

DNA

FOSSIL STROMATOLITE   SINGLE-CELLED LIFE FORM

FOSSIL MAWSONITES

FIRST LIFE
The earliest forms of life were prokaryotes. These small, single-celled life forms contained DNA, a chemical that codes genetic information. Prokaryotes developed a wide range of metabolisms (chemical reactions to generate energy). Huge fossilized mats of prokaryotic cells, called stromatolites, show how widespread they were early on in Earth's history.

VENDIAN LIFE
Multi-cellular organisms arose in the Late Precambrian, which witnessed a rapid growth of complex life forms. Fossilized remains of the Vendian fauna, discovered in South Australia, are an example of such life forms. Disc- and leaf-shaped fossils such as the Mawsonites comprise some of these organisms.

THE BURGESS SHALE

The Burgess Shale of British Columbia, Canada, is a famous rock site composed of layers of siltstone deposited on the floor of a shallow Cambrian sea. Discovered in 1909 by Charles Walcott, it contains thousands of well-preserved animal fossils, and gives a unique insight into the "Cambrian Explosion" of life.

Sponges grew on the sea floor, but the reefs of the time were mostly formed by algae

Marrella was a tiny swimming arthropod

Pikaia, *an early chordate, was a worm-like swimmer with tail fins*

Anomalocaris *was a large predatory arthropod*

Hallucigenia *was probably a bottom-dweller that fed on organic particles*

Priapulids are burrow-dwelling worms abundant in Burgess Shale times

METAZOAN DIVERSITY

The Burgess Shale shows how well metazoans (many-celled animals) diversified to fill different kinds of habitat. From the sea, animals spread through freshwater, colonized the land, and invaded the air.

DINOSAUR   BIRD   MAMMAL   ARTHROPOD

How evolution happens

As ORGANISMS change to adapt to new ways of life, they give rise to new species. The inheritance of certain features by a species' descendants is a main component of evolutionary change. The key to interpreting the fossil record is to learn about evolution.

FISHING ABOARD THE BEAGLE

THE THEORY OF EVOLUTION

The theory that living things change to suit their environments was first presented by Charles Darwin. He argued that the fittest individuals survived and their features were inherited by future generations.

VOYAGE OF THE BEAGLE

Charles Darwin developed his theory of evolution by natural selection following his travels as ship's naturalist on *HMS Beagle* during the 1830s.

Low front of shell originally shared by all Galapagos tortoises

Tortoises on wet islands feed off the ground

Higher front of shell in dry island tortoises

EVOLUTION IN ACTION

On the Galapagos Islands, giant tortoises that feed off plant growth on the ground, have shells with a low front opening. However, tortoises on dry islands have a tall front opening to their shells as there is no vegetation on the ground, and they have to reach up to chew on higher branches. On the dry islands individuals with taller front openings in their shells survived better and passed on their genes to future generations.

Tortoises on dry islands have to reach up to find food

EVOLUTION AND DIVERSIFICATION

Evolution is not as simple as was once thought – for example, organisms do not generally evolve in simple ladder-like progression. Instead, as new species evolve from old ones, they tend to branch out and diversify, forming complex patterns. Evolution also does not always lead to increasing complexity. Some living things have become less complex over time.

The Gar fish demonstrates punctuated equilibrium – the last time it changed was 60 million years ago

EVOLUTION BY JUMPS

The old view that evolution is a slow and continuous process has been challenged by fossil evidence. Many species have remained the same for a long period and then seen sudden change – this is known as "punctuated equilibrium". If conditions stay the same, so does the species. But if conditions change rapidly, the species may need to change rapidly as well.

Humans and chimpanzees evolved in the Pliocene

Chimpanzees and humans share an enlarged canal in the palate

All great apes (hominids) have an enlarged thumb and other derived characters

HUMAN

CHIMPANZEE

ORANG-UTAN

ENLARGED PALATE CANAL

LARGE OPPOSABLE THUMB

Canal passing through palate in upper jaw

Long opposable thumb gives an evolutionary advantage

DERIVED CHARACTERS

Scientists reveal evolutionary relationships by looking for shared features, called "derived characters". The presence of certain unique characters seen in one group of species but not in others shows that all the species within that group share a common ancestor. Such groups are called clades, as in the case of humans, chimpanzees, and orang-utans.

CLASSIFICATION OF LIFE

AN ACCURATE UNDERSTANDING of living things and how they have evolved relies on their being classified into groups according to their similarity. Animals are classified in groups of decreasing diversity. The diagram on the right, outlines the evolution of the major groups of vertebrates through time, from the very primitive jawless fishes to mammals. This is based on an analysis of shared features between species and their ancestors.

THE LINNAEAN SYSTEM
Devised by Karl von Linné (Carolus Linnaeus), this system subdivides all living things into ever more specific groups down to species level. Many palaeontologists prefer to use cladistic analysis to describe the relationships between species, but the Linnaean system of Latin species names remains standard throughout the scientific community. The Linnaean classification of *Tyrannosaurus rex* is shown below.

KINGDOM : Animalia
PHYLUM : Chordata
CLASS : Reptilia
ORDER : Saurischia
FAMILY : Tyrannosauridae
GENUS : Tyrannosaurus
SPECIES : Tyrannosaurus rex

THE CLADISTIC SYSTEM
Cladistic analysis shows the closeness of a relationship between a species and its most recent ancestor by a branching diagram called a cladogram. This is constructed by assessing characteristics that are shared between species and the order in which these arise.

CERATOPSIA (e.g. parrot-like beak, frill on skull)

ORNITHOPODA (e.g. beak margin lower at front of mouth)

ANKYLOSAURIA (bony armour on skull)

STEGOSAURIA (double row of bony plates on spine)

CERAPODA (short, deep skull)

THYREOPHORA (bony armour)

GENASAURA (teeth inset in jaw)

ORNITHISCHIA (bird-hipped pelvis)

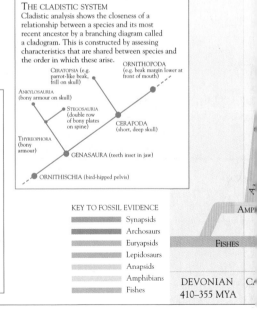

KEY TO FOSSIL EVIDENCE

Synapsids
Archosaurs
Euryapsids
Lepidosaurs
Anapsids
Amphibians
Fishes

AMP

FISHES

DEVONIAN
410–355 MYA

CA

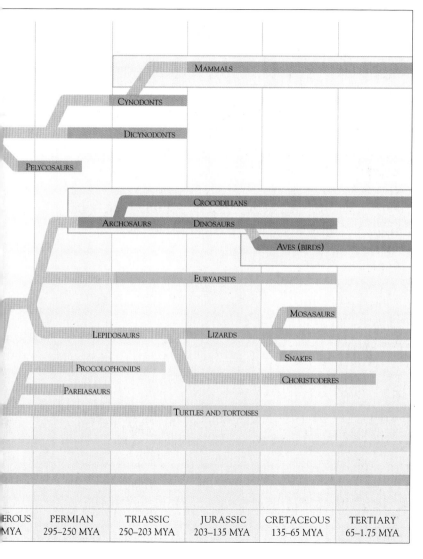

MAMMALS

CYNODONTS

DICYNODONTS

PELYCOSAURS

CROCODILIANS

ARCHOSAURS   DINOSAURS

AVES (BIRDS)

EURYAPSIDS

MOSASAURS

LEPIDOSAURS   LIZARDS

SNAKES

PROCOLOPHONIDS

CHORISTODERES

PAREIASAURS

TURTLES AND TORTOISES

EROUS MYA	PERMIAN 295–250 MYA	TRIASSIC 250–203 MYA	JURASSIC 203–135 MYA	CRETACEOUS 135–65 MYA	TERTIARY 65–1.75 MYA

GEOLOGICAL TIME

GEOLOGISTS subdivide the history of the Earth into very long time intervals called eons. Eons are, in turn, subdivided into eras, eras into periods, and periods into epochs. The oldest surviving rocks to be excavated were formed about four billion years ago, in the Archean Eon. The earliest fossils come from rocks of about this age.

ROCKS OF AGES
Where rock strata have remained undisturbed, a vertical section through the layers can reveal the rock types laid down during each time period. From these, it is possible to identify the environment (such as desert) and sometimes the age of fossils embedded in that rock, as shown on the left for rock strata at the Grand Canyon, USA.

ROCK	ENVIRONMENT	PERIOD
Shale, siltstone, mudstone	Tidal flat	Triassic
Limestone	Marine	Permian
Sandstone	Desert	
Shale	Savanna	
Mixed strata - shales, sandstones, limestones	Flood plain	Permian and Late Carboniferous
Limestone	Marine	Early Carboniferous
Limestone	Marine	Devonian
Limestone		Cambrian
Shale	Marine	
Sandstone	Marine	
Complex mixed strata	Marine and volcanic	Precambrian

CENOZOIC ERA	1.75 MYA –present
	23.5–1.75 MYA
MESOZOIC ERA	135–65 MYA
	203–135 MYA
	250–203 MYA
PALAEOZOIC ERA	295–250 MYA
	355–295 MYA
	410–355 MYA
	435–410 MYA
	500–435 MYA
	540–500 MYA
	4,600–540 MYA

4,600 MYA	4,000 MYA	3,000 MYA

QUATERNARY	0.01 MYA-present – Holocene epoch	The ice ages of the Quaternary period led to the evolution of many mammals that adapted to cold climates, such as mammoths and woolly rhinoceroses. Modern humans also evolved in this age.
	1.75-0.01 MYA – Pleistocene epoch	MACRAUCHENIA
TERTIARY	5.3-1.75 MYA Pliocene epoch	Large expanses of grassland, inhabited by grazing mammals and predatory giant birds. The first humans evolved from primate ancestors. After the end-Cretaceous extinctions, mammals evolved into large forms. Giant flightless birds also evolved.
	33.7-5.3 MYA Oligocene, Miocene epochs	
	65-33.7 MYA Paleocene, Eocene epochs	TITANIS

CRETACEOUS This was a time of flowering plants, duck-billed dinosaurs, immense ALPHADON tyrannosaurid predators, armoured ankylosaurs, and horned ceratopsians.

JURASSIC The land was dominated by huge sauropods and large predators. A wide variety of pterosaurs evolved. Mammals remained small. BAROSAURUS

TRIASSIC The age of dinosaurs began. Advanced HERRERASAURUS synapsids died out after giving rise to mammals.

PERMIAN Synapsids became the dominant land animals. The period ended with the largest mass extinction event ever, and thousands of species were lost. DIMETRODON

CARBONIFEROUS Tropical forests flourished. The first four-limbed animals and, GRAEOPHONUS later, the first reptiles moved onto the land.

DEVONIAN A time of rapid evolution, ammonoids and bony fishes diversified. Trees appeared on land, as did insects. EASTMANOSTEUS

SILURIAN Invertebrates recovered rapidly during the Silurian, and the first jawed fishes appeared. SAGENOCRINITES Primitive lycopods and myriapods became the first land organisms.

ORDOVICIAN The seas teemed with primitive fishes, trilobites, corals, and shellfish. Plants spread onto land. The period ended with mass extinctions. ESTONIOCERAS

CAMBRIAN The first animals with skeletons evolved during the Cambrian XYSTRIDURA "explosion of life". These included trilobites and jawless fishes.

PRECAMBRIAN Life arose in the oceans – first as single-celled bacteria and algae, then as soft, multicellular animals, such as jellyfish and worms. CHARNIODISCUS

| 2,000 MYA | 1,000 MYA | 500 MYA | 250 MYA | 0 |

PRECAMBRIAN TIME

THE PLANET EARTH IS about 4,600 million years old. The years from that date to 542 million years ago are known as the Precambrian. At first, the world was hot and molten. As it cooled, gases and water vapour formed the atmosphere and the oceans. Before about 3,000 million years ago, most of the Earth's surface was volcanic rock. Stable continental areas then began to form. Fossil evidence of life is first seen in rocks dated at 3,800 million years old.

VENDIAN LIFE

Impression of early jellyfish burrow or track of simple worm

Fossils in Precambrian rocks of the Vendian period are thought to be those of the earliest multicellular animals.

4,600 MYA   4,000 MYA   3,000 MYA

PRECAMBRIAN LANDMASSES

Landmasses began to form about 3,000 MYA. About 900 MYA they formed the first supercontinent, Rodinia. The movement of Rodinia southwards triggered the Verangian Ice Age. Later, Rodinia split into two halves (see map), but by the end of the Precambrian again formed a single mass.

PRECAMBRIAN LIFE
The first living cells were microscopic organisms possibly living in hot springs. By about 3,500 MYA algae may have formed.

STROMATOLITES
These layered silica or limestone structures were created by colony-forming algae.

FIRST ANIMALS
Late in the Precambrian, the first true animals and plants appeared. *Spriggina* (above) was a strange, long, tapering animal, with V-shaped segments.

Charniodiscus *looked like the modern sea pen*

FILTER FEEDER
The feather-shaped fossil of *Charniodiscus* is thought to represent an early filter-feeding animal that lived on the sea floor late in the Precambrian.

2,000 MYA | 1,000 MYA | 500 MYA | 250 MYA | 0

CAMBRIAN PERIOD

AQUATIC ANIMALS

EXPLOSION OF LIFE
Most of today's major
animal groups evolved in the
Cambrian. This huge growth
in diversity occurred only
in the seas. Soft-bodied
animals were largely
replaced by animals with
hard parts, many of whose
fossils were found in the
Burgess Shale in Canada.

METALDETES
These were early shell fossils shaped
like cones. Molluscs in coiled shells
and worms in tubes were other
early hard shelled animals.

*Metaldetes probably
resembled a sponge*

METALDETES
TAYLORI

XYSTRIDURA
Trilobites were an
enormously successful
and diverse group and
make up one third of
all fossils from the
Cambrian.
Xystridura, with
many legs and
complex eyes,
is one example
of this species.

Large eyes

*Each body segment
supported a walking leg
and a gill-bearing leg*   XYSTRIDURA

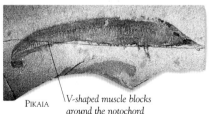

PIKAIA   \V-shaped muscle blocks
around the notochord

PIKAIA
Chordates, the group
that includes vertebrates,
evolved in the Middle Cambrian.
One of the first was *Pikaia*, a
swimming eel-like animal, 5 cm
(2 in) in length. *Pikaia* had a flexible
rod called a notochord stiffening its
body. In later animals this developed
into the backbone.

WIWAXIA

Perhaps distantly related to the molluscs, *Wiwaxia* was 3 cm (⅛ ft) long, dome shaped, and covered in scales. It had long spines, probably for self defence.

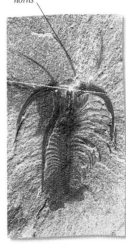

Ridged scale

Wiwaxia probably ate algae

MARRELLA

The most common arthropod in the Burgess Shale is *Marrella* – more than 13,000 specimens have been collected to date. Up to 2 cm (½₂ ft) long, this animal had a large head shield, and two pairs of long antennae.

The head shield supported large backwards-pointing horns

Indentations may have been sites of muscle attachment

Concave inner surface indicates an older individual

MOBERGELLA

Among the early shelled fossils of the Cambrian are tiny limpet-like forms, such as *Mobergella* from Scandinavia. These might not have been separate, individual animals but scale-like structures that covered the bodies of larger species. Members of another Cambrian group with hard parts, the halkieriids, were elongate with scaly bodies. It is possible that *Mobergella* may have actually been covered in halkieriid body scales.

EARTH FACTS

During the Cambrian, most of the world's landmasses were united as the supercontinent Gondwana. This was surrounded by the Iapetus Ocean. Smaller landmasses that today form Europe, North America, and Siberia lay in tropical and temperate zones.

ORDOVICIAN PERIOD

AQUATIC ANIMALS

FILTER FEEDERS

Another burst of evolution in the Ordovician gave rise to thousands of new animals. Many were filter feeders that fed on plankton. These included bivalves and corals, which formed reefs that were home to molluscs and other animals. Vertebrates with jaws may have appeared.

ESTONIOCERAS
PERFORATUM

Uncoiled final whorl of shell

STROPHOMENA

Strophomena was a small brachiopod (two-shelled animal) that lived on sand or mud.

ESTONIOCERAS

This mollusc belonged to the nautiloid group and hunted in deep waters. *Estonioceras* was 10 cm (⅓ ft) across, but some of its relatives had shells up to 5 m (16 ft) in diameter.

Shell could be locked shut by internal pegs

AQUATIC PLANTS

ALGAE AND LIFE ON LAND

Blue-green algae of the Precambrian were still widespread during the Ordovician. True algae, including round forms that resembled sponges, lived alongside other reef builders, such as corals, while green algae, the ancestors of land plants, took over freshwater habitats. Plants similar to liverworts and mosses evolved late in the Ordovician and began to colonize the land.

Honeycomb surface

MASTOPORA

This reef-forming green alga grew in rounded clusters with a characteristic honeycombed surface. Fossils, each about 8 cm (¼ ft) across, are found worldwide. Hard limestone secretions on the surface protected *Mastopora* from hungry animals.

MASTOPORA FAVUS

500–435 MYA

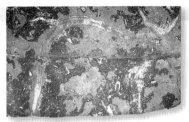

Colony about 8 cm (¼ ft) long

Serrated teeth to cut up prey

CONODONT
Conodonts were eel-like relatives of vertebrates. With large eyes, they hunted and ate small animals. *Promissum*, from South Africa, was the largest known conodont at 40 cm (1⅓ ft) in length.

ORTHOGRAPTUS
Graptolites formed colonies of linked cup-like structures called thecae, each inhabited by a soft-bodied filter-feeding animal called a zooid.

Surface strengthened by calcium carbonate

Alga 5 cm (⅙ ft) in diameter

ACANTHOCHONIA
The surface of *Acanthochonia* was made up of many diamond-shaped cells arranged in a spiral pattern. All the cells originated from a single central stem, which anchored the alga to rocks or corals.

EARTH FACTS

The Gondwanan supercontinent remained separate from the smaller landmasses, although the Iapetus Ocean had started to close. The Ordovician was a time of global cooling with a huge ice sheet covering much of the southern hemisphere towards the end.

SILURIAN PERIOD

AQUATIC ANIMALS

NEW LIFE
The end of the
Ordovician witnessed
a large-scale extinction
event. However, surviving
groups, such as rachiopods,
molluscs, and trilobites,
soon recovered and
increased in diversity
in the warm continental
seas. Invertebrates, such
as primitive sea urchins,
appeared for the first time.
Jawless fishes still thrived,
while jawed fishes
diversified. The first
land-living animals –
arthropods – evolved
from aquatic ancestors
in the Silurian.

*Small body, about 6 cm
(¼ ft) in length*

BIRKENIA ELEGANS

BIRKENIA
The small, spindle-shaped *Birkenia* lived
in European lakes and rivers. Like other
jawless fishes it lacked paired fins, making
it unstable when swimming. It probably
foraged in mud for tiny food particles.

LAND PLANTS

THE PIONEERS
The Silurian marks the
appearance of the first
true land plants. Mosses
and liverworts grew
along the edges of
ponds and streams.
Later Silurian plants
had a woody lining, for
support and for carrying
water around the body
(vascular plants).
Thus the plant could
survive further from
the water.

COOKSONIA
HEMISPHAERICA

COOKSONIA
Best known from
Silurian rocks of
southern Ireland, *Cooksonia*
was the first upright vascular
plant. Lacking leaves and
roots, it was composed of
cylindrical stems that
branched into two.

*Branching stems
formed Y-shapes*

PARKA
Green algae are simple plants
that grow close to or in water.
Parka was a green alga from
the Silurian and Devonian.

Each arm was free and could be moved

The legs could have been used for walking or for handling prey

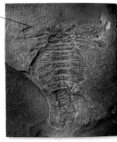

SAGENOCRINITES
Crinoids, or sea lilies, were important animals of the Silurian seas. Many species survive today in deeper waters. They collected plankton with their tentacles. *Sagenocrinites* was one of the smaller crinoids.

Stem base attached to the seafloor

PARACARCINOSOMA
Sea scorpions were Silurian arthropods – relatives of the spiders. They had long tails and large pincers. *Paracarcinosoma* was a sea scorpion 5 cm (⅙ ft) long.

Stem covered with fine leaves

BARAGWANATHIA
Closely resembling a club moss, *Baragwanathia* was a complex Silurian plant. Its "furry" stems spread across the ground and branched upwards.

Distinct rounded spore capsules grew on its surface

PARKA
DECIPIENS

BARAGWANATHIA
LONGIFOLIA

EARTH FACTS

During the Silurian, Gondwana was fringed by smaller land masses. These moved northwards and collided, producing new mountain ranges in North America and Europe. Sea levels rose as ice melted and the climate became warmer and less changeable.

DEVONIAN PERIOD

LAND ANIMALS

LIMBS ON LAND
The first vertebrates with four limbs and distinct digits evolved during this period and spread around the world. Land-living arthropods diversified and primitive insects forms appeared.

Sharp teeth suggest a diet of fishes and other animals

ACANTHOSTEGA
Among the earliest of four-limbed vertebrates was *Acanthostega* from Greenland. Like its lobe-finned fish relatives, it was a pond-dwelling predator.

AQUATIC ANIMALS

DEVONIAN DIVERSITY
Armoured jawless fishes flourished and jawed fishes were also abundant. Bony, lobe-finned fishes were diverse while ray-finned fishes gained importance. Ammonoids and horseshoe crabs also appeared.

Pointed fins

Prominent central row of bones

DIPTERUS
Lungfish such as *Dipterus* were an abundant group of the Devonian. Five species of these lobe-finned fishes survive today. *Dipterus* swam in European waters and, like all lungfish, had large crushing teeth.

LAND PLANTS

LEAVES AND ROOTS
The Devonian saw the most important steps so far in the development of land plants. Leaves and roots evolved in a number of different groups. Plant stems not only grew in length, but also in diameter. The early reed-like plants gave way to gigantic trees and species with complex leaves.

ARCHAEOPTERIS
This widespread Late Devonian plant was the first to resemble modern trees. It had an extensive root system and its trunk had branches.

Branching, fern-like leaves

ARCHAEOPTERIS

410–355 MYA

Seven toes on each foot

Used limbs to walk on land

ICHTHYOSTEGA FOSSIL
Ichthyostega was an early four-footed vertebrate. It probably hunted in shallow pools. Its multi-jointed limbs suggest that it was relatively advanced and was related to the ancestor of all later four-footed vertebrates.

Large eye for excellent vision

EASTMANOSTEUS
Placoderms were jawed fishes that included predators, armoured bottom-dwellers, and flattened ray-like forms. They were the largest vertebrates yet to evolve.

PHACOPS
Each body segment of this small trilobite supported two sets of limbs. Seven out of eight trilobite groups died out at the end of the Devonian.

PHACOPS

Clusters of spore-bearing stems

ZOSTEROPHYLLUM
Lacking roots and leaves, this was a primitive land plant. Its erect, branching stems grew not from roots, but from a complex underground rhizome (stem).

ZOSTEROPHYLLUM
LLANOVERANUM

EARTH FACTS

The Devonian world was warm and mild. The huge continent Gondwana lay over the South Pole while modern Europe and North America were positioned close to the equator. Much of the land lay under shallow seas.

CARBONIFEROUS PERIOD

LAND ANIMALS

ORIGIN OF THE AMNIOTES
Amniotes, vertebrates whose
embryos are enclosed by a
watertight membrane, evolved
in this period. Both, reptiles
and the mammal-like synapsids
appeared, while other more
primitive vertebrates diversified.
Flying insects also evolved.

WESTLOTHIANA
Primitive four-footed
vertebrates are well known from
fossils in North America and
Europe. *Westlothiana* was
discovered in Scotland, in
rocks formed in a lake fed
by hot, volcanic springs.

*Sharp teeth
suggest a
diet of
insects*

WESTLOTHIANA
LIZZIAE

AQUATIC ANIMALS

DIVERSE DEPTHS
Sharks and bony fish
dominated Carboniferous
seas, but ray-finned fish,
the actinopterygians, also
diversified greatly during this
period. Crinoids, brachiopods,
echinoderms, and swimming
molluscs inhabited the
coral reefs.

SYMMORIUM
Many of the Carboniferous sharks were bizarre
compared to modern ones. Some were
decorated with spiky crests and spines.
Stethacanthus and
Symmorium were a
few examples.

*Pointed teeth
of a predator*

LAND PLANTS

FORESTS AND FLOODPLAINS
Lush tropical forests forming
vast swamps and forested
deltas were widespread in the
Carboniferous. Clubmosses
and horsetails were important
plants of these forests, and
some grew to immense sizes.
Gymnosperms – the group
that includes conifers and
cycads – began to diversify.
Towards the end of the
period, the huge floodplains
began to shrink as the climate
became less wet.

EQUISETITES
Equisetites is an
extinct horsetail,
which came from a
group that survives
worldwide today in the
form of *Equisetum*. It
grew to a height of
around 50 cm (1½ ft)
from underground stems
(tubers), and its straight
stem carried leaves
arranged in whorls.
Equisetites dominated
the river banks.

*Fossilized tubers and
roots of* Equisetites

GRAEOPHONUS

Arachnids, the arthropod group that includes spiders, scorpions, and their relatives, are well represented in the Carboniferous fossil record and many new kinds made their first appearance at this time. *Graeophonus* was an early member of a group that survives to this day – the whip scorpions. These have six walking legs and a front pair of pincers.

Two eyes on a bump

GONIATITES

This animal is a type of swimming mollusc with a coiled shell. It was a member of a group of ammonoids that was dominant in the Palaeozoic. Like all ammonoids, *Goniatites* had gas-filled shell chambers that allowed it to float. It had complex eyes and beak-like mouthparts and lived in large swarms over reefs in shallow seas.

Growth lines, or sutures, on shell

Forked tail suggests speed

CORDAITES

This conifer-like land plant grew in Carboniferous mangrove swamps, but died out in the Permian. It had characteristic long, leathery leaves and its straight main trunk grew to a height of up to 30 m (100 ft), although other species of *Cordaites* were shrub-like. It produced seeds in loose cones.

Strap-like leaves

EARTH FACTS

The Carboniferous is known as the "age of coal" because decaying vegetation from the vast forests was transformed into coal. The main landmasses present were the two huge continents of Gondwana and Laurasia.

33

PERMIAN PERIOD

LAND ANIMALS

SYNAPSIDS
The most important
land vertebrates of the
Permian were the
primitive synapsids.
Most were small flesh-
eaters with powerful
skulls and sharp teeth.

Palate fragment with teeth

EDAPHOSAURUS
This synapsid had
a broad, rounded
body with a tall
fin on its back. It
fed on ferns and
tough Permian plants.

EDAPHOSAURUS

AQUATIC ANIMALS

SEAS OF LIFE
This period saw immense
reefs teeming with marine
life, shelled animals
called brachiopods,
and new fish groups.
However, it ended with
the biggest mass
extinction of all time.

DERBYIA
Brachiopods were shelled,
filter-feeding animals.
Their larvae could
swim, but adults
were static. *Derbyia*
was a large species
of the Carboniferous
and Permian seas.

LAND PLANTS

NAKED SEEDS
Plant communities in the
Permian were basically similar
to those of today. Clubmosses
and horsetails that
had formed the
Carboniferous forests
were replaced by
conifers, cycads
and ginkgoes –
gymnosperms or
plants that have
"naked" seeds not
enclosed within
a fruit.

*Sword-shaped
leaves*

GLOSSOPTERIS

GLOSSOPTERIS
One of the
important
Permian
gymnosperms was
Glossopteris. This
tree grew to 8 m
(26 ft) tall, and its close
relatives dominated the southern
part of the supercontinent Pangaea.

295–250 MYA

Eye socket

DIMETRODON LOOMISI SKULL

DIMETRODON
Dimetrodon was an awesome predator. This fin-backed synapsid grew to 3 m (10 ft) long. It ran fast to catch its prey. Animals like *Dimetrodon* were important because they gave rise to an entirely new group of synapsids, the therapsids.

PALAEONISCUS
Ray-finned fishes diversified in the Permian, and a major new group – the neopterygians – appeared. *Palaeoniscus* was a primitive ray-finned fish.

PALAEONISCUS
MAGNUS

Long, streamlined body suited to fast swimming

Overlapping scales

MARIOPTERIS
Found in early Permian swamps, *Mariopteris* grew to a height of around 5 m (16 ft). Some species were tree-like, while others may have been climbing plants.

Small, pointed leaflets

MARIOPTERIS
MARICATA

EARTH FACTS

Two major landmasses – Laurasia in the north and Gondwana in the south – collided late in the Permian to form the supercontinent Pangaea. The climate became hotter and drier. The south was cool, while tropical conditions prevailed in the north.

PERMIAN EXTINCTION

THE END OF THE Permian saw the greatest mass extinction of all time. Perhaps only five percent of all species survived. In the seas, trilobites, scorpions, and key coral groups disappeared. On land, synapsids and many reptile groups vanished.

FIERY END
A possible cause of the end-Permian extinction is volcanic activity. Eruptions of volcanic material may have blotted out all sunlight.

CLIMATIC CRISIS
Climate change characterized the end of the Permian. Rocks from the period indicate that cooling occurred in some areas and ice sheets built up at the poles, causing the global sea level to drop.

DESERT DEVASTATION
The vast continent of Pangaea was formed and parts of the world became drier. Deserts grew larger, and certain species of animals became extinct.

Branching colonies of bryozoans, or moss animals

Rugose corals completely disappeared

Brachiopods grew on the tops of reefs

DEATH OF A REEF

A Permian coral reef is shown healthy on the left-hand side of the image and dying – as it would have appeared during the Permian extinction – on the right-hand side. Permian reefs – made up of corals and sponges – were inhabited by thousands of different animals and plants. Lowered sea levels and reduced areas of shallow seafloor resulted in an enormous drop in the diversity of marine life.

The sponge Heliospongia *was one of the largest organisms of the Permian reef*

Animals would have died as oxygen levels dropped

Gastropods grazed on algae

TRIASSIC PERIOD

LAND ANIMALS

THE AGE OF REPTILES

This was the start of the "Age of Reptiles", with synapsids on the decline and archosaurs on the rise. The first crocodiles, pterosaurs, dinosaurs, turtles, frogs, and primitive mammals all evolved late in the Triassic.

CYNOGNATHUS

This aggressive Early Triassic predator was a member of the cynodonts – a group of advanced synapsids. It may have been warm-blooded and furry.

AQUATIC ANIMALS

SEA CHANGE

New groups of corals and molluscs evolved. The first modern sharks and rays appeared. Dolphin-shaped predators evolved from ichthyosaurs.

Diamond-shaped scales

DICELLOPYGE

Primitive ray-finned fishes like *Dicellopyge* were important predators in the Triassic. This small freshwater fish from Africa was a fast swimmer and its and jaws were armed with conical teeth.

LAND PLANTS

DOMINANT CONIFERS

The Triassic landscape was dominated by evergreen trees (conifers and other gymnosperms). Among the more modern kinds of plants, cycads became well established. Ginkgoes also became successful and at least seven genera, including the modern Ginkgo, lived during Triassic times.

Leaf fossilized in mudstone

GINKGO
BILOBA LEAF

GINKGO

This tree, which evolved in the Triassic, survives essentially unchanged to this day. A native of China, it has been planted around the world in urban gardens, partly because it grows well in heavily polluted air.

Enlarged, stabbing canine teeth

MEGAZOSTRODON
One of the earliest of all
mammals, *Megazostrodon*, was
only about 12 cm (½ ft) long
and lived in Africa. Like other
early mammals, it was probably
nocturnal and resembled a
modern shrew in appearance
and lifestyle.

Deep jaws to hold prey

Limbs were used as paddles in the water

Thick, heavy ribs

Small, delicate bones

NEUSTICOSAURUS
The sauropterygians were a group
of marine reptiles that evolved
during the Triassic. *Neusticosaurus*
was an amphibious predator that
lived in the shallow seas.

PACHYPTERIS
Seed ferns like
Pachypteris were
primitive seed
plants that grew in
swampy areas. They
had woody stems
and their tops had
fern-like fronds that carried
the seeds. *Pachypteris* grew in
tropical forests and was one
of the last seed ferns to die
out in the Cretaceous.

Typical height 2 m (6¹/2 ft)

EARTH FACTS

The vast supercontinent of
Pangaea straddled the equator
during the Triassic. Hints that it
would later split up came from the
narrow seaway that separated
North America from Europe and
another tongue of sea, the Tethys,
which encroached on Europe.

JURASSIC PERIOD

LAND ANIMALS

RULE OF THE DINOSAURS

Giant dinosaurs took over as the dominant creatures of the Jurassic. Only a few small synapsids, including early mammals, survived. Stegosaurs and sauropods were preyed upon by theropods. The first birds evolved from small dinosaurs.

PTERODACTYLUS

Pterosaurs were reptiles that developed wings and powered flight. *Pterodactylus* was a small Jurassic pterosaur that lived along the shore, feeding on fishes.

Wings and throat pouch preserved

Slender clawed toes

AQUATIC ANIMALS

JURASSIC DIVERSITY

Marine animals of the Jurassic include ammonites, belemnites, and modern-type sharks and rays. Teleosts may have grown into the biggest fishes of all time. Crinoids, relatives of today's sea lilies, were prominent.

ICHTHYOSAURUS

Advanced ichthyosaurs ("fish lizards"), swimming crocodiles, and new kinds of plesiosaurs all added to the diversity of marine reptiles in the Jurassic. *Ichthyosaurus* was a European fish lizard of this period.

Nostril was located close to the eye

Ring of bony plates

LAND PLANTS

THE AGE OF CYCADS

Cycads, conifers, and ginkgoes were important Jurassic plant groups. One group of cycads, the bennettitaleans, may have been the ancestors of flowering plants. Jurassic conifers included relatives of living pines, yews, redwoods, and cypresses. Ferns formed much of the ground cover.

CYCAS

Cycads reached their greatest diversity and abundance during the Jurassic. *Cycas*, of which about 40 species survive today, appeared in the Jurassic.

Fronds made up of many parallel leaflets

Many cycads were poisonous

Serrated teeth in lightly built skull

COMPSOGNATHUS
The chicken-sized *Compsognathus* was a predatory dinosaur from Europe. It was similar to, and shared the same habitat with, *Archaeopteryx*.

Walked on hindlimbs

ARCHAEOPTERYX
The first true bird, *Archaeopteryx*, evolved from small theropod ancestors. This famous fossil – known as the Berlin specimen – preserves impressions of the wing and tail feathers.

ASPIDORHYNCHUS
Among the new Jurassic teleosts were long-bodied predators, such as *Aspidorhynchus*. Its upper jaw was extended beyond the lower jaw, forming a prominent toothless "beak".

Triangular skull with large eyes

Sharp teeth

WILLIAMSONIA
This plant, which lived throughout the Mesozoic, was a member of the Bennettitales group. It had a robust stem that was covered in diamond-shaped scales and grew large flower-like structures.

Flowers probably pollinated by insects

EARTH FACTS

The Pangaean supercontinent split as the Atlantic opened up between the areas that today form Africa and North America. Antarctica, India, and Australia started to move away. The climate was warm with no polar ice caps.

CRETACEOUS PERIOD

LAND ANIMALS

NEW DINOSAURS
Dinosaurs remained the
dominant land animals during
the Cretaceous. New groups,
including tyrannosaurs, duck-billed
hadrosaurs, and horned dinosaurs,
spread across the north, while
birds evolved into more
modern forms.

*Lower hip
bones projected
backwards*

*Stiff tail helped
balance the
heavy body*

AQUATIC ANIMALS

MESOZOIC MARINE LIFE
Modern crustaceans evolved
among marine invertebrates.
The relatives of herrings, eels,
carps, and perches appeared.
Water lizards, turtles, and
aquatic birds also evolved.

MACROPOMA
Macropoma was a European coelacanth
(fleshy-finned fish), a group that
declined later in the period.

*Mobile skull
allowed jaws
to open wide*

LAND PLANTS

FLOWER POWER
Conifers were the
dominant trees,
while cycads and
ginkgoes declined.
Flowering plants
(the angiosperms)
arose, first as
weed-like forms.
Later birches,
willows, and
magnolias formed
forests. Ferns
remained important
wherever rainfall
was high.

BETULITES
Betulites is an extinct member of
the birch family, and a close
relative of *Betula*, the familiar
modern birch tree. Like
living birches, it grew in
temperate climates,
favouring damp
habitats.

*Leaf fossil in
ironstone
nodule*

BETULITES

135–65 MYA

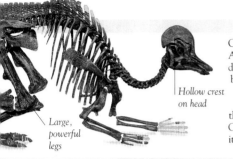

Hollow crest on head

Large, powerful legs

CORYTHOSAURUS

Among the most common Cretaceous dinosaurs were hadrosaurs – the duck-billed dinosaurs – which evolved from *Iguanodon*-like ancestors. With batteries of chewing teeth and powerful jaws they were successful browsing herbivores. *Corythosaurus* had a hollow bony crest on its head to amplify its calls.

PROTOSTEGA

Turtles first evolved in the Triassic, but forms specialized for life at sea, such as *Protostega*, did not appear until the Cretaceous.

Rubbery skin covered ribs

Strong flippers for fast swimming

Spore capsules were carried on the fronds

ONYCHIOPSIS

Ferns were important low-growing plants in the Mesozoic but became less widespread as flowering plants increased in importance during the Cretaceous. *Onychiopsis*, a small fern from the northern hemisphere, had delicate, feathery leaves and reached 50 cm (1⅔ ft) in height.

ONYCHIOPSIS
PSILOTOIDES

EARTH FACTS

By the Cretaceous, Pangaea had split into Laurasia in the north and Gondwana in the south. These continents were themselves breaking apart into the continents that exist today. Madagascar and India separated from Gondwana and moved north. Large inland seas covered parts of Laurasia.

END OF THE DINOSAURS

THE END OF THE Cretaceous saw the most famous mass extinction event of all time – although it was not the biggest in terms of species lost. All large land animals disappeared as did many marine invertebrate groups. The theropods survived as birds, but all other dinosaurs became extinct. In the seas, plesiosaurs and mosasaurs died out, as did many kinds of bivalves, swimming molluscs, and plankton.

After the Asteroid

Some evidence indicates that a large asteroid struck the Earth at this time. Experts speculate that such an impact would have thrown up enough dust to block out light from the Sun for years or even decades. Perhaps this prolonged cold, dark phase caused Cretaceous plants and animals to die off. The impact would have thrown up tidal waves that would have washed ashore on the North American continent, destroying coastal habitats. Hot debris thrown into the atmosphere by the impact may later have rained down to Earth and started huge wildfires.

Last Survivors

Triceratops and *Tyrannosaurus* were among the last of the dinosaurs, but many animal groups survived, including insects, mammals, reptiles, and fishes.

Triceratops
*was one of the
very last dinosaurs*

PALAEOCENE & EOCENE EPOCHS

LAND ANIMALS

LARGE LANDLUBBERS
At the start of the Palaeocene, there were no large animals on the land. But they soon began to evolve from the small survivors of the Cretaceous extinction. Bats, rodents, and true primates made their appearance, together with many birds, crocodiles, lizards, snakes, turtles, and frogs.

PALAEOCHIROPTERYX
Bats probably evolved from tree-climbing ancestors that leapt to catch their insect prey. Early true bats, such as *Palaeochiropteryx* from Eocene Europe, had wings formed from enlarged hands.

AQUATIC ANIMALS

SEA MAMMALS
Modern forms of marine life became established. Fishes took on now-familiar forms. The first penguins appeared including giant forms. Aquatic mammals such as whales and seacows evolved.

WETHERELLUS
This Eocene mackerel was around 25 cm (1 ft) in length. Mackerels are fast-swimming marine fishes that belong to a group called the scombroids.

LAND PLANTS

TROPICAL TIMES
The world was dominated by tropical forests. Even Europe had tropical swamps where ferns, horsetails, and palms formed the undergrowth and vines and citrus trees grew overhead. Trees included forms as diverse as hazel, chestnut, magnolia, poplar, and walnut. Towards the end of the Eocene, the world cooled. Deciduous and coniferous trees became dominant at higher latitudes and tropical forests retreated to the equatorial regions.

Wide jaws lined with rows of pointed teeth

NIPA
BURTINII

NIPA
This palm, which survives only in the mangrove swamps of southeast Asia, was widespread in the Northern Hemisphere. Its coconut-like seeds grew at its base.

Rounded fruit with protective woody shell

GASTORNIS

Gastornis was a giant, flightless, land bird of Palaeocene and Eocene North America and Europe. It stood 2.1 m (7 ft) high and had short, largely useless wings, but its long, stout legs would have made it a fast runner and powerful kicker. Its massive, deep beak was very strong, suggesting that it could break open bones.

Beak well suited for crushing

BASILOSAURUS

One of the best-known prehistoric whales is *Basilosaurus*, a gigantic predator that grew to more than 20 m (66 ft) in length. It had a big skull with massive teeth for slicing prey. Its relatives were ancestors of modern whales.

Large brain, though smaller than that of living whales

Figs were an important food for animals

FICUS

Ficus, or figs, are widespread flowering plants and are part of the same group as oaks. They can be trees, shrubs, or climbers. Their fossils are first seen in Eocene rocks.

Ficus fruit with woody covering

FICUS

EARTH FACTS

The climate cooled late in the Eocene. North America and Europe were still linked but a seaway separated Europe from Asia. India and Africa were isolated island continents, while Australia broke away from Antarctica late in the Eocene.

OLIGOCENE & MIOCENE EPOCHS

LAND ANIMALS

THE MODERN AGE
Many modern animals
evolved during this period.
Monkeys and apes replaced
primitive primates. Mammals
similar to today's horses,
elephants, and camels and
new forms of carnivores,
birds and reptiles also arose.

AEGYPTOPITHECUS
This primate from
Egypt was about
the size of a tame
cat. It resembled
a modern monkey
and probably climbed
in trees feeding on
fruit and leaves.

HIPPARION
With the spread of
grasslands in the
Miocene, horses
such as *Hipparion*
emerged as
important
herbivores.

AQUATIC ANIMALS

FAMILIAR WATERS
By the Miocene, well-
known types of fishes such
as mackerels, flatfish, and
advanced sharks, including
the Great White, swam the
seas, while carp, catfish, and
other groups evolved in fresh
water. Modern whales and
the first seals evolved.

LEUCISCUS
PACHECOI

LEUCISCUS
The freshwater fish
Leuciscus appeared in the
Oligocene and survives
to this day in North
America, Asia, Europe,
and Africa.

These Leuciscus *died as
their home lake dried up*

LAND PLANTS

TEMPERATE LANDS
The tropical forests of the
Eocene gave way to drier
grasslands. The lower
temperatures of the Oligocene
allowed temperate woodlands
to spread across the continents.
The warmer and drier
conditions of the Miocene
coincided with the evolution
of grasses, which spread
across the landscape,
forming vast savanna and
prairie environments in
the south.

*Typical winged fruit
of* Acer *preserved
in limestone*

ACER
The maples (*Acer*) and
their relatives first evolved
in the Oligocene, and
many species survive today
in temperate forests
around the
world. These
deciduous trees
grow to 25 m
(82 ft) in height.   ACER

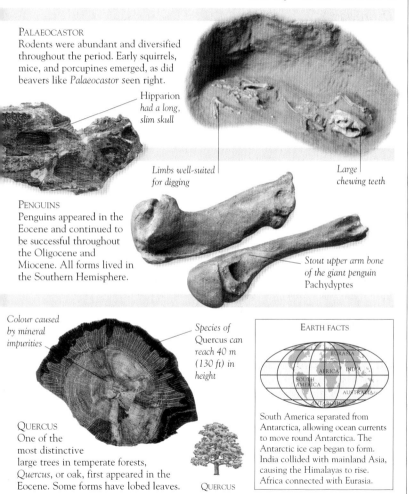

PALAEOCASTOR
Rodents were abundant and diversified throughout the period. Early squirrels, mice, and porcupines emerged, as did beavers like *Palaeocastor* seen right.

Hipparion *had a long, slim skull*

Limbs well-suited for digging

Large chewing teeth

PENGUINS
Penguins appeared in the Eocene and continued to be successful throughout the Oligocene and Miocene. All forms lived in the Southern Hemisphere.

Stout upper arm bone of the giant penguin Pachydyptes

Colour caused by mineral impurities

Species of Quercus *can reach 40 m (130 ft) in height*

QUERCUS
One of the most distinctive large trees in temperate forests, *Quercus*, or oak, first appeared in the Eocene. Some forms have lobed leaves.

QUERCUS

EARTH FACTS

EURASIA

AFRICA | INDIA

SOUTH AMERICA

AUSTRALIA

ANTARCTICA

South America separated from Antarctica, allowing ocean currents to move round Antarctica. The Antarctic ice cap began to form. India collided with mainland Asia, causing the Himalayas to rise. Africa connected with Eurasia.

PLIOCENE EPOCH

LAND ANIMALS

GRASSLAND GRAZERS
Pliocene animals were similar to today's forms. Hoofed mammals, such as horses, elephants, and antelopes diversified. Large cats hunted the plains and forests and humans evolved from chimp-like ancestors.

TETRALOPHODON
LONGIROSTRUS

TETRALOPHODON
During this time, advanced elephant forms, closely related to today's species, spread worldwide. *Tetralophodon* was an elephant that lived in Africa, Asia, and Europe.

AQUATIC ANIMALS

WHALE DIVERSITY
By the Pliocene, modern whales such as sperm whales, humpbacks, killer whales, and many modern dolphin species had evolved. Numerous fishes and animals unique to the Caribbean Sea also evolved during this time.

BALAENA
The bowhead whale (*Balaena*) grows to 65 ft (20 m) in length and has been hunted to near-extinction by humans. Its ear bone often drops away from the carcass.

BALAENA | Fossilized ear bone

LAND PLANTS

RETREATING TROPICS
Conditions became drier and cooler during the Pliocene and arid grasslands spread, replacing the more wooded savannas of the Miocene. As a result, grazing animals flourished at the expense of browsers. Tropical plants started to disappear from high latitudes and bands of cooler-adapted forests, made up of conifers, birches, and other trees, began to spread across the northern regions.

GRASSES
Grasses are a very important group of plants today. They provide shelter and food for countless animal species. The spread and diversification of grasses started in the Miocene and continued through the Pliocene as the climate became drier.

Grasses produce huge quantities of pollen and seed

Body about 1.2 m (4 ft) long

Short tail

Retractable claws, like those of a living cat

Deep, powerful lower jaw

SMILODON
The famous sabre-toothed cat, *Smilodon*, lived in the Americas. It hunted horses, camels, and other hoofed mammals that thrived during the epoch. *Smilodon* probably killed its prey by biting it at the throat.

MACRONES
All the familiar kinds of living fishes had evolved by the Pliocene. *Macrones* was a fish that resembled the catfish of today.

Sensitive barbels grew from the upper jaw

Long, toothed skull, ideal for a diet of invertebrates

Macrones were about 50 cm (1½ ft) long

LIQUIDAMBAR
These trees, sometimes called sweetgum, grew to around 25 m (82 ft) in height. They formed an important part of Pliocene forests worldwide.

Distinctive star-shaped five-lobed leaf

Leaves were shed in the autumn

LIQUIDAMBAR EUROPEANUM

EARTH FACTS

In the Pliocene, a land bridge formed between North and South America. Animals could move from one continent to the other. India continued to push the Himalayas higher. The climate grew cooler and Antarctica froze.

PLEISTOCENE EPOCH

LAND ANIMALS

MAMMALS AND HUMANS
During the Pleistocene, temperatures dropped in the northern hemisphere. Numerous large, fur-covered mammals, such as new mammoths, giant rhinos, cave lions, and giant deer, evolved. New human species emerged in Africa, Europe, and Asia.

HOMO SAPIENS
Our own species – *Homo sapiens* – emerged in Africa. It soon spread to Europe and Asia and even crossed over to the Americas and Australasia.

AQUATIC ANIMALS

COLD WATERS
Marine invertebrate life in the Pleistocene was largely unchanged from the Miocene and Pliocene. However, corals and other reef animals were affected as sea levels fell. The colder climate worldwide meant that cold-water seabirds and marine mammals were far more widely distributed.

GREAT AUK
The great auk, *Pinguinus impennis*, was a flightless seabird that inhabited the seas of the northern hemisphere as far south as north Africa and Florida, USA. Like the modern-day penguin (left), the great auk chased its prey underwater. The last great auks died by 1860.

LAND PLANTS

GRASSLANDS AND TAIGA
Grasslands developed in the northern latitudes. These also supported lichens, mosses, dwarf sedges, and miniature willow and birch. Taiga – a new kind of coniferous forest – colonized the area between the cold northern grasslands (steppes) and the temperate deciduous forests further south. Tropical forests retreated, and the South American and African rainforests may have existed in small "islands".

PICEA
Spruces (*Picea*) are pine trees that formed much of the taiga – the vast forests that spread through the northern hemisphere in the Pleistocene. More than 30 species of spruce exist today.

Cones release winged seeds

Woody cone covered with bracts in diamond pattern

1.75–0.01 MYA

Small brain

Some skeletons have marks indicating that they were hunted by prehistoric people

Strong, heavy, column-like limbs

DIPROTODON
Herds of this giant marsupial roamed the Australian grasslands of the Pleistocene. This herbivore had large chewing teeth set into thick, heavy jaws. *Diprotodon* declined as Australia became drier and was replaced by the large grazing kangaroos of today.

Short feet suited for bearing the animal's weight

HYDRODAMALIS
Steller's sea cow (*Hydrodamalis gigas*) was a marine mammal related to the modern dugong. It lived in the Arctic seas, protected from the icy water by layers of fat beneath its bark-like skin. It survived into the Holocene and was hunted to extinction by 1767.

Blunt and stump-like flippers

Ranunculus spread across North America, Europe, and Asia

Buttercups can have yellow, white, red, or blue flowers

RANUNCULUS
Buttercups (*Ranunculus*) are flowering plants that grow in temperate grassland, wetland, and woodland environments. They are among the oldest groups of flowering plants and were widespread in the Pleistocene. About 2,000 members of the buttercup family are found today.

EARTH FACTS

Northern North America, Europe, and Asia were covered by ice. Southern South America, Australia, and Antarctica were also icier than today. Dry land linked North America to eastern Asia and Australia to New Guinea.

HOLOCENE EPOCH

LAND ANIMALS

THE GREATEST DIVERSITY EVER
With the formation of the
continents as they exist now, and
the clearly differentiated climatic
zones, Earth witnessed the greatest
biodiversity than at any other
time in the past. However,
increasing human presence and
pollution has taken its toll on
animal life and natural habitats.

*Prominent curved beak
and naked facial skin*

DODO
The dodo was a giant
flightless pigeon that
lived on the island of
Mauritius in the Indian
Ocean. Hunted mercilessly,
it was extinct by about 1680.

AQUATIC ANIMALS

WATER LOSSES
In the Holocene seas some species of
seals and sea cows have been hunted
to extinction. Whaling has almost
wiped out certain whale species
and industrial fishing has
changed the balance of life
in the seas. The waters
are also polluted.

SALMON
Today wild salmon are hunted
for sport, while some species
are farmed. Salmon numbers have
been hit by water pollution
and by the construction of
dams, which prevent the
fish from migrating upstream
to breed.

LAND PLANTS

HUMAN INFLUENCE
At the start of the Holocene,
elm, birch, and conifer woodland
colonized much of the northern
hemisphere. Vast tracts of
these woodlands, as well as
wetlands and tropical forests,
were later cleared by humans
for farming cereal crops. Other
apparently natural habitats,
such as moorlands, heaths, and
grasslands are actually created
and maintained by human
activity, such as deliberate
burning and grazing of livestock.

*Branching, leafy
thallus (body)*

OAK MOSS
Oak moss is a lichen – an alga and a fungus growing
together. Some scientists believe that lichens may have
been the first multi-cellular organisms on Earth. Today,
many lichens are dying off as a result of pollution.

0.01 MYA – present

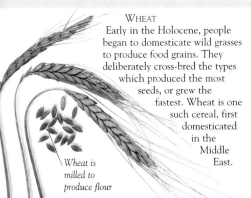

GIANT PANDA
Giant pandas are
Asian bears that
live on a diet of
bamboo. Only
one out three
species survives
today and it
is highly
endangered.

DOLLY THE SHEEP
Advances in genetics
now allow biologists to
manipulate genetic
material and clone
(duplicate) embryos.
Dolly the sheep, born
in 1997, was the
world's first successfully
cloned animal.

BLUE WHALE
The invention of the explosive harpoon
in the late 1800s enabled humans to hunt
the blue whale, the largest animal that
has ever lived,
to near-
extinction.
It is still
endangered.

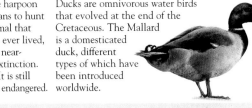

DUCKS
Ducks are omnivorous water birds
that evolved at the end of the
Cretaceous. The Mallard
is a domesticated
duck, different
types of which have
been introduced
worldwide.

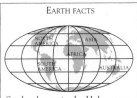

WHEAT
Early in the Holocene, people
began to domesticate wild grasses
to produce food grains. They
deliberately cross-bred the types
which produced the most
seeds, or grew the
fastest. Wheat is one
such cereal, first
domesticated
in the
Middle
East.

*Wheat is
milled to
produce flour*

EARTH FACTS

Sea levels rose in the Holocene as
the large ice caps retreated. Global
warming continues this trend today.
The land bridge that linked Asia
with North America was
submerged and New Guinea was
separated from Australia.

INTRODUCTION

55

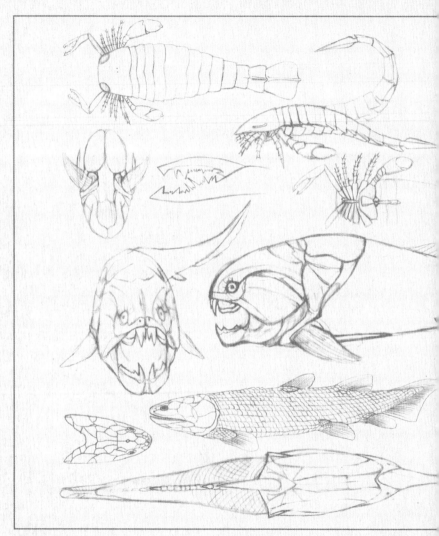

FISHES AND INVERTEBRATES

STARTING WITH a strange collection of invertebrates (animals without backbones), this section moves on to a fantastic variety of fishes, the first animals to have backbones. Little fishes with ever-open mouths, armoured and spiny fishes, sharks, and finally, lobe-finned fishes, an ancient group that is ancestral to humans, are all exhibited here.

TRILOBITES

BEFORE FISHES BECAME dominant, the seas teemed with trilobites. They were among the earliest arthropods (creatures that possess external skeletons) and ranged in size from microscopically tiny, to species that were larger than a dish. With over 15,000 species, trilobites outnumber any other known extinct creature.

TRILOBITE BODY PLAN
Trilobite means "three-lobed", which describes its body's lengthwise division into three parts. A tough outer casing protected the body. After a trilobite died, the casing often broke apart into the three lobes.

A knobbly shield guarded the head

Middle lobe, flanked by two side lobes

DEFENCE
Phacops curled up in a tight ball or burrowed if attacked. The 12 plates of its thorax (middle region) overlapped like a Venetian blind to protect the legs and underside. Fishes were probably *Phacops*'s worst enemies.

PHACOPS ROLLED
UP IN DEFENCE

Tail

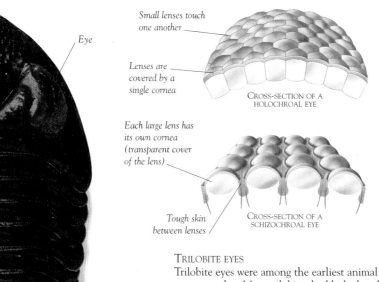

Eye

Small lenses touch
one another

Lenses are
covered by a
single cornea

CROSS-SECTION OF A
HOLOCHROAL EYE

Each large lens has
its own cornea
(transparent cover
of the lens)

Tough skin
between lenses

CROSS-SECTION OF A
SCHIZOCHROAL EYE

TRILOBITE EYES

Trilobite eyes were among the earliest animal
eyes to evolve. Most trilobites had holochroal
eyes. These resembled the compound eyes of
insects with up to 15,000 six-sided lenses
packed like a honeycomb, and they gave
a fuzzy image. Some other trilobites had
schizochroal eyes with many separated, large
round lenses that produced a sharper image.

Flexible middle
region made up
of many segments

PHACOPS

PHACOPS

- Group: Trilobita
- Order: Phacopida
- Time: Devonian period
  (410–355 MYA)
- Size: 4.5 cm (1¼ in) long
- Diet: Edible particles
- Habitat: Warm, shallow seas

SEA SCORPIONS

EURYPTERIDS (SEA SCORPIONS) were the largest-ever arthropods. They belong to the chelicerates ("pincered creatures"), a group that includes spiders and scorpions. Among the largest sea scorpions was *Pterygotus*, which lived more than 400 million years ago, and could grow longer than a man. Before hunting fish evolved, sea scorpions were among the most dominant hunters of shallow seas.

Larg

Small eye

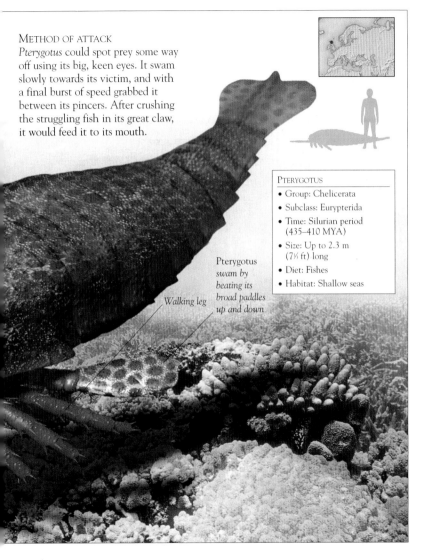

METHOD OF ATTACK

Pterygotus could spot prey some way off using its big, keen eyes. It swam slowly towards its victim, and with a final burst of speed grabbed it between its pincers. After crushing the struggling fish in its great claw, it would feed it to its mouth.

Pterygotus swam by beating its broad paddles up and down

Walking leg

PTERYGOTUS

- Group: Chelicerata
- Subclass: Eurypterida
- Time: Silurian period (435–410 MYA)
- Size: Up to 2.3 m (7½ ft) long
- Diet: Fishes
- Habitat: Shallow seas

AMMONITES AND BELEMNITES

THE COILED SHELLS called ammonites were named after Ammon, an Egyptian god with coiled horns; while the long, tapering belemnites were named from the Greek word for darts. Both groups were cephalopods – soft bodied molluscs – and they lived in the sea.

ECHIOCERAS
The ammonite *Echioceras* lived in shallow seas around the world in Jurassic times. In life, its tentacled head poked out of the shell's open end as it searched for food.

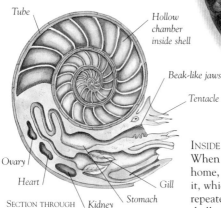

Tube

Hollow chamber inside shell

Beak-like jaws

Tentacle

Ovary

Heart

Gill

SECTION THROUGH AN AMMONITE

Kidney

Stomach

INSIDE AN AMMONITE
When the young ammonite outgrew its home, it built a bigger chamber next to it, which it moved into. This process was repeated as the ammonite grew, and a shell with many chambers was created.

ECHIOCERAS
- Group: Ammonitida
- Family: Echioceratidae
- Time: Jurassic period (203–135 MYA)
- Size: 6 cm (2½ in) wide
- Diet: Tiny living creatures
- Habitat: Shallow seas

Loosely coiled shell, with many turns known as whorls

ECHIOCERAS

Mantle or front of the body

Head region

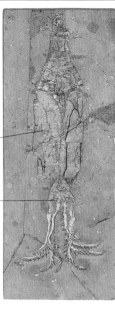

BELEMNOTEUTHIS

Belemnites, such as *Belemnoteuthis*, were squid-like creatures with large brains and big eyes. From the head end sprang ten tentacles armed with suckers and hooks, with which it grappled small sea creatures to its beak. *Belemnoteuthis* moved its body forwards by squirting jets of water. It lived in a Late Jurassic sea that once existed where Europe stands today.

Ribs strengthened the shell

INSIDE A BELEMNITE
This *Cylindroteuthis* fossil shows the main parts of a belemnite's internal shell. The chambered front end helped the body float while the tapering rear end fitted into a hard, narrow guard.

Chambered front end of the body

Long, pointed guard or pen

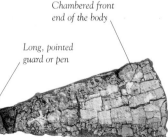

EVOLVING INSECTS

THE FIRST INSECTS were tiny, wingless arthropods that lived in the Devonian. By 320 million years ago, some insects had developed wings. The flowering plants of the Cretaceous provided food for butterflies and bees. By 220 million years ago, termites were forming colonies; they were followed by ants, bees, and wasps. The world now teems with millions of insect species.

HYDROPHILUS

Fine veins stiffened the wings

MEGANEURA FOSSIL

Hard wing case preserved in a fossil

WINGS AS SHIELDS
Beetles almost identical to this *Hydrophilus* fossil still swim in ponds today. Their forewings form hard protective cases.

HAWK-LIKE HUNTERS
Meganeura was a gigantic, primitive dragonfly with two pairs of wings that were 70-cm (27-in) wide. It hunted insects above tropical forests in the Late Carboniferous. Its swivelling eyes were like headlamps, sharp enough to allow it to spot and pounce on flying prey.

Six jointed legs, as found in other insects

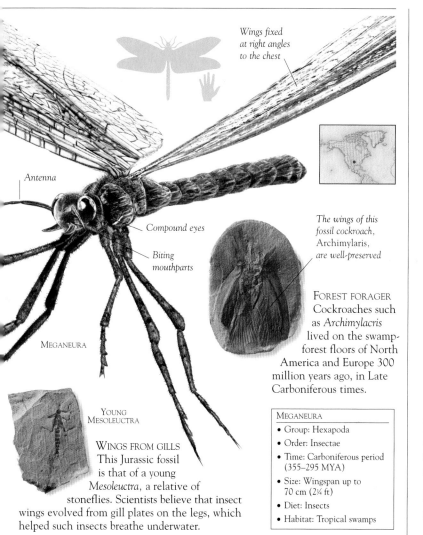

Wings fixed
at right angles
to the chest

Antenna

Compound eyes

Biting
mouthparts

MEGANEURA

The wings of this
fossil cockroach,
Archimylaris,
are well-preserved

FOREST FORAGER
Cockroaches such
as *Archimylacris*
lived on the swamp-
forest floors of North
America and Europe 300
million years ago, in Late
Carboniferous times.

YOUNG
MESOLEUCTRA

WINGS FROM GILLS
This Jurassic fossil
is that of a young
Mesoleuctra, a relative of
stoneflies. Scientists believe that insect
wings evolved from gill plates on the legs, which
helped such insects breathe underwater.

MEGANEURA
- Group: Hexapoda
- Order: Insectae
- Time: Carboniferous period
  (355–295 MYA)
- Size: Wingspan up to
  70 cm (2¼ ft)
- Diet: Insects
- Habitat: Tropical swamps

VERTEBRATES CLADOGRAM

ALL VERTEBRATES possess an internal skeleton. The evolution of the skeleton allowed vertebrates to support their weight on land better than any other animal group. Vertebrates have grown to sizes and taken to lifestyles that are more complex than other animals.

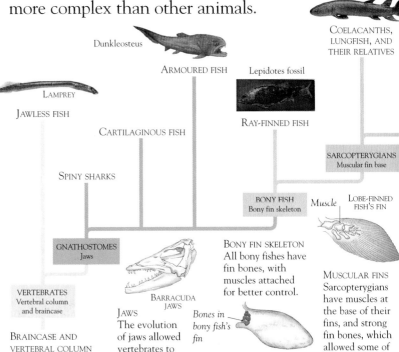

Eusthenopteron

Dunkleosteus

ARMOURED FISH

Lepidotes fossil

COELACANTHS, LUNGFISH, AND THEIR RELATIVES

LAMPREY

JAWLESS FISH

RAY-FINNED FISH

CARTILAGINOUS FISH

SARCOPTERYGIANS
Muscular fin base

SPINY SHARKS

BONY FISH
Bony fin skeleton

Muscle

LOBE-FINNED FISH'S FIN

GNATHOSTOMES
Jaws

BARRACUDA
JAWS

BONY FIN SKELETON
All bony fishes have fin bones, with muscles attached for better control.

VERTEBRATES
Vertebral column and braincase

JAWS
The evolution of jaws allowed vertebrates to eat a varied diet.

Bones in bony fish's fin

BRAINCASE AND VERTEBRAL COLUMN
These structures protect the brain and main nervous system.

MUSCULAR FINS
Sarcopterygians have muscles at the base of their fins, and strong fin bones, which allowed some of them to clamber on to land.

Vertebral column and skull in a simple vertebrate

Mastodonsaurus from the Late Triassic

Diadectes

Domestic chicken

In cladistic terms, birds are reptiles

TEMNOSPONDYLS

DIADECTOMORPHS

SYNAPSIDS

REPTILES

SEYMOURIAMORPHS

LEPOSPONDYLS AND LISSAMPHIBIANS

AMNIOTES
Amniotic membrane

REPTILIOMORPHS
Reduced premaxillae

CHICKEN EGG

The amniotic membrane

TETRAPODS
Limbs with distinct digits

The premaxillae are two bones that form the tip of the snout

SKULL OF REPTILIOMORPH

Digit

FORELIMB OF PERMIAN TEMNOSPONDYL ERYOPS

REDUCED PREMAXILLAE
The premaxillae are proportionally smaller in the reptiliomorphs than they are in other tetrapods.

AMNIOTIC MEMBRANE
The embryos of amniotes are protected by a watertight amniotic membrane. The evolution of this membrane allowed amniotes to dispense with the aquatic larval stage present in primitive tetrapods, and to colonize the land away from bodies of water.

LIMBS WITH DIGITS
Sarcopterygians with distinct limbs and digits are called tetrapods. These vertebrates evolved in the Devonian from aquatic or amphibious predators that later adapted to life on land.

VERTEBRATE EVOLUTION
A major part of vertebrates' evolution took place in water. Primitive jawless fishes were the earliest vertebrates. They were superseded by jawed vertebrates. The evolution of muscular fins and limbs allowed lobe-finned fishes to take to the land. Tetrapods evolved during the Devonian. By the Carboniferous, they had radiated into aquatic, amphibious, and terrestrial groups.

TOWARDS THE FIRST FISHES

THE EARLIEST sea creatures were sponges with a single type of cell in their bodies. Gradually, cells became specialized and bodies more complex, giving rise to bilaterians – creatures with left and right sides. About 535 million years ago, bilaterians called chordates developed a stiffening rod (notochord) that would eventually become a proper skeleton. These became the first fishes.

Inlet for food and water

COTHURNOCYSTIS
Cothurnocystis was a strange, boot-like animal. Its tail might have had a notochord, and the small slits in its body might have filtered food. It had a hard outer shell like a sea urchins.

COTHURNOCYSTIS

Hard protective covering on the body

Hard plates framing the head

Slits for expelling waste

COTHURNOCYSTIS FOSSIL
A *Cothurnocystis* fossil lies embedded in an ancient piece of Scottish rock. *Cothurnocystis* belonged to the carpoids – small, oddly flattened creatures that lived on Early Palaeozoic seabeds – and may have been the ancestors of fishes.

HEAD CHORDATES

The little eel-like cephalochordate ("head chordate") called *Branchiostoma* living today is probably the best clue to the ancestors of fishes. Cephalochordates do not have a head but a swelling at the front end that hints at the beginnings of a brain. In 1999, Chinese scientists found a much older fish-like creature, *Haikouella*, that had a brain, eyes, heart, and gill filaments.

Haikouella lived 530 million years ago, and may have been among the first creatures with a skull.

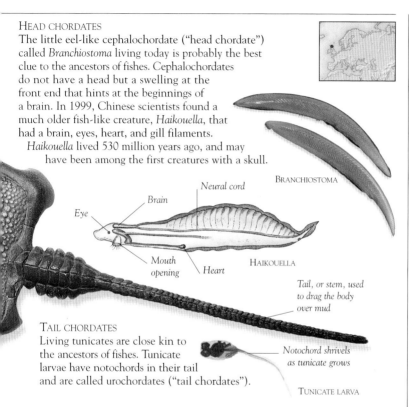

BRANCHIOSTOMA

Neural cord

Brain

Eye

Mouth opening

Heart

HAIKOUELLA

Tail, or stem, used to drag the body over mud

TAIL CHORDATES

Living tunicates are close kin to the ancestors of fishes. Tunicate larvae have notochords in their tail and are called urochordates ("tail chordates").

Notochord shrivels as tunicate grows

TUNICATE LARVA

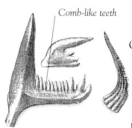

Comb-like teeth

COTHURNOCYSTIS

- Group: Cothurnocystis
- Family: Cornuta
- Time: Ordovician period (500–435 MYA)
- Size: 5 cm (⅙ ft) wide
- Diet: Edible particles
- Habitat: Muddy sea floor

CONODONT TEETH

These tiny fossils are from the eel-like conodonts that lived 300 million years ago. They had large eyes, and teeth inside the throat.

JAWLESS FISHES

AGNATHANS ("WITHOUT JAWS") were the most primitive fishes. Their mouths were fixed open because they lacked jaws, they had no bony internal skeleton, and they lacked paired fins. Early jawless fishes lived in the seas, but they later invaded rivers and lakes. They swam by waggling their tails, and sucked in small food particles from the mud or water around them.

Backswept horns helped with balance

The long lower lobe of the tail lifted the fish as it swam

PTERASPIS

Bony armour protected it from sea scorpions and other predators

VERTEBRATE PIONEER
Sacabamsbapis was a tadpole-shaped fish that lived 450 million years ago. It swam by waggling its tail, but had no fins, which would have made braking and steering very difficult. Two tiny, headlamp-like eyes gazed from the front of its armoured head as it sucked in water and food through its ever-open mouth.

Large bony plates protected the head and chest

SACABAMSBAPIS

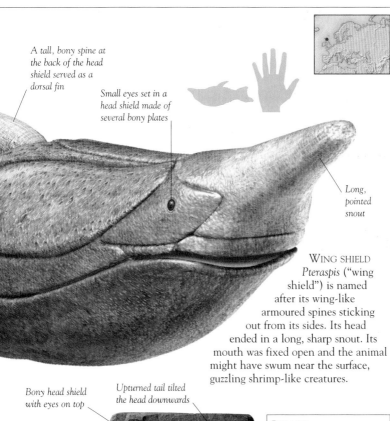

A tall, bony spine at the back of the head shield served as a dorsal fin

Small eyes set in a head shield made of several bony plates

Long, pointed snout

WING SHIELD
Pteraspis ("wing shield") is named after its wing-like armoured spines sticking out from its sides. Its head ended in a long, sharp snout. Its mouth was fixed open and the animal might have swum near the surface, guzzling shrimp-like creatures.

Bony head shield with eyes on top

Upturned tail tilted the head downwards

BETTER BALANCE
Cephalaspis was an advanced jawless fish that had a big, bony head with sense organs on the sides and top, a mouth below the head, and paired flaps that provided lift and balance.

PTERASPIS
• Group: Agnatha
• Order: Heterostraci
• Time: Devonian period (410–355 MYA)
• Size: 20 cm (¼ ft) long
• Diet: Tiny water animals
• Habitat: Shallow seas

FISHES AND INVERTEBRATES

ARMOURED FISHES

PLACODERMS ("PLATED SKINS") were primitive jawed fishes named after the protective bony plates on their head and body. Some lived in the sea, some in fresh water, and they ranged in size from a few centimetres up to 8 m (26 ft) – the first fishes to grow to such a large size. Placoderms were a very successful group. It is possible that they may have shared a common ancestor with sharks.

BOTHRIOLEPIS

Each jointed "arm" was a fin inside a bony tube

Preserved head and trunk shields

ROCK SLAB CONTAINING MANY FOSSILS OF BOTHRIOLEPIS

FISHES WITH "ARMS"
Bothriolepis was amongst the strangest of placoderms. Up to 1 m (3¼ ft) in length, it possessed jointed "arms" made of bony tubes that enclosed its long, narrow pectoral fins. It might have used these arms to dig for food in the mud or to even drag itself over dry land as it migrated from one pool to another.

FLAT OUT
The flat-bodied fish *Gemuendina* belonged to an ancient group of placoderms called rhenanids. Much like living rays, it swam with rippling movements of its broad, wing-like pectoral fins. A short, bony shield guarded its foreparts and tiny bony plates ran down its slender tail. It thrust out its jaws and caught shellfish for food.

GEMUENDINA FOSSIL IN FINE-GRAINED ROCK

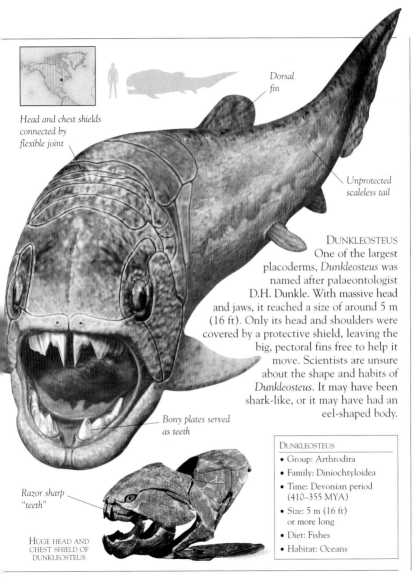

Head and chest shields
connected by
flexible joint

Dorsal
fin

Unprotected
scaleless tail

DUNKLEOSTEUS
One of the largest
placoderms, *Dunkleosteus* was
named after palaeontologist
D.H. Dunkle. With massive head
and jaws, it reached a size of around 5 m
(16 ft). Only its head and shoulders were
covered by a protective shield, leaving the
big, pectoral fins free to help it
move. Scientists are unsure
about the shape and habits of
Dunkleosteus. It may have been
shark-like, or it may have had an
eel-shaped body.

Bony plates served
as teeth

Razor sharp
"teeth"

HUGE HEAD AND
CHEST SHIELD OF
DUNKLEOSTEUS

DUNKLEOSTEUS
• Group: Arthrodira
• Family: Diniochtyloidea
• Time: Devonian period
  (410–355 MYA)
• Size: 5 m (16 ft)
  or more long
• Diet: Fishes
• Habitat: Oceans

SHARKS AND RAYS

SHARKS HAVE BEEN among the top ocean predators for over 400 million years. Their basic features – a streamlined shape and jaws bristling with razor-sharp fangs – have changed little in this time, although many different kinds of shark-like fishes have evolved. These include rat fish, skates, and rays. Sharks and their relatives are known as Chondrichthyes ("cartilage fishes") because their skeletons are made of cartilage.

Streamlined, torpedo-shaped body

CLADOSELACHE
Well-preserved fossils of *Cladoselache*, one of the earliest known sharks, have been found in Late Devonian rocks. This carnivore hunted fishes, squid, and crustaceans.

CLADOSELACHE

The fin rays radiated like the rays of the Sun

SUN RAY
The stingray *Heliobatis* ("Sun ray") was a flat-bodied, freshwater fish that lived in North America about 50 million years ago. Up to 30 cm (1 ft) in length, its flat, round body had a long whip-like tail armed with spines.

CLADOSELACHE
- Group:Elasmobranchii
- Family: Cladoselachidae
- Time: Devonian period (410–355 MYA)
- Size: Up to 2 m (6½ ft) long
- Diet: Fish and crustaceans
- Habitat: Seas

WIDESPREAD PREDATORS
Hybodus was a blunt-headed shark that was widespread in the Mesozoic. It had prominent fin spines and distinctive scales. Growing to a length of 2.5 m (8 ft), it closely resembled modern sharks although its jaws were different, carrying two types of teeth. Pointed teeth in front were used to seize fishes, while blunt teeth at the back were used to crush bones.

Barbed spines on the head of male Hybodus

Large pectoral fins helped the shark to manoeuvre

HYBODUS

Snout blunter than modern sharks

SHARP TOOTH OF A SHARK

FLAT TOOTHPLATE OF A RAY

Large pectoral fins

SHARK OR RAY?
Prehistoric sharks and rays are often identified from their teeth because their gristly skeletons did not easily fossilize. Sharks had sharp teeth while rays had flat toothplates.

Spine-covered "tower"

SPINY CHEST
Stethacanthus ("spiny chest"), was a small shark that lived 360 million years ago. The male carried a bizarre tower on its flat, spiny back.

STETHACANTHUS

75

SPINY SHARKS

ACANTHODIANS OR "SPINY SHARKS" may have pre-dated placoderms as the first fishes with jaws. They got their name from their shark-like bodies with upturned tails, and the sharp spines at the tip of their fins. Although their cartilage backbone reminds us of a shark's, acanthodians had a braincase, gills, and other features more like those of bony fishes that are common today.

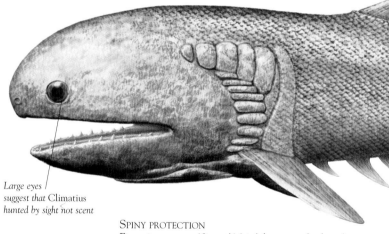

Large eyes suggest that Climatius *hunted by sight not scent*

Distinctive ridges on surface

SPINY PROTECTION

Fin spines up to 40 cm (16 in) long are the best known remains of the spiny shark *Gyracanthus*. Fossils of this well-defended animal are found in Carboniferous rocks of North America and Europe. Some acanthodians had spines that were half their body length as protection against large, fierce predators.

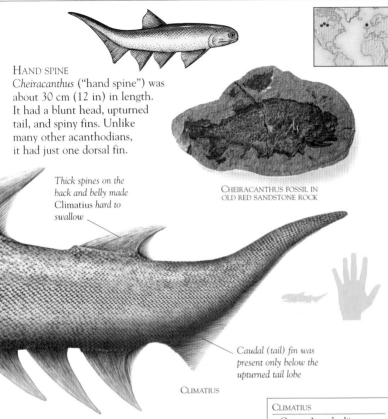

HAND SPINE

Cheiracanthus ("hand spine") was about 30 cm (12 in) in length. It had a blunt head, upturned tail, and spiny fins. Unlike many other acanthodians, it had just one dorsal fin.

Thick spines on the back and belly made Climatius *hard to swallow*

CHEIRACANTHUS FOSSIL IN OLD RED SANDSTONE ROCK

Caudal (tail) fin was present only below the upturned tail lobe

CLIMATIUS

INCLINED FISH

Climatius ("inclined or slanted fish") was named after its upward tilted tail. This small river fish was a member of the Climatiiformes, the earliest group of acanthodians. It had big eyes and sharp teeth suggesting that it was an active hunter. It is likely that *Climatius* zoomed low over the beds of seas or rivers in search of prey – tiny fishes and crustaceans.

CLIMATIUS
- Group: Acanthodii
- Family: Climatiidae
- Time: Silurian – Devonian periods (435–355 MYA)
- Size: 7.5 cm (¼ ft) long
- Diet: Small fish and crustaceans
- Habitat: Rivers

EARLY RAY-FINNED FISHES

BONY FISHES ARE the most numerous and diverse of all living vertebrates and more than 20,000 of them belong to one giant group known as actinopterygians or "ray fins". They are named after the straight bony rays that jut out from their body and stiffen the fins. The earliest known ray fins lived 410 million years ago.

LIVING FOSSILS
Bichirs are ray-finned fishes that live in Africa. They can be traced back to ancestors that lived 400 million years ago.

HAND FIN
Cheirolepis ("hand fin") was one of the earliest ray-finned fishes. Only parts of its backbone were actually made of bone – the rest was made of gristle and so not often preserved in fossils. This wide-jawed fish was a keen hunter, swimming fast to catch prey in freshwater pools and streams.

Relatively large eyes

Long jaws equipped with many tiny teeth

Pectoral fins on fleshy lobes

REDFIELDIUS
About 20 cm (8 in) in length, *Redfieldius* lived about 210 million years ago. Its group, the redfieldiids, are thought to have evolved in Australia or South Africa and then spread to North Africa and North America in Early Mesozoic times.

LEPISOSTEUS

This freshwater predator, about 70 cm (28 in) long, had dorsal and anal fins placed close to its tail. Despite its "old-fashioned" enamelled scales, it was more advanced than the first ray-finned fishes. Fifty million years ago, *Lepisosteus* would have lurked in shallow waters of what is now Wyoming, USA.

LEPISOSTEUS FOSSIL FROM THE EOCENE

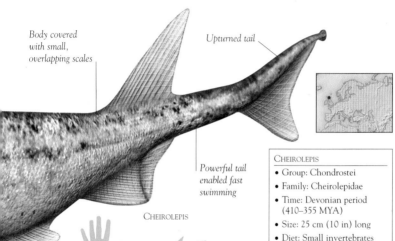

Body covered with small, overlapping scales

Upturned tail

Powerful tail enabled fast swimming

CHEIROLEPIS

CHEIROLEPIS
- Group: Chondrostei
- Family: Cheirolepidae
- Time: Devonian period (410–355 MYA)
- Size: 25 cm (10 in) long
- Diet: Small invertebrates
- Habitat: Fresh water

STURGEON

Best known for producing eggs that people eat as caviar, sturgeons are living "prehistoric" ray-finned fishes. The two dozen kinds alive today live in northern seas and swim up rivers to lay eggs. Several species are endangered by fishing, dam construction, and pollution.

ADVANCED RAY-FINNED FISHES

IMPROVED TYPES of ray-finned fishes called the neopterygians ("new fins") began to appear in Mesozoic times. Their mouths could open wider and had tooth plates to grind up food. Changes in the fins and tail made them better swimmers. The most advanced of this group were the teleosts or "complete bones".

Body made inflexible by thick layer of scales

SCURFY SCALES
Lepidotes ("covered in scurfy scales") was a bony fish nearly as long as a human. Like early ray-finned fishes, its body had a coat of thick and hard scales, although it was far bigger in size. *Lepidotes* swam in shallow coastal waters, hunting for shellfish. However, it too was sometimes eaten by a fish-eating dinosaur called *Spinosaur*.

Relatively deep body

LEPIDOTES

Leptolepides, *a teleost fossil of the Late Jurassic*

PRIMITIVE TELEOST
As big as a human hand, *Leptolepides* was a bony fish that lived about 150 million years ago. It swam in shoals in tropical lagoons where Germany now stands. It is the ancestor of carp and other modern teleosts.

LEPIDOTES

- Group: Neopterygii
- Family: Semionotidae
- Time: Triassic – Cretaceous periods (250–65 MYA)
- Size: Up to 1.7 m (5½ ft) long
- Diet: Shellfish
- Habitat: Lakes and shallow seas

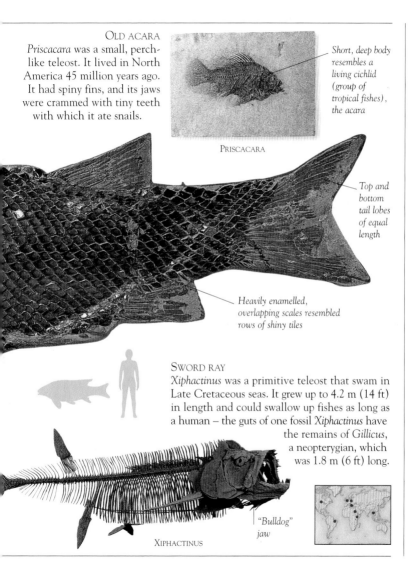

OLD ACARA

Priscacara was a small, perch-like teleost. It lived in North America 45 million years ago. It had spiny fins, and its jaws were crammed with tiny teeth with which it ate snails.

Short, deep body resembles a living cichlid (group of tropical fishes), the acara

PRISCACARA

Top and bottom tail lobes of equal length

Heavily enamelled, overlapping scales resembled rows of shiny tiles

SWORD RAY

Xiphactinus was a primitive teleost that swam in Late Cretaceous seas. It grew up to 4.2 m (14 ft) in length and could swallow up fishes as long as a human – the guts of one fossil *Xiphactinus* have the remains of *Gillicus*, a neopterygian, which was 1.8 m (6 ft) long.

"Bulldog" jaw

XIPHACTINUS

LOBE-FINNED FISHES

THE BONY FISHES OF 400 million years ago belonged to two large groups – lobe fins and ray fins. Lobe-finned fishes, or sarcopterygians, had fins that sprouted from fleshy lobes. Many also had a type of lung in addition to gills and so could breathe in air. There were two main groups of lobe fins – lungfish and crossopterygians. The latter group included the coelacanths ("hollow spines") and rhipidistians ("fan sails"), which have an important place in evolutionary history.

PANDER'S FISH
In the 1990s, scientists made an important discovery about the Late Devonian fan sail *Panderichthys*. Their studies revealed that this freshwater rhipidistian was one of the closest known ancestors of four-limbed vertebrates.

RIDGED UPPER AND
LOWER TOOTHPLATES
OF CERATODUS

HORN TEETH
Ceratodus ("horn teeth") was a lungfish that lived in the Age of Dinosaurs. It had gills, but could also breathe through its nostrils at the water surface, using its swim bladder as a kind of lung.

Broad, flat head of Panderichthys with eyes located on top

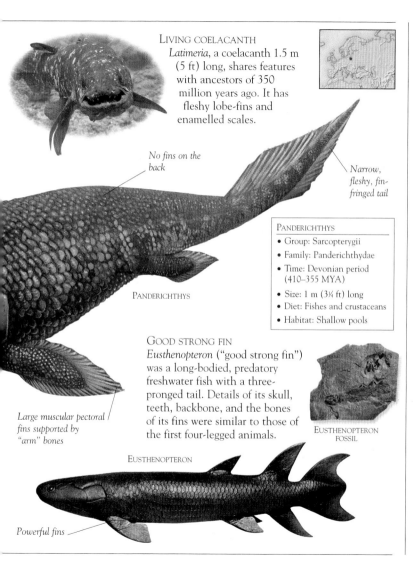

LIVING COELACANTH
Latimeria, a coelacanth 1.5 m
(5 ft) long, shares features
with ancestors of 350
million years ago. It has
fleshy lobe-fins and
enamelled scales.

*No fins on the
back*

*Narrow,
fleshy, fin-
fringed tail*

PANDERICHTHYS

PANDERICHTHYS
- Group: Sarcopterygii
- Family: Panderichthydae
- Time: Devonian period
  (410–355 MYA)
- Size: 1 m (3¼ ft) long
- Diet: Fishes and crustaceans
- Habitat: Shallow pools

GOOD STRONG FIN
Eusthenopteron ("good strong fin")
was a long-bodied, predatory
freshwater fish with a three-
pronged tail. Details of its skull,
teeth, backbone, and the bones
of its fins were similar to those of
the first four-legged animals.

EUSTHENOPTERON
FOSSIL

*Large muscular pectoral
fins supported by
"arm" bones*

EUSTHENOPTERON

Powerful fins

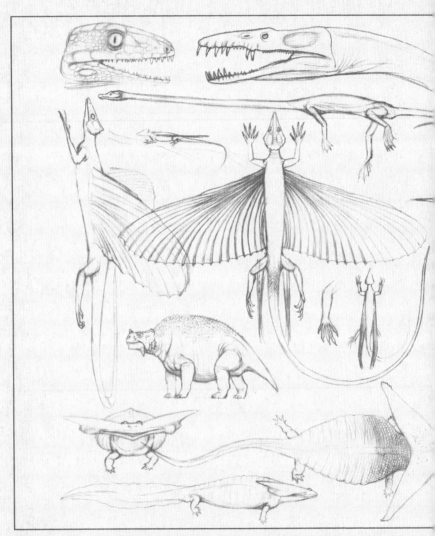

AMPHIBIANS AND REPTILES

ABOUT 360 MILLION years ago, a fish with lungs crawled ashore on stubby fins. So vertebrates began their great adventure on dry land. From early amphibians that laid small, unprotected eggs in water, eventually reptiles began to breed on land with eggs that were protected by a shell. An incredible variety of prehistoric reptiles began to rule land, sea, and air.

EARLY TETRAPODS AND AMPHIBIANS CLADOGRAM

TETRAPODS, the limb-bearing vertebrates, gradually adapted to life on land. They evolved stronger limbs, each with five digits, and some of the skull bones seen in their fish ancestors were lost. They also developed a stronger link between their hips and vertebrae.

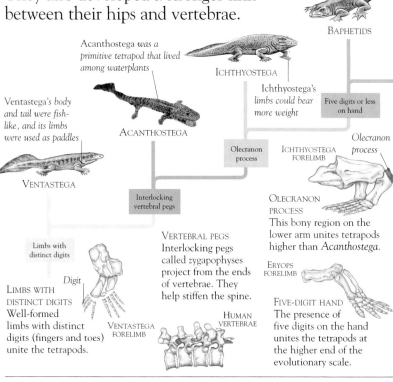

Eucritta *from the Carboniferous*

BAPHETIDS

Acanthostega *was a primitive tetrapod that lived among waterplants*

ICHTHYOSTEGA

Ichthyostega's limbs could bear more weight

Five digits or less on hand

Ventastega's body and tail were fish-like, and its limbs were used as paddles

ACANTHOSTEGA

Olecranon process

ICHTHYOSTEGA FORELIMB

VENTASTEGA

Olecranon process

Interlocking vertebral pegs

OLECRANON PROCESS
This bony region on the lower arm unites tetrapods higher than *Acanthostega*.

Limbs with distinct digits

Digit

LIMBS WITH DISTINCT DIGITS
Well-formed limbs with distinct digits (fingers and toes) unite the tetrapods.

VERTEBRAL PEGS
Interlocking pegs called zygapophyses project from the ends of vertebrae. They help stiffen the spine.

VENTASTEGA FORELIMB

ERYOPS FORELIMB

FIVE-DIGIT HAND
The presence of five digits on the hand unites the tetrapods at the higher end of the evolutionary scale.

HUMAN VERTEBRAE

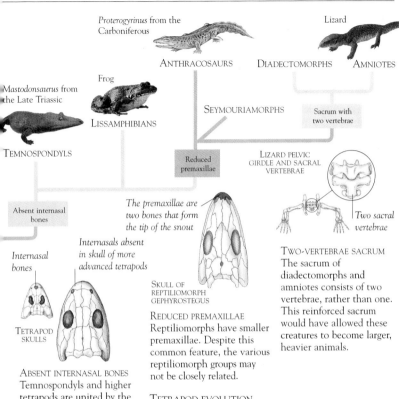

Proterogyrinus from the Carboniferous

Lizard

ANTHRACOSAURS   DIADECTOMORPHS   AMNIOTES

Frog

Mastodonsaurus from the Late Triassic

SEYMOURIAMORPHS

Sacrum with two vertebrae

LISSAMPHIBIANS

TEMNOSPONDYLS

Reduced premaxillae

LIZARD PELVIC GIRDLE AND SACRAL VERTEBRAE

Absent internasal bones

The premaxillae are two bones that form the tip of the snout

Two sacral vertebrae

Internasal bones

Internasals absent in skull of more advanced tetrapods

SKULL OF REPTILIOMORPH GEPHYROSTEGUS

TWO-VERTEBRAE SACRUM
The sacrum of diadectomorphs and amniotes consists of two vertebrae, rather than one. This reinforced sacrum would have allowed these creatures to become larger, heavier animals.

TETRAPOD SKULLS

REDUCED PREMAXILLAE
Reptiliomorphs have smaller premaxillae. Despite this common feature, the various reptiliomorph groups may not be closely related.

ABSENT INTERNASAL BONES
Temnospondyls and higher tetrapods are united by the absence of the internasal bones. The factors that caused these bones to be lost remain unknown.

TETRAPOD EVOLUTION
Primitive tetrapods with multiple digits appear to have been largely restricted to watery environments. The fossil record shows that after tetrapods with five-fingered hands evolved in the Carboniferous, they diversified rapidly and gave rise to most of the major groups within 30 million years. All tetrapods that are not amniotes were formerly called amphibians. However, many fossil animals that have been called amphibians were not in fact related to each other.

EARLY TETRAPODS

THE TETRAPODS, meaning "four feet", are a group that include all vertebrates with four limbs and distinct digits (fingers and toes). Early tetrapods were tied to life in water. They had paddle-like limbs, gills, and tail fins. They also possessed many features inherited by later types: digits, limbs with wrist and elbow joints, and vertebrae with interlocking pegs, which seemed to have all evolved in the water.

Bony rays supported the tail fins

Early tetrapods were quite large – between 50 cm (20 in) and 1 m (40 in) long

Hindlimbs were directed sideways and backwards, to help in swimming

ELGINERPETON

Paddle-like limbs

TETRAPOD ORIGINS
Among the earliest tetrapods is *Elginerpeton* from Devonian Scotland. The very first tetrapods, which include *Obruchevichthys* from Latvia and *Metaxygnathus* from Australia, are from the late Devonian (about 365 MYA). Footprints found in Australia show that four-footed animals were walking on land even at this time.

ACANTHOSTEGA
- Group: Labyrinthodontia
- Order: Acanthostegidae
- Time: Devonian period (410–355 MYA)
- Size: 1 m (3⅓ ft) long
- Diet: Insects, fish, smaller animals of its own kind
- Habitat: Lakes and ponds

Patterned skull surface seen in all early limbed vertebrates

ACANTHOSTEGA
SKULL

FISH-LIKE SKULL
The skull of *Acanthostega* was designed for grabbing fishes and other aquatic prey. This well-preserved skull is similar to that of the lobe-finned fishes, ancestors of the earliest limbed vertebrates.

ACANTHOSTEGA
Tetrapods like *Ichthyostega* and *Acanthostega* from Late Devonian Greenland were aquatic predators with fish-like features, including a tail fin, gill bones, and paddle-like hindlimbs. Intriguingly, their multiple digits suggest that the evolution of limbs and digits first occurred in the water, and not on land. *Acanthostega* might have ventured onto land, although its limbs were not suited to walking.

Acanthostega had a stiff spine with interlocking pegs on the vertebrae

The eight fingers were probably webbed together to form a paddle

Large eyes directed upwards and sideways

EVOLUTION OF DIGITS
Digits evolved from the fin bones of lobe-finned fishes. The early vertebrates often had more than five digits. More advanced tetrapods may have five digits because this is best suited for walking.

Numerous small bones form the fin skeletons of lobe-finned fishes

ICHTHYOSTEGA
FIN/HAND

TEMNOSPONDYLS

THESE WERE A LARGE group of animals that lived in the water, land, or on both. Most early temnospondyls were aquatic, but some were land-living predators with short, scaly bodies and stout limbs. Some later land temnospondyls had armour on their backs: some that stayed in the water became huge predators.

MASTODONSAURUS

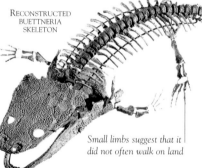

RECONSTRUCTED BUETTNERIA SKELETON

Small limbs suggest that it did not often walk on land

METOPOSAURS

Related to *Mastodonsaurus*, the metoposaurs were a group of large, mostly aquatic temnospondyls. All metoposaurs, including this *Buettneria* from Late Triassic North America, had large, flat skulls.

MASS DEATHS

Some temnospondyls perished in hundreds and were preserved in mass death fossils, as seen below in the case of *Trimerorhachis*, a Permian temnospondyl from North America.

TRIMERORHACHIS MASS-DEATH FOSSIL

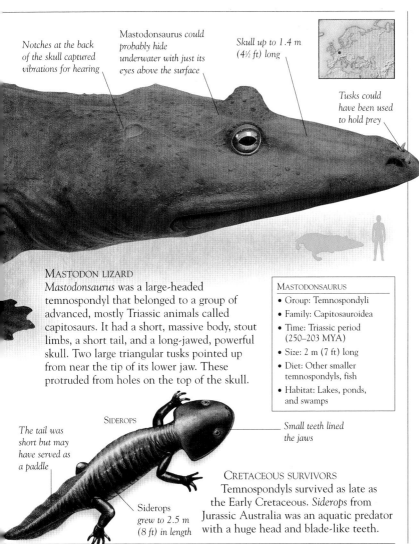

Notches at the back of the skull captured vibrations for hearing

Mastodonsaurus *could probably hide underwater with just its eyes above the surface*

Skull up to 1.4 m (4½ ft) long

Tusks could have been used to hold prey

MASTODON LIZARD

Mastodonsaurus was a large-headed temnospondyl that belonged to a group of advanced, mostly Triassic animals called capitosaurs. It had a short, massive body, stout limbs, a short tail, and a long-jawed, powerful skull. Two large triangular tusks pointed up from near the tip of its lower jaw. These protruded from holes on the top of the skull.

MASTODONSAURUS
- Group: Temnospondyli
- Family: Capitosauroidea
- Time: Triassic period (250–203 MYA)
- Size: 2 m (7 ft) long
- Diet: Other smaller temnospondyls, fish
- Habitat: Lakes, ponds, and swamps

SIDEROPS

Small teeth lined the jaws

The tail was short but may have served as a paddle

Siderops grew to 2.5 m (8 ft) in length

CRETACEOUS SURVIVORS

Temnospondyls survived as late as the Early Cretaceous. *Siderops* from Jurassic Australia was an aquatic predator with a huge head and blade-like teeth.

LIFE IN A SWAMP FOREST

DURING THE CARBONIFEROUS period, several new kinds of terrestrial vertebrates evolved. Lush, forested swamps with an atmosphere rich in oxygen, favoured the growth of giant arthropods, as well as different species of amphibious, aquatic, and land-dwelling predators.

GIANT ARTHROPODS
With a wingspan of 70 cm (27 in) Meganeura was the largest flying insect ever. Other giant arthropods included scorpions and flat-bodied millipedes.

Eryops *was an aquatic hunter*

AQUATIC HUNTERS
Various large predators haunted the dark waters of the Carboniferous forests, including amphibious temnospondyls called eryopids ("long-faces") that survived into the Permian period. Their long, flat skulls had numerous sharp teeth suggesting that they were aquatic hunters. Eyes and nostrils were located on the top of the head, and were the only part of their body exposed while they stalked prey.

Early reptiles, such as Hylonomus, foraged in the leaf litter for insects

CARBONIFEROUS PLANTS

A number of plant groups, including clubmosses, horsetails, and ferns, formed the swamp forests. The largest clubmosses, such as *Lepidodendron*, reached 50 m (165 ft) in height, while the biggest horsetails grew to 15 m (50 ft). Today such plants are usually a few metres high.

ERYOPS

- Group: Temnospondyli
- Family: Eryopidae
- Time: Carboniferous period (355–295 MYA)
- Size: 2 m (6½ ft) long
- Diet: Fish, amphibious tetrapods
- Habitat: Swamps and lakes

Eryops may have crawled onto the shore or onto fallen tree trunks to bask or rest

COAL FORMATION

The broken stems, branches, and leaves of Carboniferous plants would have lain in the waters. The decaying tissues built up in layers as peat. Later, this became compressed and fossilized to produce lignite and eventually, coal.

LEPOSPONDYLS AND LISSAMPHIBIANS

LEPOSPONDYLS WERE A group of tetrapods that probably included the ancestors of lissamphibians, the group that includes frogs and salamanders. They lived in a warm, humid world. Some were well-adapted for life on land, while others were aquatic. Today there are more lissamphibian than mammal species.

SNAKE-LIKE AÏSTOPODS

One of the most bizarre groups of Paleozoic tetrapods were the limbless aïstopods, eel-like animals with more than 200 vertebrae.

Snake-like body with no sign of limbs

AÏSTOPOD AORNERPETON

BOOMERANG HEAD

Diplocaulus from the Permian of Texas was one of the most unusual lepospondyls. The "boomerang" shape of the skull was formed by hornlike extensions from the back of the skull. There were several bizarre features found among nectrideans (salamander-like nepospondyls) – for example, some later species grew extremely elongated snouts.

LISSAMPHIBIAN DIVERSITY

Lissamphibians have evolved into a wide variety of forms. Frogs have dramatically reduced skeletons – they lack ribs and a tail, and have a few vertebrae. Salamanders first appeared in the Jurassic, and modern groups, such as giant salamanders, are known from the Eocene. The worm-like caecilians also originated in the Jurassic.

GIANT SALAMANDER ANDRIAS

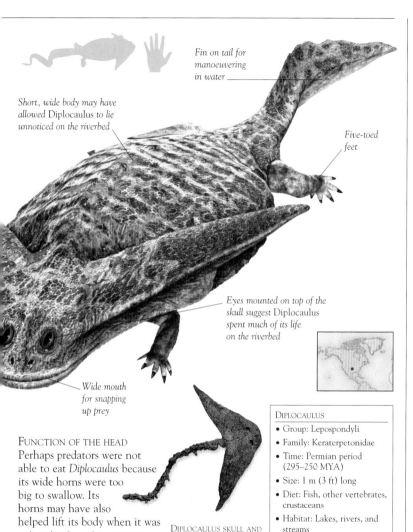

Fin on tail for manoeuvering in water

Short, wide body may have allowed Diplocaulus to lie unnoticed on the riverbed

Five-toed feet

Eyes mounted on top of the skull suggest Diplocaulus spent much of its life on the riverbed

Wide mouth for snapping up prey

FUNCTION OF THE HEAD
Perhaps predators were not able to eat *Diplocaulus* because its wide horns were too big to swallow. Its horns may have also helped lift its body when it was swimming in a river current.

DIPLOCAULUS SKULL AND VERTEBRAE

DIPLOCAULUS
- Group: Lepospondyli
- Family: Keraterpetonidae
- Time: Permian period (295–250 MYA)
- Size: 1 m (3 ft) long
- Diet: Fish, other vertebrates, crustaceans
- Habitat: Lakes, rivers, and streams

REPTILIOMORPHS

THE REPTILIOMORPHS include the amniotes – the group that includes reptiles – and the ancestors of amniotes. Although some reptiliomorphs were amphibious or aquatic, generally their skeletons became steadily better suited for carrying weight on land. Some reptiliomorphs have been found preserved in environments well away from water.

Tail was probably long and used in swimming

Barrel-shaped body

The back of the skull had large chewing muscles

Diadectes had a stout skull

Strong fingers to dig up plants

Front teeth were spoon-shaped

DIADECTES

Powerful limbs sprawled sideways

FIRST HERBIVORES

Diadectomorphs were reptile-like animals with short, strong limbs. *Diadectes* from North America and Europe is the best known of the diadectomorphs. Their teeth show that they were the first land vertebrates to evolve plant-eating habits.

BIZARRE AQUATIC PREDATOR
Crassigyrinus from the Early Carboniferous of Scotland is regarded by some as a reptiliomorph. It was about 2 m (6 ft) long, with a massive head and tiny limbs. Several of its features were very primitive, perhaps because of its specialization as an aquatic predator.

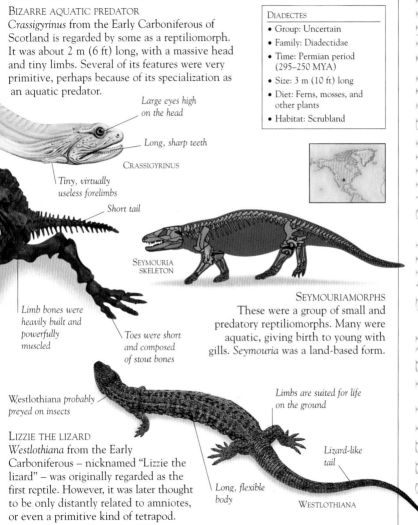

DIADECTES
- Group: Uncertain
- Family: Diadectidae
- Time: Permian period (295–250 MYA)
- Size: 3 m (10 ft) long
- Diet: Ferns, mosses, and other plants
- Habitat: Scrubland

Large eyes high on the head

Long, sharp teeth

CRASSIGYRINUS

Tiny, virtually useless forelimbs

Short tail

SEYMOURIA SKELETON

SEYMOURIAMORPHS
These were a group of small and predatory reptiliomorphs. Many were aquatic, giving birth to young with gills. *Seymouria* was a land-based form.

Limb bones were heavily built and powerfully muscled

Toes were short and composed of stout bones

Westlothiana probably preyed on insects

Limbs are suited for life on the ground

LIZZIE THE LIZARD
Westlothiana from the Early Carboniferous – nicknamed "Lizzie the lizard" – was originally regarded as the first reptile. However, it was later thought to be only distantly related to amniotes, or even a primitive kind of tetrapod.

Lizard-like tail

Long, flexible body

WESTLOTHIANA

INTRODUCING AMNIOTES

THE AMNIOTES WERE animals that dominated life on land in the Late Carboniferous. They were the first creatures to protect their unborn babies in an amniotic egg, which survived on land. Amniotes comprise two groups: synapsids (mammals and their relatives) and reptiles. Many later did away with the eggshell and retained their embryos inside the body.

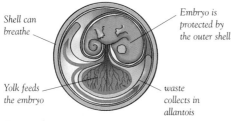

Shell can breathe

Embryo is protected by the outer shell

Yolk feeds the embryo

waste collects in allantois

AMNIOTE EGGS
Amniotic eggs have a shell that can let gases in and out. It protects the embryo from drying out on land. The embryo is fed by the yolk, and a sac called the allantois stores waste.

SKULL OF PALEOTHYRIS

EARLY FOSSIL AMNIOTES
Certain skeletal features unique to synapsids and reptiles, such as their teeth, allow scientists to recognize early fossil amniotes without direct proof that they laid amniotic eggs.

The rotten tree stumps that trapped Hylonomus mostly belonged to Sigillaria, a giant clubmoss

Hylonomus was attracted by millipedes and other insects that fell into the hollow

Trapped at the bottom of the hollow tree stump, Hylonomus died of starvation

Hylonomus *and other
early reptiles had jaws
with muscles that were
more powerful than
earlier tetrapods*

*Stout skull
and sharp
pointed teeth*

*Repeated floods left mud
deposits at the base of a
tree. The sediments built up
and were later compressed
into rock.*

HYLONOMUS

- Group: Captorhinomorpha
- Family: Protorothyrididae
- Time: Carboniferous period
  (355–295 MYA)
- Size: 20 cm (⅔ ft) long
- Diet: Millipedes and other
  arthropods
- Habitat: Tropical forest floors

LIFE AND DEATH
OF HYLONOMUS
The early reptile *Hylonomus*
("forest mouse") comes from a
famous fossil site called Joggins
in Nova Scotia, Canada. Here
specimens were preserved with
full skeletons including the
smallest bones. This remarkable
preservation occurred because
the remains were fossilized
inside forest-floor traps formed
from rotten tree stumps.

REPTILES CLADOGRAM

REPTILES DOMINATED Earth during the Palaeozoic and Mesozoic. First to appear were parareptiles, the ancestors of turtles, followed by the earliest reptiles that were tiny insectivores. Diapsids, including lizards and snakes, evolved late in the Carboniferous. The late Permian saw the rise of the archosaurs: dinosaurs, birds, pterosaurs, and crocodiles.

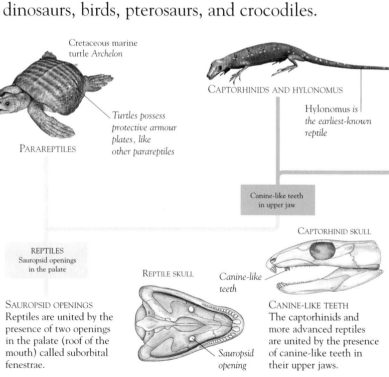

Cretaceous marine turtle *Archelon*

CAPTORHINIDS AND HYLONOMUS

Hylonomus is the earliest-known reptile

Turtles possess protective armour plates, like other parareptiles

PARAREPTILES

Canine-like teeth in upper jaw

CAPTORHINID SKULL

REPTILES
Sauropsid openings in the palate

REPTILE SKULL

Canine-like teeth

SAUROPSID OPENINGS
Reptiles are united by the presence of two openings in the palate (roof of the mouth) called suborbital fenestrae.

Sauropsid opening

CANINE-LIKE TEETH
The captorhinids and more advanced reptiles are united by the presence of canine-like teeth in their upper jaws.

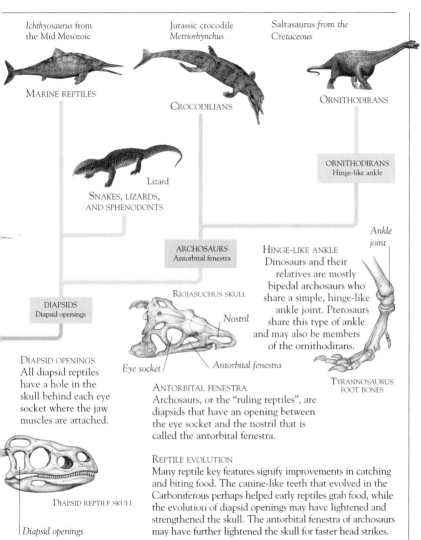

Ichthyosaurus from the Mid Mesozoic

MARINE REPTILES

Jurassic crocodile *Metriorhynchus*

CROCODILIANS

Saltasaurus *from the Cretaceous*

ORNITHODIRANS

Lizard

SNAKES, LIZARDS, AND SPHENODONTS

ORNITHODIRANS
Hinge-like ankle

Ankle joint

ARCHOSAURS
Antorbital fenestra

RIOJASUCHUS SKULL

Nostril

DIAPSIDS
Diapsid openings

HINGE-LIKE ANKLE
Dinosaurs and their relatives are mostly bipedal archosaurs who share a simple, hinge-like ankle joint. Pterosaurs share this type of ankle and may also be members of the ornithodirans.

Eye socket

Antorbital fenestra

TYRANNOSAURUS
FOOT BONES

DIAPSID OPENINGS
All diapsid reptiles have a hole in the skull behind each eye socket where the jaw muscles are attached.

ANTORBITAL FENESTRA
Archosaurs, or the "ruling reptiles", are diapsids that have an opening between the eye socket and the nostril that is called the antorbital fenestra.

DIAPSID REPTILE SKULL

Diapsid openings

REPTILE EVOLUTION
Many reptile key features signify improvements in catching and biting food. The canine-like teeth that evolved in the Carboniferous perhaps helped early reptiles grab food, while the evolution of diapsid openings may have lightened and strengthened the skull. The antorbital fenestra of archosaurs may have further lightened the skull for faster head strikes.

PARAREPTILES

THIS GROUP OF unusual reptiles includes small lizard-like forms as well as larger animals. Unlike most reptiles, many parareptiles lack holes, called fenestrae, at the back of their skulls. Many parareptiles appear to have been herbivorous, while others probably ate insects and other arthropods.

Conical defensive spikes covering back

PROCOLOPHONIDS

The procolophonids were parareptiles that lived worldwide from the Late Permian to the Late Triassic. They were shaped like chunky lizards, with broad-cheeked skulls and backward-pointing spikes on their cheeks.

Short tail

Large eyes suggest good vision

Strong limbs perhaps used for digging

FRAGMENTED PROCOLOPHON FOSSIL

SCUTOSAURUS

Robust, rounded body

Skull surface covered in bumps

ARMOURED SKULL
Elginia was a Late Permian parareptile that had a pair of long horns and a head covered in spikes.

Short legs and toes suggest that Procolophon *was not a fast runner*

ELGINIA SKULL

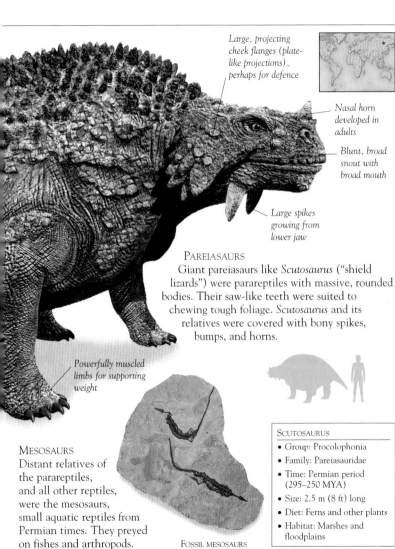

Large, projecting cheek flanges (plate-like projections), perhaps for defence

Nasal horn developed in adults

Blunt, broad snout with broad mouth

Large spikes growing from lower jaw

PAREIASAURS

Giant pareiasaurs like *Scutosaurus* ("shield lizards") were parareptiles with massive, rounded bodies. Their saw-like teeth were suited to chewing tough foliage. *Scutosaurus* and its relatives were covered with bony spikes, bumps, and horns.

Powerfully muscled limbs for supporting weight

MESOSAURS

Distant relatives of the parareptiles, and all other reptiles, were the mesosaurs, small aquatic reptiles from Permian times. They preyed on fishes and arthropods.

FOSSIL MESOSAURS

SCUTOSAURUS
- Group: Procolophonia
- Family: Pareiasauridae
- Time: Permian period (295–250 MYA)
- Size: 2.5 m (8 ft) long
- Diet: Ferns and other plants
- Habitat: Marshes and floodplains

TURTLES

TURTLES, OR CHELONIANS, are unique
reptiles that first appeared in the Triassic
as small amphibious omnivores (eaters of a
varied diet, including plants and animals).
During the Mesozoic, they diverged into land-
dwelling herbivores, freshwater omnivores and
predators, and giant, fully marine creatures
with a diet of sponges and jellyfish. Today
they flourish as more than 250 species.

*The largest
meiolaniids had
skulls more than
30 cm (12 in)
wide*

MEIOLANIID
SKULL

*Large side
horns, perhaps
used in fighting*

*Nostrils high
up on the
snout*

HORNED LAND TURTLES
The meiolaniids were a group
of giant land turtles that lived
from the Cretaceous to the
recent past. Large horns on their
skulls meant that they could not
pull their heads into their shells.

MARINE GIANT
Seagoing turtles first evolved in the Early
Cretaceous, and are just one of many groups
that developed into giant forms. *Archelon*,
among the biggest of all, reached nearly
4 m (13 ft) long – twice the length of a large
modern marine turtle. Turtles never grew much
larger than this because they still needed to
come ashore and lay eggs, and this meant they
had to be able to support their weight on land.

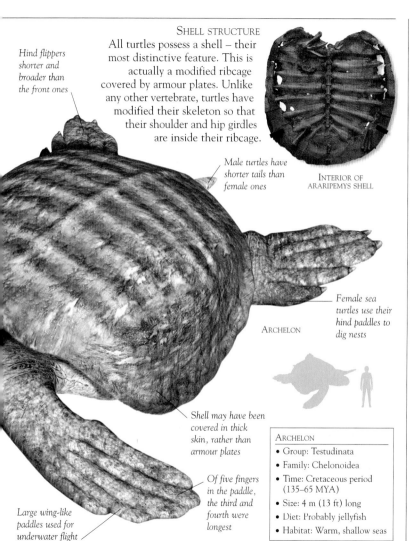

Hind flippers shorter and broader than the front ones

SHELL STRUCTURE

All turtles possess a shell – their most distinctive feature. This is actually a modified ribcage covered by armour plates. Unlike any other vertebrate, turtles have modified their skeleton so that their shoulder and hip girdles are inside their ribcage.

Male turtles have shorter tails than female ones

INTERIOR OF ARARIPEMYS SHELL

Female sea turtles use their hind paddles to dig nests

ARCHELON

Shell may have been covered in thick skin, rather than armour plates

Of five fingers in the paddle, the third and fourth were longest

Large wing-like paddles used for underwater flight

ARCHELON
• Group: Testudinata
• Family: Chelonoidea
• Time: Cretaceous period (135–65 MYA)
• Size: 4 m (13 ft) long
• Diet: Probably jellyfish
• Habitat: Warm, shallow seas

DIVERSIFYING DIAPSIDS

Late in the Permian, the
diapsids – the reptilian group
that includes lizards, archosaurs,
and marine ichthyosaurs and
plesiosaurs – underwent a burst
of evolution. Evolving from small
insect-eating ancestors of the
Carboniferous, the diapsids soon
produced gliders, swimmers, and
diggers. Many of the new diapsids were
grouped together as the neodiapsids.

*Each wing was
supported by
22 curving,
rod-like bones*

*Serrated
crest*

*The back of the skull resembles
that of lizards, which once led
experts to think that lizards
descended from younginiforms*

Long, narrow snout

YOUNGINA
SKULL

*Sharp, conical teeth
for catching insects*

COELUROSAURAVUS
- Group: Diapsida
- Family: Coelurosauravidae
- Time: Permian period
  (295–250 MYA)
- Size: 60 cm (2 ft) long
- Diet: Insects
- Habitat: Open forest

YOUNGINA AND RELATIVES
The younginiforms were among the most primitive
neodiapsids. They were agile Permian reptiles with
short necks and large holes at the back of the skull.
Some were aquatic, but most were land dwellers.

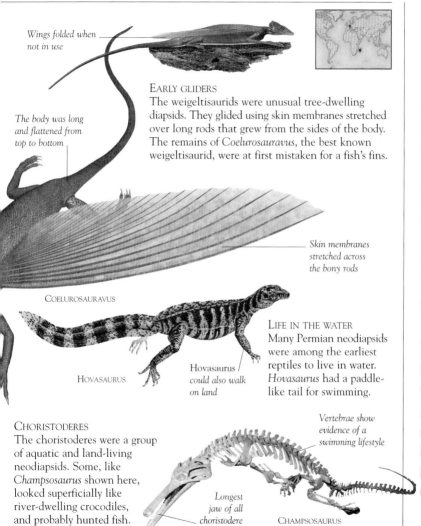

Wings folded when not in use

The body was long and flattened from top to bottom

EARLY GLIDERS

The weigeltisaurids were unusual tree-dwelling diapsids. They glided using skin membranes stretched over long rods that grew from the sides of the body. The remains of *Coelurosauravus*, the best known weigeltisaurid, were at first mistaken for a fish's fins.

Skin membranes stretched across the bony rods

COELUROSAURAVUS

HOVASAURUS

Hovasaurus could also walk on land

LIFE IN THE WATER

Many Permian neodiapsids were among the earliest reptiles to live in water. *Hovasaurus* had a paddle-like tail for swimming.

CHORISTODERES

The choristoderes were a group of aquatic and land-living neodiapsids. Some, like *Champsosaurus* shown here, looked superficially like river-dwelling crocodiles, and probably hunted fish.

Vertebrae show evidence of a swimming lifestyle

Longest jaw of all choristodere

CHAMPSOSAURUS

MOSASAURS

SEA LIZARDS called mosasaurs ruled the continental seas of the Cretaceous. These creatures grew to more than 15 m (49 ft) long and were among the most awesome marine predators of all time. With their strong jaws, mosasaurs preyed on fishes, turtles, and plesiosaurs.

Deep but narrow tail like a living sea snake's

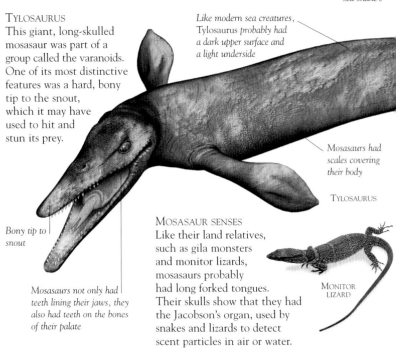

TYLOSAURUS
This giant, long-skulled mosasaur was part of a group called the varanoids. One of its most distinctive features was a hard, bony tip to the snout, which it may have used to hit and stun its prey.

Like modern sea creatures, Tylosaurus probably had a dark upper surface and a light underside

Mosasaurs had scales covering their body

TYLOSAURUS

Bony tip to snout

Mosasaurs not only had teeth lining their jaws, they also had teeth on the bones of their palate

MOSASAUR SENSES
Like their land relatives, such as gila monsters and monitor lizards, mosasaurs probably had long forked tongues. Their skulls show that they had the Jacobson's organ, used by snakes and lizards to detect scent particles in air or water.

MONITOR LIZARD

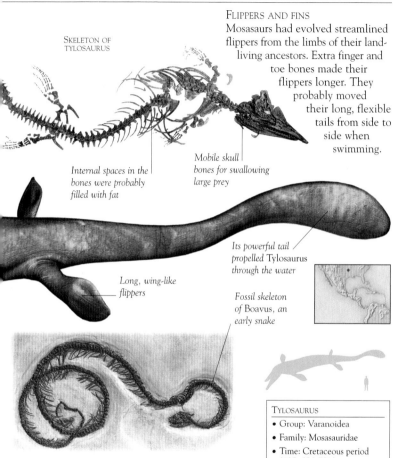

SKELETON OF
TYLOSAURUS

FLIPPERS AND FINS
Mosasaurs had evolved streamlined flippers from the limbs of their land-living ancestors. Extra finger and toe bones made their flippers longer. They probably moved their long, flexible tails from side to side when swimming.

Internal spaces in the bones were probably filled with fat

Mobile skull bones for swallowing large prey

Its powerful tail propelled Tylosaurus through the water

Long, wing-like flippers

Fossil skeleton of Boavus, an early snake

MOSASAURS AND SNAKES
Some experts argue that snakes and early mosasaurs both had the same swimming ancestor. Other experts argue that snakes are not related to mosasaurs and that the similarities are superficial.

TYLOSAURUS
- Group: Varanoidea
- Family: Mosasauridae
- Time: Cretaceous period (135–65 MYA)
- Size: 11 m (36 ft) long
- Diet: Turtles, fish, and other mosasaurs
- Habitat: Shallow seas

PLACODONTS AND NOTHOSAURS

THESE TWO GROUPS of creatures were marine reptiles. They were related to plesiosaurs and formed part of a larger group called the sauropterygia. Placodonts and nothosaurs were largely restricted to the warm, shallow seas of Triassic Europe, northern Africa, and Asia and most were about 1 m (3 ft) long.

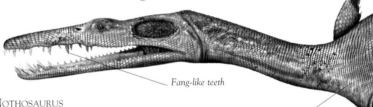

Fang-like teeth

NOTHOSAURUS

Nothosaurs were amphibious predators. The best known of them is *Nothosaurus*, of which eight species have been found in Europe and the Middle East. In the Early Triassic *Nothosaurus* lived in a shallow sea over what is now Israel.

Shoulder and chest bones formed large, flattened plates

NOTHOSAURUS

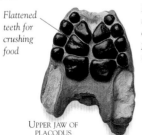

Flattened teeth for crushing food

Peg-like teeth stuck out of the front of the jaws

SHELLFISH DIET

Some placodonts, such as *Placodus*, had peg-like teeth, which they probably used to pluck shellfish from the sea floor.

The lower jaw teeth were wide and rounded

UPPER JAW OF PLACODUS

LOWER JAW OF PLACODUS

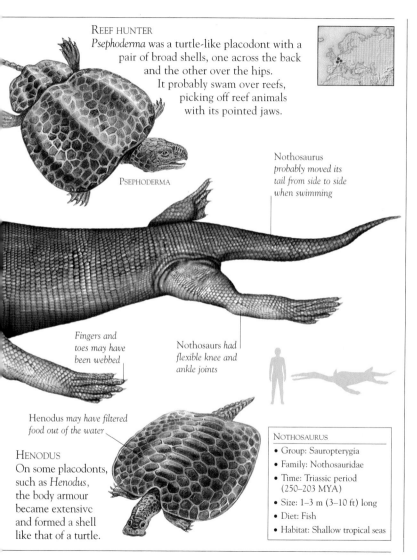

REEF HUNTER
Psephoderma was a turtle-like placodont with a pair of broad shells, one across the back and the other over the hips. It probably swam over reefs, picking off reef animals with its pointed jaws.

PSEPHODERMA

Nothosaurus
probably moved its
tail from side to side
when swimming

Fingers and
toes may have
been webbed

Nothosaurs had
flexible knee and
ankle joints

Henodus may have filtered
food out of the water

HENODUS
On some placodonts, such as *Henodus*, the body armour became extensive and formed a shell like that of a turtle.

NOTHOSAURUS

- Group: Sauropterygia
- Family: Nothosauridae
- Time: Triassic period (250–203 MYA)
- Size: 1–3 m (3–10 ft) long
- Diet: Fish
- Habitat: Shallow tropical seas

SHORT-NECKED PLESIOSAURS

PLESIOSAURS WERE MARINE REPTILES that belonged to the sauropterygia group. All plesiosaurs had four wing-like flippers, which they probably used to "fly" underwater in a similar way to marine turtles or penguins. While many plesiosaurs had long necks and small skulls, others, the pliosaurs, were short-necked and had enormous skulls.

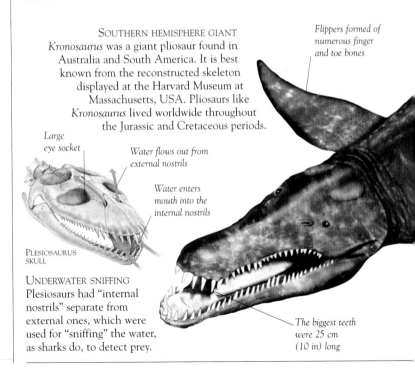

SOUTHERN HEMISPHERE GIANT
Kronosaurus was a giant pliosaur found in Australia and South America. It is best known from the reconstructed skeleton displayed at the Harvard Museum at Massachusetts, USA. Pliosaurs like *Kronosaurus* lived worldwide throughout the Jurassic and Cretaceous periods.

Flippers formed of numerous finger and toe bones

Large eye socket

Water flows out from external nostrils

Water enters mouth into the internal nostrils

PLESIOSAURUS SKULL

UNDERWATER SNIFFING
Plesiosaurs had "internal nostrils" separate from external ones, which were used for "sniffing" the water, as sharks do, to detect prey.

The biggest teeth were 25 cm (10 in) long

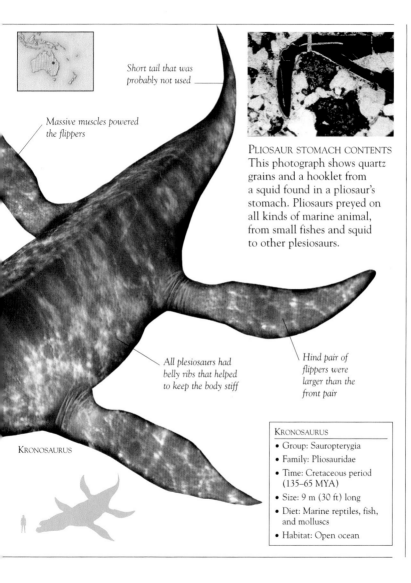

Short tail that was probably not used

Massive muscles powered the flippers

PLIOSAUR STOMACH CONTENTS
This photograph shows quartz grains and a hooklet from a squid found in a pliosaur's stomach. Pliosaurs preyed on all kinds of marine animal, from small fishes and squid to other plesiosaurs.

All plesiosaurs had belly ribs that helped to keep the body stiff

Hind pair of flippers were larger than the front pair

KRONOSAURUS

KRONOSAURUS
- Group: Sauropterygia
- Family: Pliosauridae
- Time: Cretaceous period (135–65 MYA)
- Size: 9 m (30 ft) long
- Diet: Marine reptiles, fish, and molluscs
- Habitat: Open ocean

LONG-NECKED PLESIOSAURS

WHILE SOME PLESIOSAURS were large-headed predators, others had small skulls and very long necks. One group of plesiosaurs, the elasmosaurs, had necks of up to 5 m (16 ft) long. Most long-necked plesiosaurs fed on fishes and molluscs, though some may have eaten sea-floor invertebrates; others perhaps preyed on other marine reptiles. Both short- and long-necked plesiosaurs became extinct at the very end of the Cretaceous.

LONG NECKS
Elasmosaurus had 72 vertebrae in its neck, more than any other plesiosaur, or indeed any other animal. Studies suggest that its neck was fairly flexible, but experts are still unsure about the way it was used.

Light skull with interlocking teeth

PLATE LIZARD

Elasmosaurus was a Late Cretaceous
representative of the elasmosaurs, a group
of long-necked plesiosaurs that originated
in the Jurassic. Its name means "plate lizard"
and comes from the plate-like shoulder
bones that covered its chest and formed its
arm sockets. The huge muscles that powered
its flippers were anchored to these bones.

ELASMOSAURUS

- Group: Plesiosauria
- Family: Elasmosauridae
- Time: Cretaceous period
  (135–65 MYA)
- Size: 14 m (46 ft) long
- Diet: Fish and swimming
  molluscs
- Habitat: Shallow seas

Flippers with
pointed tips

ICHTHYOSAURS

THESE MESOZOIC MARINE REPTILES resemble sharks or dolphins. Fossils preserved with impressions of skin show that ichthyosaurs such as *Ichthyosaurus* had a triangular dorsal fin and a forked, vertical tail like a shark's. While smaller ichthyosaurs were about 1 m (3 ft) long, giant ichthyosaurs grew to over 20 m (65 ft), making them the largest marine reptiles ever.

SHARK-SHAPED REPTILE
Many fossils of *Ichthyosaurus*, the best known ichthyosaur, have been found in Jurassic rocks in England and Germany.

Small, pointed teeth

Nostril was positioned close to the eye

ICHTHYOSAURUS

Long, slim jaws

This ichthyosaur fossil is preserved with the babies

BIRTH AND BABIES
Some ichthyosaurs have been found with the bones of babies preserved in their abdominal region. At first, experts thought that these babies were stomach contents.

FOSSIL OF PREGNANT STENOPTERYGIUS

HOW DID ICHTHYOSAURS SWIM?
Ichthyosaurs probably used their forked
tails to propel themselves through the
water. They flapped their powerful
shoulders and wing-shaped flippers
and "flew" underwater.

FOSSIL OF
STENOPTERYGIUS

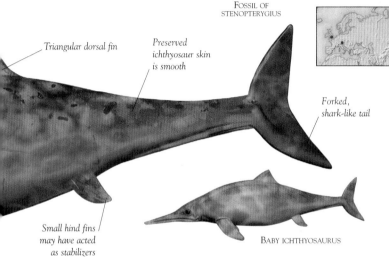

Triangular dorsal fin

_Preserved
ichthyosaur skin
is smooth_

_Forked,
shark-like tail_

_Small hind fins
may have acted
as stabilizers_

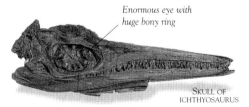

BABY ICHTHYOSAURUS

_Enormous eye with
huge bony ring_

SKULL OF
ICHTHYOSAURUS

BIG EYES AND DEEP DIVING
Ichthyosaurs had huge eye sockets filled by a ring of
bones, which supported the massive eyeball. Their
large eyes suggest that ichthyosaurs may have been
able to hunt prey at night or in deep, murky waters.

ICHTHYOSAURUS
- Group: Ichthyopterygia
- Family: Ichthyosauridae
- Time: Jurassic period
  (203–135 MYA)
- Size: 3 m (10 ft) long
- Diet: Fish and squid
- Habitat: Open ocean

EARLY RULING REPTILE GROUPS

ARCHOSAURS – THE GROUP OF animals that includes crocodiles, dinosaurs, and birds – belong to a larger group called the archosauromorphs or "ruling reptile forms". Out of the many archosauromorph groups evolved the lizard-like meat-eating prolacertiforms, and the plant-eating trilophosaurs and rhynchosaurs.

GIRAFFE-NECKED FISHER
The Triassic reptile *Tanystropheus* had a neck twice as long as its body. Most of its fossils are found in marine rocks, so it may have swam or caught fish at the water's edge.

Lizard-like body shape

Tanystropheus had long legs

Toes may have been webbed for swimming

All trilophosaurs were less than 1m (3 ft) in length

TRILOPHOSAURS
This was an archosauromorph with a robust skull and beak-like snout tip. It had broad teeth for slicing and chewing tough plants.

Long limbs suited to running and digging

SKELETON OF TRILOPHOSAURUS

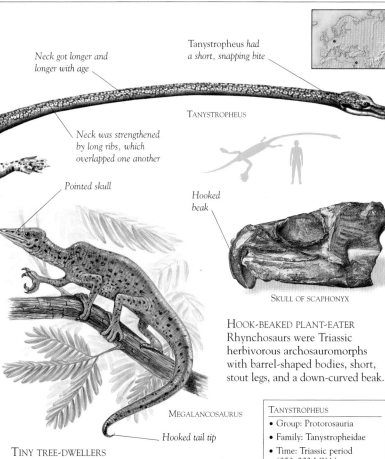

Neck got longer and longer with age

Tanystropheus *had a short, snapping bite*

TANYSTROPHEUS

Neck was strengthened by long ribs, which overlapped one another

Pointed skull

Hooked beak

SKULL OF SCAPHONYX

HOOK-BEAKED PLANT-EATER
Rhynchosaurs were Triassic herbivorous archosauromorphs with barrel-shaped bodies, short, stout legs, and a down-curved beak.

MEGALANCOSAURUS

Hooked tail tip

TINY TREE-DWELLERS
A group of prolacertiforms, the megalancosaurs, probably lived in the trees. They were small – less than 30 cm (1 ft) long – and resembled living chameleons. Their small, pointed teeth suggest that these reptiles ate insects.

TANYSTROPHEUS
- Group: Protorosauria
- Family: Tanystropheidae
- Time: Triassic period (250–203 MYA)
- Size: 3 m (10 ft) long
- Diet: Fish and crustaceans
- Habitat: Shallow seas and shorelines

CROCODILE-GROUP REPTILES

ARCHOSAURS – CROCODILES, PTEROSAURS, dinosaurs, and their relatives – diversified into many groups during the Triassic. Early on, archosaurs split into two groups, both of which have living members today. Ornithodirans included pterosaurs, dinosaurs, and birds. Crocodylotarsians included numerous extinct groups and crocodiles.

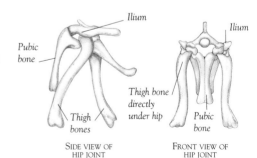

Long, slender tail

Powerful leg bones suggest that Prestosuchus could run at high speeds

DEEP-SKULLED GIANTS
Many crocodile-group reptiles were land-living predators, called rauisuchians. Some were huge, reaching lengths of up to 10 m (33 ft). *Prestosuchus* was from Triassic Brazil. Similar rauisuchians lived in Europe, Argentina, and elsewhere.

HOW RAUISUCHIANS WALKED
Rauisuchians had a stance that was similar to that of the dinosaurs, with their legs held beneath the body. The flexibility of the backbone shows that they ran with a bounding gait.

Ilium

Ilium

Pubic bone

Thigh bone directly under hip

Thigh bones

Pubic bone

SIDE VIEW OF HIP JOINT

FRONT VIEW OF HIP JOINT

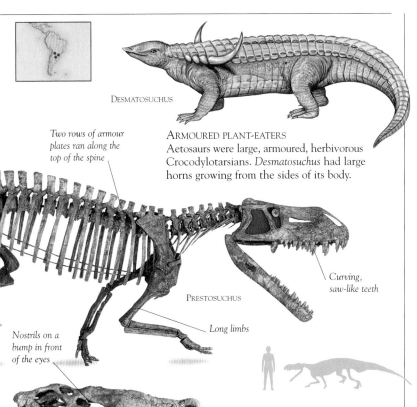

DESMATOSUCHUS

Two rows of armour plates ran along the top of the spine

ARMOURED PLANT-EATERS
Aetosaurs were large, armoured, herbivorous Crocodylotarsians. *Desmatosuchus* had large horns growing from the sides of its body.

PRESTOSUCHUS

Curving, saw-like teeth

Long limbs

Nostrils on a bump in front of the eyes

ANCIENT CROCODILES
Phytosaurs such as *Machaeroprosopus* were primitive, amphibious crocodilians of the Late Triassic that had evolved long before crocodiles.

Long, powerful jaws with sharp, pointed teeth

PRESTOSUCHUS
- Group: Rauisuchia
- Family: Rauisuchidae
- Time: Triassic period (250–203 MYA)
- Size: 5 m (16 ft) long
- Diet: Large vertebrates
- Habitat: Scrubland, open woodland

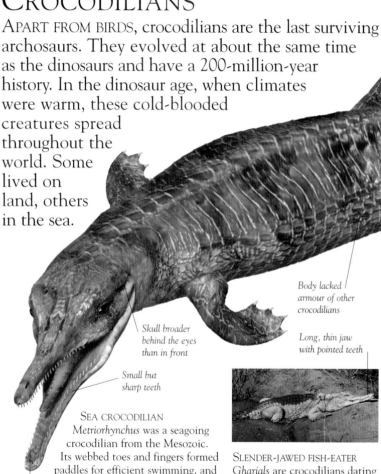

CROCODILIANS

APART FROM BIRDS, crocodilians are the last surviving archosaurs. They evolved at about the same time as the dinosaurs and have a 200-million-year history. In the dinosaur age, when climates were warm, these cold-blooded creatures spread throughout the world. Some lived on land, others in the sea.

Body lacked armour of other crocodilians

Skull broader behind the eyes than in front

Long, thin jaw with pointed teeth

Small but sharp teeth

SEA CROCODILIAN
Metriorhynchus was a seagoing crocodilian from the Mesozoic. Its webbed toes and fingers formed paddles for efficient swimming, and its jaws bristled with razor-sharp teeth for seizing fishes and squid.

Slender jaws

SLENDER-JAWED FISH-EATER
Gharials are crocodilians dating back 50 million years. They are now only found in India.

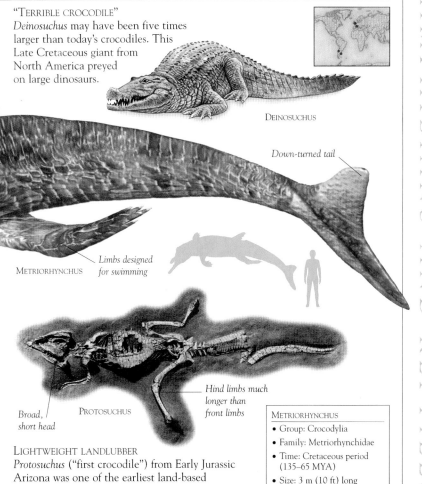

"TERRIBLE CROCODILE"

Deinosuchus may have been five times larger than today's crocodiles. This Late Cretaceous giant from North America preyed on large dinosaurs.

DEINOSUCHUS

Down-turned tail

METRIORHYNCHUS

Limbs designed for swimming

Broad, short head

PROTOSUCHUS

Hind limbs much longer than front limbs

LIGHTWEIGHT LANDLUBBER

Protosuchus ("first crocodile") from Early Jurassic Arizona was one of the earliest land-based crocodilians. About 1 m (3 ft) in length, this agile hunter could run semi-upright on its long hind legs, and was able to catch speedy lizards and mammals.

METRIORHYNCHUS
- Group: Crocodylia
- Family: Metriorhynchidae
- Time: Cretaceous period (135–65 MYA)
- Size: 3 m (10 ft) long
- Diet: Fish
- Habitat: Seas

EARLY PTEROSAURS

PTEROSAURS WERE flying archosaurs that may have been closely related to dinosaurs. A pterosaur's wings were made of skin that stretched from the end of its incredibly long fourth finger to its body and back legs. Fossils show that some pterosaurs had furry bodies and may have been warm-blooded. Early pterosaurs were small compared to later types, with a wingspan of up to 3 m (10 ft).

Fossil skeleton of Dimorphodon

PRIMITIVE PTEROSAURS
Dimorphodon was an Early Jurassic pterosaur, notable for its huge skull and large, pointed teeth at the front of its jaw.

EXCELLENT FLIERS
Pterosaurs had large eyes with excellent vision. The parts of the brain responsible for sight and control of movement were well developed and similar to those of modern birds.

Short wrist bones of early pterosaurs

INSECT CATCHERS
ANUROGNATHUS
Anurognathids had short, high skulls, sharply pointed teeth and long, slim wings. These features suggest that they were fast-flying predators that fed on insects.

ANUROGNATHUS

- Group: Pterosauria
- Family: Rhamphorhynchoidea
- Time: Jurassic period (203–135 MYA)
- Size: Wingspan 50 cm (1½ ft)
- Diet: Insects, possibly lacewings
- Habitat: Seashores, riverside, and woodland

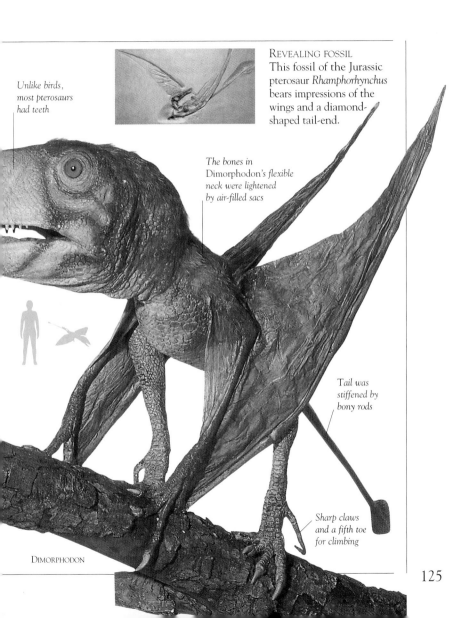

Unlike birds, most pterosaurs had teeth

REVEALING FOSSIL
This fossil of the Jurassic pterosaur *Rhamphorhynchus* bears impressions of the wings and a diamond-shaped tail-end.

The bones in Dimorphodon's *flexible neck were lightened by air-filled sacs*

Tail was stiffened by bony rods

Sharp claws and a fifth toe for climbing

DIMORPHODON

DIMORPHODON

THE MOST STRIKING feature of *Dimorphodon* ("two-form tooth") was its enormous puffin-like head. It had a short neck, and a long tail that ended in a diamond shape. The tail could only be moved near the base, helping to steer the animal. *Dimorphodon* had two types of teeth – long front ones and small cheek teeth. It may have been a clumsy walker.

Leathery wings

Large, toothed beak

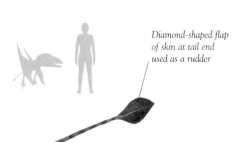

Diamond-shaped flap of skin at tail end used as a rudder

DIMORPHODON
• Group: Rhamphorhynchoidea
• Family: Dimorphodontidae
• Time: Jurassic period (203–135 MYA)
• Size: 1.4 m (4 ft) long
• Diet: Small animals and fish
• Habitat: Shores, river banks

OPPORTUNISTIC HUNTER

Remains of *Dimorphodon* and related pterosaurs have been found in former sea and riverside areas, so they may have lived in a variety of habitats. This group probably preyed on small animals, such as insects, lizards and other small reptiles, fishes, and crustaceans. Experts do not know whether they caught their prey on the wing, or while standing on all fours. It is possible that *Dimorphodon* spent most of its time on cliffs or branches, from which it launched itself into flight.

127

ADVANCED PTEROSAURS

PTERODACTYLOIDS WERE advanced pterosaurs that came to rule the Cretaceous skies. However, by the end of this period, only one or two species survived. Pterosaurs may have died out as newly evolving waterbirds took over their habitats.

WINGS AND NO TEETH
Pteranodon, meaning "wings and no teeth", is one of the most famous pterosaurs that inhabited North America. It had a large head crest and the shape of its lower jaw suggests that it had a pouch under its bill like a pelican's.

Long, backward-pointing crest

MALES AND FEMALES
Different specimens of *Pteranodon* have differently shaped head crests. Some have a large, very prominent crest – others a small crest. These two kinds have been found together, so it seems that they are males and females of the same species. The males are probably the ones with the bigger crests, which they used to attract females.

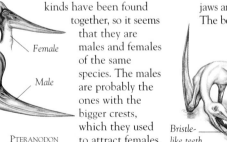

Female

Male

PTERANODON
STERNBERGI

PTERODAUSTRO
Some pterodactyloids had long jaws and hundreds of slim teeth. The best example is *Pterodaustro* from South America. Its lower jaws were filled with about 1,000 bristle-like teeth through which it strained out plankton from the water.

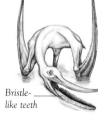

Bristle-like teeth

128

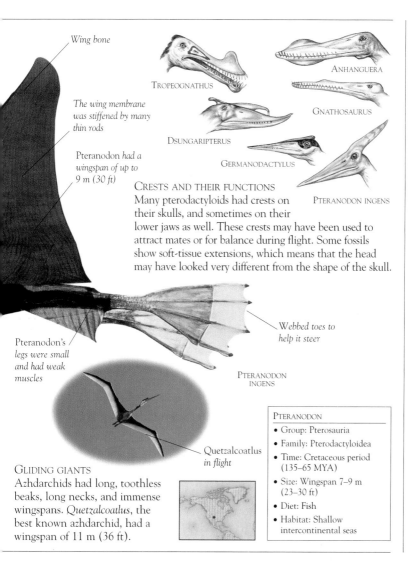

Wing bone

TROPEOGNATHUS

ANHANGUERA

GNATHOSAURUS

The wing membrane was stiffened by many thin rods

DSUNGARIPTERUS

GERMANODACTYLUS

Pteranodon had a wingspan of up to 9 m (30 ft)

CRESTS AND THEIR FUNCTIONS

PTERANODON INGENS

Many pterodactyloids had crests on their skulls, and sometimes on their lower jaws as well. These crests may have been used to attract mates or for balance during flight. Some fossils show soft-tissue extensions, which means that the head may have looked very different from the shape of the skull.

Webbed toes to help it steer

Pteranodon's legs were small and had weak muscles

PTERANODON INGENS

PTERANODON

- Group: Pterosauria
- Family: Pterodactyloidea
- Time: Cretaceous period (135–65 MYA)
- Size: Wingspan 7–9 m (23–30 ft)
- Diet: Fish
- Habitat: Shallow intercontinental seas

Quetzalcoatlus in flight

GLIDING GIANTS

Azhdarchids had long, toothless beaks, long necks, and immense wingspans. *Quetzalcoatlus*, the best known azhdarchid, had a wingspan of 11 m (36 ft).

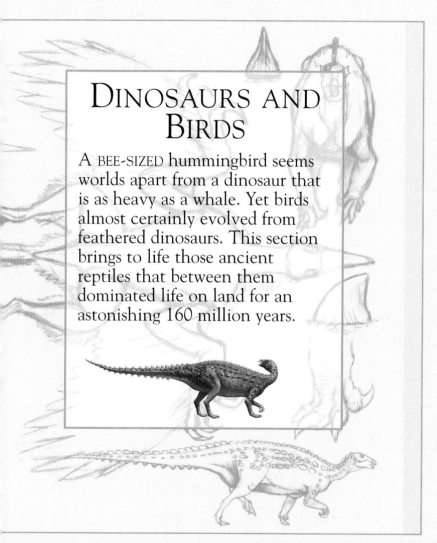

DINOSAURS AND BIRDS

A BEE-SIZED hummingbird seems worlds apart from a dinosaur that is as heavy as a whale. Yet birds almost certainly evolved from feathered dinosaurs. This section brings to life those ancient reptiles that between them dominated life on land for an astonishing 160 million years.

WHAT ARE DINOSAURS?

ABOUT 225 MILLION YEARS AGO, a new group of reptiles appeared on Earth. Like all reptiles, they had waterproof, scaly skin and young that hatched from eggs. These were the dinosaurs. For the next 160 million years they ruled the Earth, before finally becoming extinct.

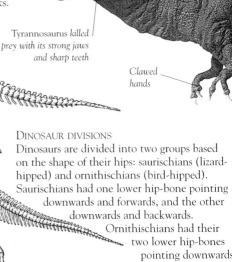

Powerful neck muscles were needed for ripping flesh from prey

LAND LEGS
Dinosaurs were land animals – they could not swim or fly. All dinosaurs had four limbs, but many, such as this *Tyrannosaurus*, walked on only their two back legs, leaving the front legs free for other tasks.

Tyrannosaurus *killed prey with its strong jaws and sharp teeth*

Clawed hands

TYRANNOSAURUS
(LIZARD-HIPPED)

DINOSAUR DIVISIONS
Dinosaurs are divided into two groups based on the shape of their hips: saurischians (lizard-hipped) and ornithischians (bird-hipped). Saurischians had one lower hip-bone pointing downwards and forwards, and the other downwards and backwards. Ornithischians had their two lower hip-bones pointing downwards and backwards.

IGUANODON
(BIRD-HIPPED)

Period	Millions of years ago	Examples of dinosaurs from each period
CRETACEOUS	135-65	Triceratops
JURASSIC	203-135	Stegosaurus
TRIASSIC	250-203	Herrerasaurus

TIME LINES
Dinosaurs lived through three periods in the Earth's history – Triassic, Jurassic, and Cretaceous. Different species of dinosaur lived and died throughout these three periods. Each species may have survived for only 2-3 million years.

Waterproof skin was covered in scales

Muscular tail balanced the front of the body

LIVING REPTILES
Modern reptiles, such as this iguana, have many features in common with dinosaurs, such as scaly skin and sharp claws. But many scientists believe that birds, rather than modern reptiles, are the closest living relatives of the dinosaurs.

Powerful legs

133

TYPES OF DINOSAUR

DINOSAUR DESIGNS were varied
and spectacular. A group of dinosaurs
called the sauropods were the largest
land animals that ever lived. The
smallest dinosaurs were chicken-
sized. Some dinosaurs had armoured
skin for protection;
others could run
fast to escape
being hunted.

DINOSAUR TERROR
Tyrannosaurus and
other fierce meat
eaters had huge,
sharp teeth with
which they killed
prey.

HERBIVORES
There were many more
herbivores (plant eaters) than
carnivores (meat eaters) in the
dinosaur world. A herbivore
called *Stegosaurus* had a sharp
beak for cropping leaves
off plants.

ONE OF THE BIGGEST
Heavier than eight elephants and more than
24 m (80 ft) long, *Barosaurus*, a sauropod, was
one of the biggest dinosaurs.

Compsognathus
reached just below
Barosaurus' *ankle*

Barosaurus' *tail
was about 13 m
(42 ft) long*

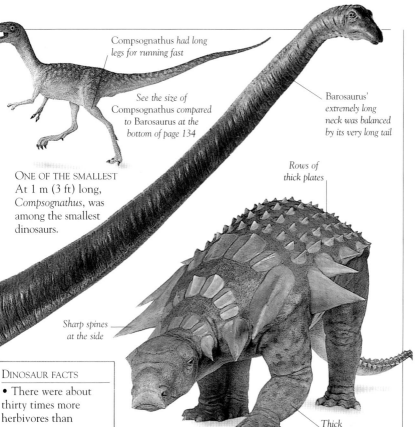

Compsognathus *had long legs for running fast*

See the size of Compsognathus *compared to Barosaurus at the bottom of page 134*

Barosaurus' *extremely long neck was balanced by its very long tail*

Rows of thick plates

ONE OF THE SMALLEST
At 1 m (3 ft) long, *Compsognathus*, was among the smallest dinosaurs.

Sharp spines at the side

DINOSAUR FACTS

• There were about thirty times more herbivores than carnivores.

• The fastest dinosaurs were the theropods, which ran on two legs.

• Dinosaurs did not fly or live in the sea.

• The sauropods were the largest dinosaurs.

Thick legs

SPIKY PROTECTION
The plant-eating, slow-moving ankylosaurs had armoured skin for protection from sharp-toothed meat eaters. *Edmontonia* had bony plates and spikes on its skin. It lived at the same time and in the same places as *Tyrannosaurus*, so it needed all the protection its armour could give.

MORE TYPES OF DINOSAUR

WE WILL NEVER KNOW how many kinds of dinosaur existed over the 160 million years of their existence. We do know that some fossils belong not to the dinosaurs but to swimming and flying relatives.

Strong plant-chewing jaws

Arms sometimes used for walking

IGUANODON

Flexible neck

Long jaws

A hooked claw on each hand

Baryonyx walked on two legs

BARYONYX

VERY COMMON
Iguanodon was a common dinosaur. In one location, between 1878-81, coal miners in Belgium dug up more than 39 *Iguanodon* skeletons.

VERY RARE
Baryonyx is one of the rarest dinosaurs known. Only one specimen of this hook-clawed meat eater has been found so far.

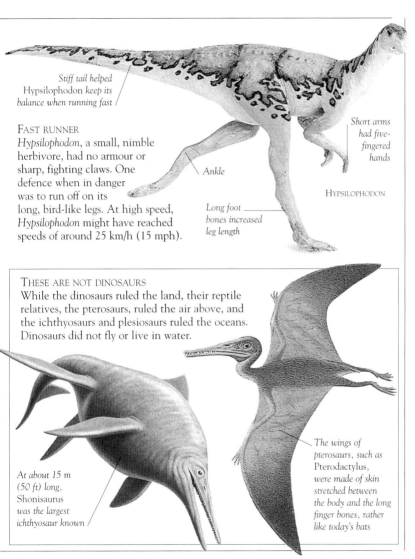

Stiff tail helped Hypsilophodon *keep its balance when running fast*

FAST RUNNER
Hypsilophodon, a small, nimble herbivore, had no armour or sharp, fighting claws. One defence when in danger was to run off on its long, bird-like legs. At high speed, Hypsilophodon might have reached speeds of around 25 km/h (15 mph).

Ankle

Short arms had five-fingered hands

HYPSILOPHODON

Long foot bones increased leg length

THESE ARE NOT DINOSAURS
While the dinosaurs ruled the land, their reptile relatives, the pterosaurs, ruled the air above, and the ichthyosaurs and plesiosaurs ruled the oceans. Dinosaurs did not fly or live in water.

At about 15 m (50 ft) long, Shonisaurus was the largest ichthyosaur known

The wings of pterosaurs, such as Pterodactylus, were made of skin stretched between the body and the long finger bones, rather like today's bats

DINOSAUR ANATOMY

THE SIZE AND SHAPE of a dinosaur's head, body, and legs help us to tell one dinosaur from another, and also tell us how the body parts were used. From the skeleton inside to the scaly skin outside, each part of a dinosaur helps build a picture of these amazing animals.

BODY POWER

The shoulder and pelvic muscles were crucial areas of power for light, fast runners as well as slow, heavy plodders. The largest dinosaurs were not always the mightiest. Some of the smallest dinosaurs were powerful runners.

BRACHIOSAURUS

Neck muscles

Pelvic muscles

Shoulder muscles

Rib-cage

Elbow joint

PROTECTIVE CAGE

Like all dinosaurs, *Brachiosaurus* had a cage, formed from vertebrae, ribs, and sheets of muscle, to protect the vital internal organs.

Thigh bone

Shin bone

Wrist joint

Toe bone

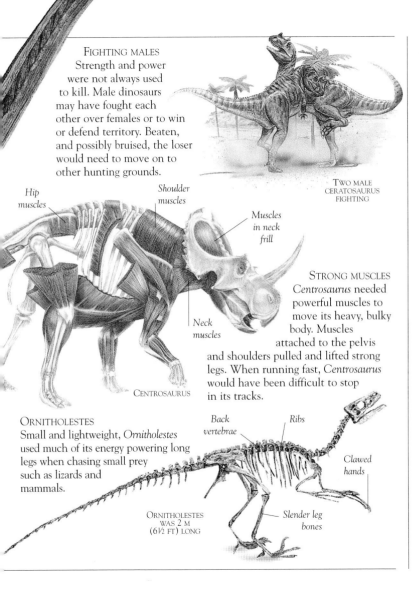

FIGHTING MALES
Strength and power were not always used to kill. Male dinosaurs may have fought each other over females or to win or defend territory. Beaten, and possibly bruised, the loser would need to move on to other hunting grounds.

TWO MALE CERATOSAURUS FIGHTING

Hip muscles

Shoulder muscles

Muscles in neck frill

Neck muscles

CENTROSAURUS

STRONG MUSCLES
Centrosaurus needed powerful muscles to move its heavy, bulky body. Muscles attached to the pelvis and shoulders pulled and lifted strong legs. When running fast, *Centrosaurus* would have been difficult to stop in its tracks.

ORNITHOLESTES
Small and lightweight, *Ornitholestes* used much of its energy powering long legs when chasing small prey such as lizards and mammals.

Back vertebrae

Ribs

Clawed hands

ORNITHOLESTES WAS 2 M (6½ FT) LONG

Slender leg bones

HEADS

CRESTS, FRILLS, and horns adorned the heads of many dinosaurs. These helped dinosaurs identify one another or were used for signalling. A dinosaur with more spectacular headgear may have won in a fight for dominance, while horns may have been used by herbivores to ward off hungry carnivores.

Large eye socket

Toothless jaws

BIRD BEAK
Gallimimus ate plants, insects, and lizards with its long, toothless beak. Its large-eyed skull looks very much like that of a big bird.

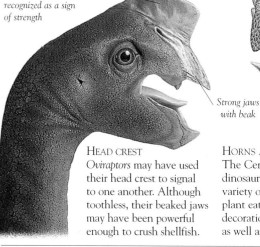

The size of the head crest may have been recognized as a sign of strength

OVIRAPTOR

Strong jaws with beak

CENTROSAURUS
HEAD

HEAD CREST
Oviraptors may have used their head crest to signal to one another. Although toothless, their beaked jaws may have been powerful enough to crush shellfish.

HORNS AND FRILLS
The Ceratopsian group of dinosaurs had heads with a variety of frills and horns. These plant eaters probably used such decorations to frighten off attackers as well as to attract a mate.

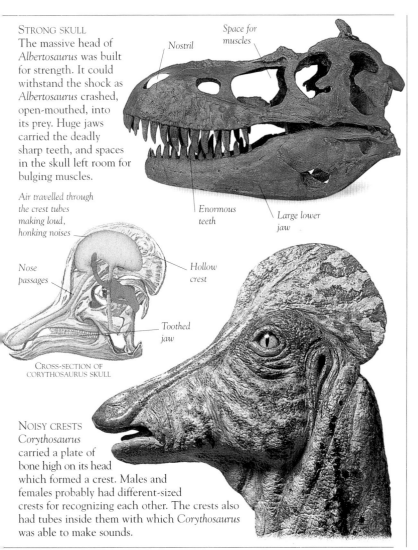

STRONG SKULL

The massive head of *Albertosaurus* was built for strength. It could withstand the shock as *Albertosaurus* crashed, open-mouthed, into its prey. Huge jaws carried the deadly sharp teeth, and spaces in the skull left room for bulging muscles.

Nostril

Space for muscles

Enormous teeth

Large lower jaw

Air travelled through the crest tubes making loud, honking noises

Nose passages

Hollow crest

Toothed jaw

CROSS-SECTION OF CORYTHOSAURUS SKULL

NOISY CRESTS

Corythosaurus carried a plate of bone high on its head which formed a crest. Males and females probably had different-sized crests for recognizing each other. The crests also had tubes inside them with which *Corythosaurus* was able to make sounds.

NECKS

FOR DINOSAURS, the neck was a vital channel between the head and body. It carried food to the stomach and air to the lungs; nerves passed on messages to and from the brain and body, and blood travelled through the arteries and veins. All of these life-lines, as well as muscles, were supported by the neck vertebrae.

BAROSAURUS
NECK VERTEBRA

LONG AND FLEXIBLE

Plant-eating, long-necked dinosaurs like *Barosaurus*, probably used their flexible necks to browse on leaves from a large area of low-lying foliage, while standing still. But if they needed to, they could have reached up to the leaves in tall trees.

Muscles were attached to spines on the vertebrae

Barosaurus' neck was 9 m (29½ ft) long

STRONG AND LIGHT

The long neck of *Diplodocus* was made up of 15 vertebrae. These bones had deep hollows inside them to make them lightweight, although they remained very strong. A notch on top of the vertebra carried a strong ligament which supported the neck in the way that wires support a suspension bridge.

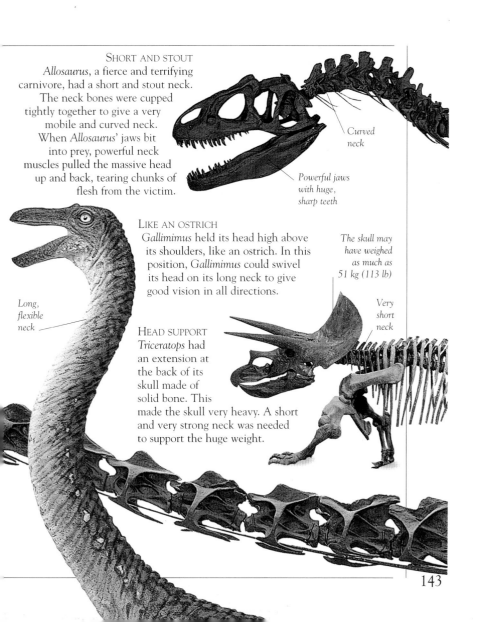

SHORT AND STOUT
Allosaurus, a fierce and terrifying
carnivore, had a short and stout neck.
The neck bones were cupped
tightly together to give a very
mobile and curved neck.
When *Allosaurus'* jaws bit
into prey, powerful neck
muscles pulled the massive head
up and back, tearing chunks of
flesh from the victim.

Curved
neck

Powerful jaws
with huge,
sharp teeth

LIKE AN OSTRICH
Gallimimus held its head high above
its shoulders, like an ostrich. In this
position, *Gallimimus* could swivel
its head on its long neck to give
good vision in all directions.

The skull may
have weighed
as much as
51 kg (113 lb)

Long,
flexible
neck

Very
short
neck

HEAD SUPPORT
Triceratops had
an extension at
the back of its
skull made of
solid bone. This
made the skull very heavy. A short
and very strong neck was needed
to support the huge weight.

DINOSAUR LIMBS

Femur
(thigh bone)

DINOSAURS HELD their legs directly beneath the body, unlike other reptiles, which crawl with their legs held out from the sides. Huge plant-eating dinosaurs, such as *Diplodocus*, walked on all fours, while most carnivores, such as *Albertosaurus*, walked on the two back legs, leaving the front limbs free for catching prey.

IGUANODON
FOOT BONE

Knee

Muscle

Ankle

Metatarsals

Toe

MYSTERIOUS DINOSAUR

Almost all that is known of *Deinocheirus* is this huge pair of arms and hands. These forelimbs are 2.4 m (8 ft) long. It is thought that Deinocheirus belonged to a group of dinosaurs called ornithomimosaurs. The huge hands would have been used to catch and hold prey.

Long, slender arms

Fingers have 26-cm (⅔ ft) claws

Three clawed fingers on each hand

FLESH AND BONE

The rear legs of *Albertosaurus* were powered by large muscles which pulled on the bones to make them move. The metatarsal foot bones worked as part of the leg, giving a longer stride.

144

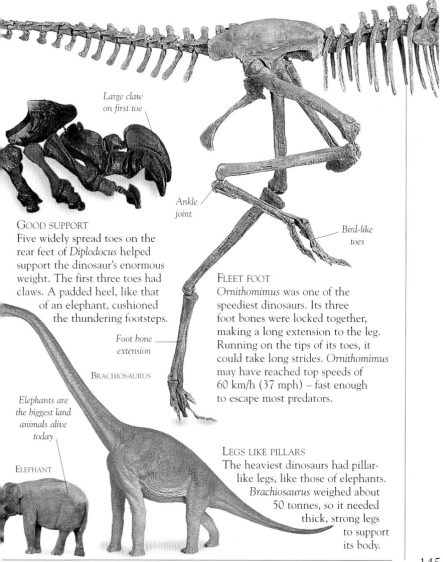

Large claw on first toe

Ankle joint

Bird-like toes

GOOD SUPPORT
Five widely spread toes on the rear feet of *Diplodocus* helped support the dinosaur's enormous weight. The first three toes had claws. A padded heel, like that of an elephant, cushioned the thundering footsteps.

Foot bone extension

BRACHIOSAURUS

Elephants are the biggest land animals alive today

ELEPHANT

FLEET FOOT
Ornithomimus was one of the speediest dinosaurs. Its three foot bones were locked together, making a long extension to the leg. Running on the tips of its toes, it could take long strides. *Ornithomimus* may have reached top speeds of 60 km/h (37 mph) – fast enough to escape most predators.

LEGS LIKE PILLARS
The heaviest dinosaurs had pillar-like legs, like those of elephants. *Brachiosaurus* weighed about 50 tonnes, so it needed thick, strong legs to support its body.

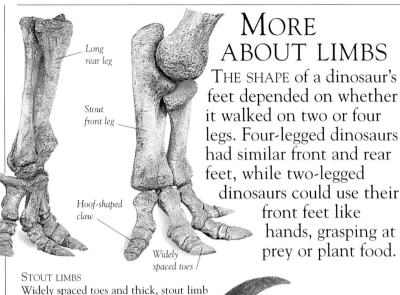

Long rear leg

Stout front leg

Hoof-shaped claw

Widely spaced toes

MORE ABOUT LIMBS

THE SHAPE of a dinosaur's feet depended on whether it walked on two or four legs. Four-legged dinosaurs had similar front and rear feet, while two-legged dinosaurs could use their front feet like hands, grasping at prey or plant food.

STOUT LIMBS

Widely spaced toes and thick, stout limb bones helped *Triceratops* spread the weight of its massive body. The shorter forelimbs carried the weight of *Triceratops*' huge head. Much of the body weight was supported by the long and powerful rear legs. Short and stubby toes on all four feet ended in hoof-shaped claws.

The claw was the first part of Baryonyx to be discovered, giving the dinosaur the nickname "Claws"

GIANT CLAW

The powerful carnivore *Baryonyx* had one of the largest dinosaur claws known. The curved talon, which was 31 cm (1 ft) long, formed a huge weapon on *Baryonyx*'s hand.

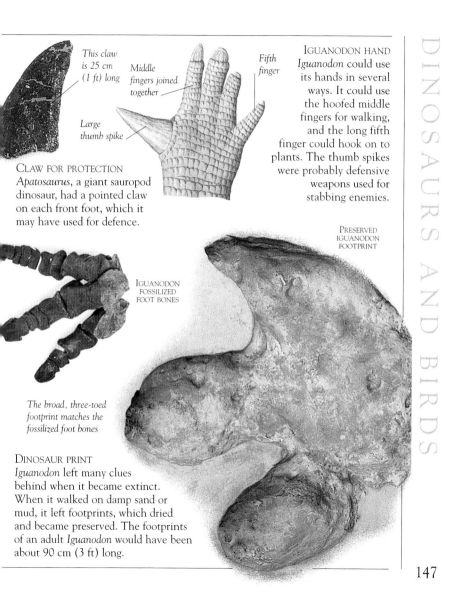

This claw is 25 cm (1 ft) long

Middle fingers joined together

Large thumb spike

Fifth finger

IGUANODON HAND
Iguanodon could use its hands in several ways. It could use the hoofed middle fingers for walking, and the long fifth finger could hook on to plants. The thumb spikes were probably defensive weapons used for stabbing enemies.

CLAW FOR PROTECTION
Apatosaurus, a giant sauropod dinosaur, had a pointed claw on each front foot, which it may have used for defence.

PRESERVED
IGUANODON
FOOTPRINT

IGUANODON
FOSSILIZED
FOOT BONES

The broad, three-toed footprint matches the fossilized foot bones

DINOSAUR PRINT
Iguanodon left many clues behind when it became extinct. When it walked on damp sand or mud, it left footprints, which dried and became preserved. The footprints of an adult *Iguanodon* would have been about 90 cm (3 ft) long.

TAILS

DINOSAUR TAILS had
many uses, and tail
bones can tell us a lot
about them. The giant
sauropods had long, tapering,
flexible tails, while two-legged
dinosaurs had tail bones that
were locked stiffly to help give
balance. Tails that ended in
lumps and spikes were used
as weapons.

*Slender head perched
on long neck*

*Tail bones
tightly locked
together*

BALANCING ACT
Scientists once believed that
Parasaurolophus used its thick tail for
swimming by sweeping it from side to side
like a fish's tail. But they now think that the
tail counterbalanced the front of the body.

TAIL WHIP
When defending itself, *Diplodocus* used its long tail like a
huge whip to swipe at its attacker. The tail had 73 bones
joined together, and made a powerful weapon with
its thin, whiplike ending.

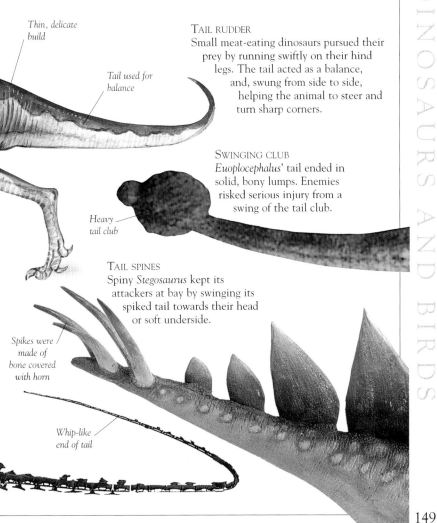

Thin, delicate build

Tail used for balance

TAIL RUDDER

Small meat-eating dinosaurs pursued their prey by running swiftly on their hind legs. The tail acted as a balance, and, swung from side to side, helping the animal to steer and turn sharp corners.

SWINGING CLUB

Euoplocephalus' tail ended in solid, bony lumps. Enemies risked serious injury from a swing of the tail club.

Heavy tail club

TAIL SPINES

Spiny *Stegosaurus* kept its attackers at bay by swinging its spiked tail towards their head or soft underside.

Spikes were made of bone covered with horn

Whip-like end of tail

149

SKIN

TOUGH SCALY SKIN is a trademark of all reptiles and dinosaurs were no exception. Fossilized imprints of their skin shows patterns of big and small bumps. Some dinosaurs had spikes and scutes (plates or lumps of bone) embedded in their skin to give them protection.

SKIN SHAPE
Bony scutes, such as this one, were inset in the skin of *Polacanthus*, an early relative of the ankylosaurs.

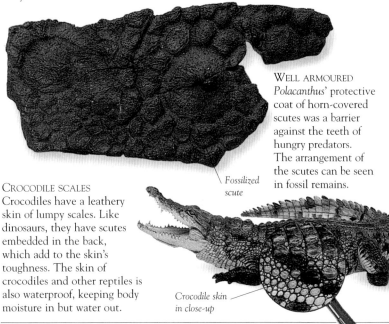

WELL ARMOURED
Polacanthus' protective coat of horn-covered scutes was a barrier against the teeth of hungry predators. The arrangement of the scutes can be seen in fossil remains.

Fossilized scute

CROCODILE SCALES
Crocodiles have a leathery skin of lumpy scales. Like dinosaurs, they have scutes embedded in the back, which add to the skin's toughness. The skin of crocodiles and other reptiles is also waterproof, keeping body moisture in but water out.

Crocodile skin in close-up

ARMOUR-PLATED
Ankylosaurs were among the most heavily protected of all dinosaurs. Large, plate-like scutes lay side by side on the upper part of its body.

SPIKES AND SCUTES
As well as scutes, the ankylosaur *Euoplocephalus* had thorn-shaped spikes across its shoulders for added effect.

Shoulder spike

EUOPLOCEPHALUS

FOSSIL ANKYLOSAUR SCUTE

Scutes were ridged in the middle

WRAPPED IN SKIN
In rare cases, a dinosaur's dead body dried up and shrivelled instead of rotting away. This *Edmontosaurus* fossil has the skin impression preserved and wrapped around the skeleton.

Small bumps

SKIN PATTERN
Corythosaurus had no protective armour. Its skin, a mosaic of small bumpy scales, was wrinkled and folded around the moving parts of the body.

This fossil is 65 million years old

SENSES

WELL-DEVELOPED SIGHT, smell, and hearing were crucial to the dinosaurs' daily survival in a hostile world. Hunting dinosaurs tracked prey by following noises and scents. Dinosaurs that lived in groups protected their young by listening and watching for predators.

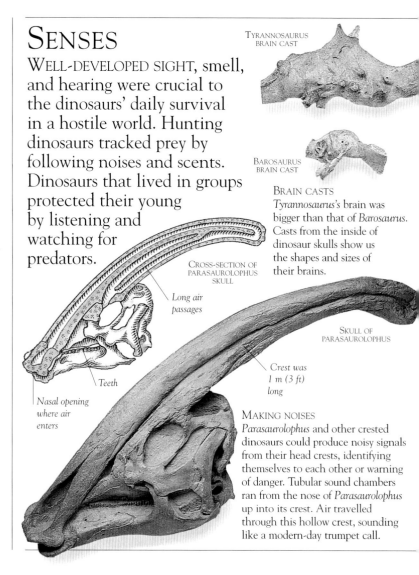

TYRANNOSAURUS
BRAIN CAST

BAROSAURUS
BRAIN CAST

BRAIN CASTS
Tyrannosaurus's brain was bigger than that of *Barosaurus*. Casts from the inside of dinosaur skulls show us the shapes and sizes of their brains.

CROSS-SECTION OF
PARASAUROLOPHUS
SKULL

Long air
passages

SKULL OF
PARASAUROLOPHUS

Teeth

Nasal opening
where air
enters

Crest was
1 m (3 ft)
long

MAKING NOISES
Parasaurolophus and other crested dinosaurs could produce noisy signals from their head crests, identifying themselves to each other or warning of danger. Tubular sound chambers ran from the nose of *Parasaurolophus* up into its crest. Air travelled through this hollow crest, sounding like a modern-day trumpet call.

COLOUR

VIEW FROM LEFT

VIEW FROM RIGHT

BLACK AND WHITE

VIEW FROM LEFT

VIEW FROM RIGHT

DOUBLE VISION

We do not know if dinosaurs could see in colour, but the position of the eyes affected the kind of image seen. Eyes on the sides of the head, common in herbivores, sent two different pictures to the brain.

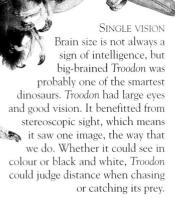

SINGLE VISION

Brain size is not always a sign of intelligence, but big-brained *Troodon* was probably one of the smartest dinosaurs. *Troodon* had large eyes and good vision. It benefitted from stereoscopic sight, which means it saw one image, the way that we do. Whether it could see in colour or black and white, *Troodon* could judge distance when chasing or catching its prey.

COLOUR

BLACK AND WHITE

153

WARM AND COLD BLOOD

REPTILES ARE COLD-BLOODED, which means that they depend on the sun's heat for warmth. Warm-blooded animals, such as mammals, produce heat from food energy within their body. Although dinosaurs were reptiles, much of their behaviour was like mammals. Scientists have wondered whether certain dinosaurs were indeed warm-blooded.

Skin "sail" was supported by spines projecting from the vertebrae

Blood vessels

CROSS-SECTION OF MAMMAL BONE

Blood vessels

CROSS-SECTION OF REPTILE BONE

BLOOD AND BONES
Dinosaurs had bones more like mammals than reptiles. Mammal bones contain far more blood vessels than reptile bones.

Side view of plate

Cross-section of plate

STEGOSAURUS BACK PLATE FOSSILS

SAIL BACK
Spinosaurus had a large "sail", which may have been used for temperature control, absorbing the sun's warmth in the morning and cooling down in the breeze later in the day. *Stegosaurus* may have used its back plates in a similar way.

SPINOSAURUS

COLD-BLOODED SUNBATHER

A typical cold-blooded creature, such as a lizard, spends hours sunbathing to raise the body's temperature to a level where it can work effectively. To avoid overheating, the lizard can cool off in the shade. When it is cold at night, or in the winter, reptiles are inactive.

LIZARD SUNBATHING

Long jaws with small, pointed teeth for catching and eating fishes

Spinosaurus was about 12 m (40 ft) long

High blood pressure was needed to reach a brain 15 m (50 ft) above the ground

BLOOD PRESSURE

Tall dinosaurs needed high blood pressure to pump blood to their brain. But down at the level of their lungs, such high pressure would be fatal. Warm-blooded animals have a twin pressure system. Perhaps dinosaurs had a similar system.

Feathered coat

VELOCIRAPTOR

GOOD EXAMPLE

Velociraptor is one of the best arguments for dinosaurs being warm-blooded animals. Fast and agile, *Velociraptor* had a lifestyle better suited to warm-blooded killers like wolves, than to reptiles like lizards.

BRACHIOSAURUS

DINOSAUR LIFESTYLES

ALTHOUGH DINOSAURS died out 65 million years ago, we know a lot about their lifestyles. Some were herbivores, some carnivores, and others omnivores. Some dinosaurs lived in herds or families and cared for their young. But whether they were warm- or cold-blooded has yet to be established.

CARNIVORES
Most carnivores had deadly sharp teeth and claws. Some hunted in packs; some hunted alone; while others may have scavenged on dead animals which were possibly killed by disease.

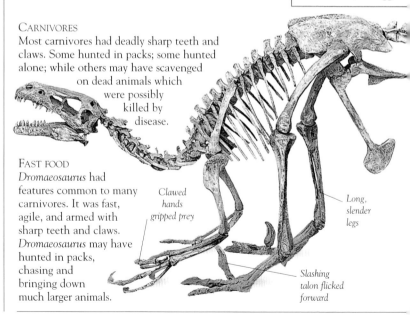

FAST FOOD
Dromaeosaurus had features common to many carnivores. It was fast, agile, and armed with sharp teeth and claws. *Dromaeosaurus* may have hunted in packs, chasing and bringing down much larger animals.

Clawed hands gripped prey

Long, slender legs

Slashing talon flicked forward

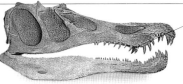

BARYONYX
From the side, *Baryonyx's* skull appears crocodile shaped. *Baryonyx* may have used its long and narrow snout for catching fish.

Sharp, serrated teeth lined the long jaws

Lethal claw

CUTTING CLAW
Like *Dromaeosaurus*, *Deinonychus* had a lethal weapon – a 15-cm (½ ft) long curved claw on each foot. When *Deinonychus* caught prey, it flicked the claw forwards to cut deep into its victim.

TERRIBLE TEETH
The teeth of carnivorous dinosaurs were sharp with serrated (sawlike) edges for cutting through flesh and bones.

LOWER JAW OF
ALBERTOSAURUS

MEATY DIET
Tyrannosaurus was one of the fiercest carnivores. With its powerful body and massive head, it overwhelmed victims, delivering a fatal, biting blow with its deadly jaws.

Small "hands" could tear food apart

HERBIVORES

PLANT-EATING DINOSAURS had to eat large amounts of plants to fuel their bodies. Some herbivores' teeth were shaped for chopping or crushing. Other herbivores had sharp beaks for snipping leaves and twigs. Once eaten, these plants may have taken days to digest.

GRINDING GUT
Barosaurus did not chew its food – it swallowed tough leaves and twigs whole. In a part of its stomach, stones called gastroliths ground the food for digestion.

SMOOTH STONES
Gastroliths have been found near the skeletons of several dinosaurs.

HERBIVORE FACTS

• All ornithischian dinosaurs were herbivores.

• Some herbivores had up to 960 teeth.

• There were no flowers for dinosaurs to eat until about 125 million years ago.

• Herds of herbivores may have migrated during dry seasons to find fresh food supplies.

• Some of the plants the dinosaurs ate, such as pine trees, ferns, and cycads, still grow today.

PLANT PULP
Edmontosaurus had hundreds of tough teeth packed together in its upper and lower jaws. The two sets of teeth worked together like a pair of coarse files, grinding leaves, fruits, and seeds.

Lever for muscle attachment

EDMONTOSAURUS LOWER JAW

Toothless front of jaw

PARASAUROLOPHUS

Teeth packed together

Parasaurolophus had hundreds of teeth for chewing tough ferns

Serrated cutting edge

Root of tooth

LEAF CUTTERS
The teeth of sauropods such as *Rebbachisaurus* were designed for cutting rather than chewing

TOUGH TO EAT
We can see which plants were available to dinosaurs by studying plant fossils. Herbivores such as *Parasaurolophus* had strong teeth for chewing tough plants such as ferns and conifers.

MAGNOLIA

GINKGO

MONKEY PUZZLE CONIFER

DINOSAUR MENU
Many of the plants the dinosaurs ate can be seen in gardens and parks today.

EGGS, NESTS, AND YOUNG

DINOSAURS laid eggs, like most other reptiles as well as birds. Scientists have discovered dinosaur nesting sites which show that some young were cared for by adults in their nests until they were old enough to leave. Other dinosaurs used the same nesting sites year after year.

EGG FIND
Dinosaur eggs were first discovered in the 1920s in fossil nests in Mongolia. Once believed to be from *Proceratops*, the eggs are now known to belong to *Oviraptor*.

Fossil egg with broken eggshell fragments

Hard snout for breaking out of egg

SMALL EGGS
These fossilized sauropod eggs, which are only 15 cm (½ ft) in diameter, could have produced young that grew to an adult length of 12 m (39 ft). It probably took sauropods several years to reach their adult size.

HOME LIFE

Female *Maiasaura* laid about 25 eggs in a nest that was dug in the ground and lined with leaves and twigs. Young *Maiasaura* were about 30 cm (12 in) long when they hatched. They were reared in the nest until they grew to about 1.5 m (5 ft), when they would be old enough to start fending for themselves.

FOSSILIZED MAIASAURA EGG AND SKELETON OF YOUNG

Maiasaura *hatchlings were very weak*

EGGSHELLS

It was once thought that dinosaur eggs were soft and leathery, like those of snakes and other reptiles. Microscopic studies now show that dinosaur eggshells were hard and brittle like those of birds. The eggs of pterosaurs, on the other hand, seem to have had reptilian leathery shells.

Eggs left empty and broken

THE FIRST DINOSAURS

SEVERAL GROUPS of reptiles existed before the dinosaurs appeared. One group was the thecodonts. These were the ancestors of the dinosaurs, and they probably also gave rise to the pterosaurs and the crocodiles. Like the first dinosaurs, thecodonts were large carnivores which had straighter legs than other reptiles. The earliest known dinosaur, *Eoraptor*, first appeared 228 million years ago.

A VERY EARLY DINOSAUR *Eoraptor* may have been the first dinosaur. It was discovered in 1992 in Argentina. *Eoraptor* had a crocodile-like skull with sharp, curved teeth.

Jaws were lined with sharp teeth

Long, stiff tail

Long tail acted as a counterbalance to the front of the body

STAURIKOSAURUS

Staurikosaurus was about 2 m (6½ ft) long.

FAST HUNTER
Speedy *Staurikosaurus* was one of the first carnivorous dinosaurs. It had long, tooth-lined jaws for catching its prey, which it chased on its long and slender back legs.

Long, bird-like back legs

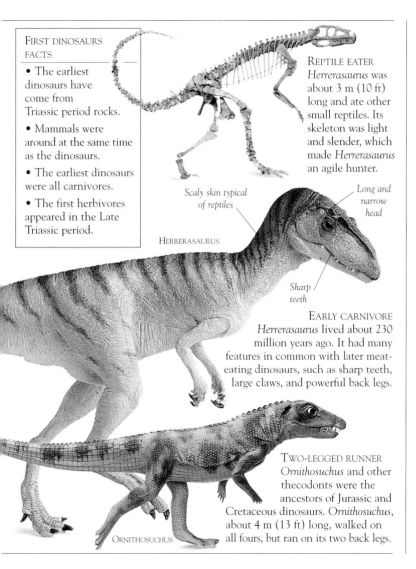

FIRST DINOSAURS FACTS

• The earliest dinosaurs have come from Triassic period rocks.

• Mammals were around at the same time as the dinosaurs.

• The earliest dinosaurs were all carnivores.

• The first herbivores appeared in the Late Triassic period.

HERRERASAURUS

Scaly skin typical of reptiles

Long and narrow head

Sharp teeth

REPTILE EATER
Herrerasaurus was about 3 m (10 ft) long and ate other small reptiles. Its skeleton was light and slender, which made *Herrerasaurus* an agile hunter.

EARLY CARNIVORE
Herrerasaurus lived about 230 million years ago. It had many features in common with later meat-eating dinosaurs, such as sharp teeth, large claws, and powerful back legs.

ORNITHOSUCHUS

TWO-LEGGED RUNNER
Ornithosuchus and other thecodonts were the ancestors of Jurassic and Cretaceous dinosaurs. *Ornithosuchus*, about 4 m (13 ft) long, walked on all fours, but ran on its two back legs.

DINOSAUR EXTINCTION

AROUND 65 MILLION YEARS AGO, the dinosaurs became extinct. At the same time, other creatures, such as the sea and air reptiles, also died out. There are many theories for this extinction. But, as with so many facts about dinosaurs, no-one really knows for sure what happened.

ASTEROID THEORY
At the end of the Cretaceous, a giant asteroid struck Earth. The impact resulted in a dust cloud which circled the globe, blocking out the sunlight and bringing cold, stormy weather.

TYRANNOSAURUS

SLOW DEATH
Some experts are of the opinion that dinosaurs died out over a few million years.

MAGNOLIA

FLOWERS
Certain poisonous flowering plants may have contributed to the extinction of the dinosaurs. Herbivorous dinosaurs that ate these plants may have died. Many carnivores, which fed on herbivores, would then have died because of lack of prey to hunt and eat.

VOLCANO THEORY
Many volcanoes were active during the Cretaceous period. There were vast lava flows in the area which is now India. This would have poured huge amounts of carbon dioxide into the air, causing overheating, acid rain, and the destruction of the protective ozone layer.

Megazostrodon was a mammal which lived in the Triassic period.

Crocodiles have not changed much in appearance over the years

MAMMALS
Mammals appeared during the Triassic period, when they lived alongside the dinosaurs. They became the dominant land animals after the dinosaurs' extinction.

SURVIVING REPTILES
Crocodiles were around before the dinosaurs, and are still alive today. The reason these reptiles survived while the dinosaurs died out is a complete mystery.

165

DINOSAURS TODAY

THE REMAINS OF DINOSAURS have been discovered on every continent. New dinosaur fossils are being discovered constantly by scientists, amateur fossil hunters, or even by accident in building sites and mines. This map shows the major dinosaur finds.

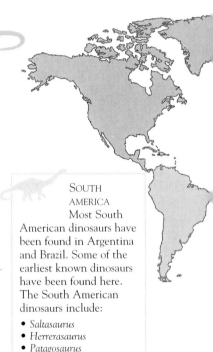

NORTH AMERICA
Expeditions are always being organized to search for dinosaurs in North America, since rocks from the dinosaur age are exposed over vast areas. The dinosaurs discovered here include:

- *Allosaurus*
- *Triceratops*
- *Deinonychus*
- *Camarasaurus*
- *Parasaurolophus*
- *Corythosaurus*
- *Stegosaurus*
- *Apatosaurus*
- *Coelophysis*

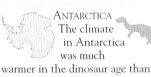

ANTARCTICA
The climate in Antarctica was much warmer in the dinosaur age than it is today. The bones of several small Cretaceous period dinosaurs have been found here, including a relative of the small ornithopod *Hypsilophodon*.

SOUTH AMERICA
Most South American dinosaurs have been found in Argentina and Brazil. Some of the earliest known dinosaurs have been found here. The South American dinosaurs include:

- *Saltasaurus*
- *Herrerasaurus*
- *Patagosaurus*
- *Staurikosaurus*
- *Piatnitzkyosaurus*

EUROPE

It was here in the 19th century that the first dinosaur fossils were collected and recorded, and where the name "dinosaur" was first used. Dinosaurs found in Europe include:

- *Hypsilophodon*
- *Iguanodon*
- *Plateosaurus*
- *Baryonyx*
- *Compsognathus*
- *Eustreptospondylus*

ASIA

Many exciting discoveries of dinosaurs have been made in the Gobi Desert. Scientists are still making new discoveries in China and India. Dinosaurs found in Asia include:

- *Velociraptor*
- *Oviraptor*
- *Protoceratops*
- *Tuojiangosaurus*
- *Mamenchisaurus*
- *Gallimimus*

AUSTRALIA AND NEW ZEALAND

There have been many fossil finds in Australia, and one in New Zealand. There are probably many sites rich in dinosaur fossils in these countries, but they have yet to be found. Dinosaurs found in these countries include:

- *Muttaburrasaurus*
- *Leaellynosaura*
- *Austrosaurus*
- *Rhoetosaurus*
- *Minmi*

AFRICA

Africa is a rich source of dinosaur fossils. A site in Tanzania has held some major discoveries. Dinosaurs found in Africa include:

- *Spinosaurus*
- *Brachiosaurus*
- *Barosaurus*
- *Massospondylus*

DINOSAURS CLASSIFIED

THE CLASSIFICATION OF DINOSAURS is controversial and continually being revised. In this chart, dinosaurs are subdivided into three main groups – Herrerasauria, Saurischia, and Ornithischia. Birds (Aves) also now come under dinosaurs as they share many basic features.

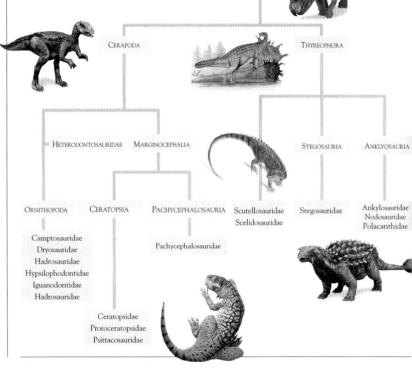

ORNITHISCHIA

CERAPODA

THYREOPHORA

HETERODONTOSAURIDAE   MARGINOCEPHALIA

STEGOSAURIA   ANKLYOSAURIA

ORNITHOPODA   CERATOPSIA   PACHYCEPHALOSAURIA   Scutellosauridae   Stegosauridae   Ankylosauridae
Scelidosauridae   Nodosauridae
Polacanthidae

Camptosauridae
Dryosauridae
Hadrosauridae
Hypsilophodontidae
Iguanodontidae
Hadrosauridae

Pachycephalosauridae

Ceratopsidae
Protoceratopsidae
Psittacosauridae

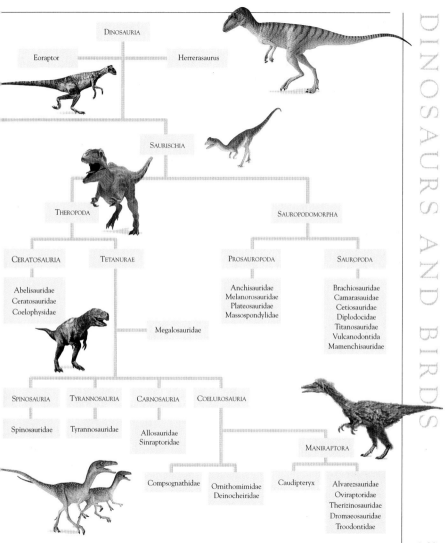

DINOSAURIA

Eoraptor — Herrerasaurus

SAURISCHIA

THEROPODA

SAUROPODOMORPHA

CERATOSAURIA

TETANURAE

PROSAUROPODA

SAUROPODA

Abelisauridae
Ceratosauridae
Coelophysidae

Anchisauridae
Melanorosauridae
Plateosauridae
Massospondylidae

Brachiosauridae
Camarasauidae
Cetiosauridae
Diplodocidae
Titanosauridae
Vulcanodontida
Mamenchisauridae

Megalosauridae

SPINOSAURIA

TYRANNOSAURIA

CARNOSAURIA

COELUROSAURIA

Spinosauridae

Tyrannosauridae

Allosauridae
Sinraptoridae

MANIRAPTORA

Compsognathidae

Ornithomimidae
Deinocheiridae

Caudipteryx

Alvarezsauridae
Oviraptoridae
Therizinosauridae
Dromaeosauridae
Troodontidae

169

ABOUT SAURISCHIANS

THERE WERE two main
groups of saurischians –
the theropods and the
sauropodomorphs. The
largest dinosaurs, and
some of the smallest, were
saurischians. This group
differed from ornithischians
mainly because of the shape
of the hip-bones.

*Sharp-toothed
jaws typical of the
meat-eating
theropods*

SAUROPODOMORPHS
Members of the sauropodomorph
group were mainly herbivorous and
quadrupedal (walked on four legs).
The sauropodomorphs included
the longest of all dinosaurs,
Seismosaurus, which
was about 40 m
(130 ft) long.

TYRANNOSAURUS

BRACHIOSAURUS – A
SAUROPODOMORPH

THEROPODS
All theropods were carnivores, and were bipedal
(walked on two legs only). One of the smallest
dinosaurs, *Compsognathus*, and the largest ever
land-based carnivore, *Tyrannosaurus*,
belonged in the theropod group.

COMPSOGNATHUS

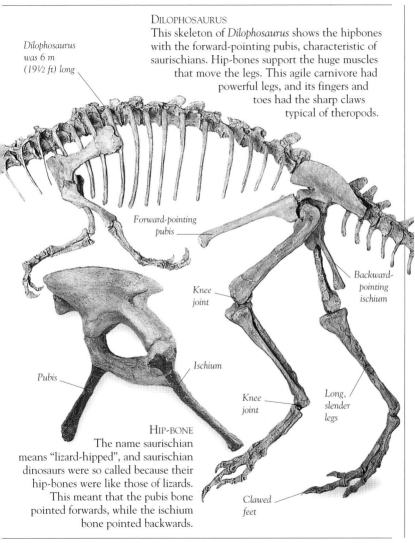

Dilophosaurus was 6 m (19½ ft) long

DILOPHOSAURUS

This skeleton of *Dilophosaurus* shows the hipbones with the forward-pointing pubis, characteristic of saurischians. Hip-bones support the huge muscles that move the legs. This agile carnivore had powerful legs, and its fingers and toes had the sharp claws typical of theropods.

Forward-pointing pubis

Knee joint

Backward-pointing ischium

Ischium

Pubis

Knee joint

Long, slender legs

HIP-BONE

The name saurischian means "lizard-hipped", and saurischian dinosaurs were so called because their hip-bones were like those of lizards. This meant that the pubis bone pointed forwards, while the ischium bone pointed backwards.

Clawed feet

171

THEROPODS

THIS GROUP comprised the killers of the dinosaur world. Often large and ferocious, these carnivores usually walked on their clawed rear feet. Theropod means "beast feet", but their feet were very bird-like. Each foot had three toes for walking on, with long foot bones that added to the length of the legs. Sharp-clawed hands were often used for attacking and catching hold of prey.

EARLY THEROPOD
Dilophosaurus lived during the early part of the Jurassic period. An agile predator, it was one of the first large carnivorous dinosaurs.

Tail

FOSSIL FIND
Coelophysis hunted lizards and small dinosaurs. But in this fossilized *Coelophysis* skeleton, there are skeletons of young of the same species among the ribs, indicating that *Coelophysis* was also a cannibal.

Coelophysis was 3 m (10 ft) long.

Bones of young in ribcage

THEROPOD FACTS

• All theropods were carnivores.

• *Coelophysis* was one of the first theropods, living about 220 million years ago.

• *Tyrannosaurus* was one of the last theropods, living 65 million years ago.

• Many theropods had no fourth or fifth fingers.

• At least five vertebrae supported the pelvis of theropods.

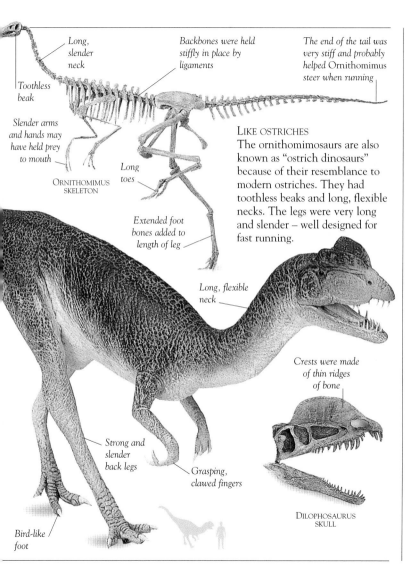

Long, slender neck

Backbones were held stiffly in place by ligaments

The end of the tail was very stiff and probably helped Ornithomimus steer when running

Toothless beak

Slender arms and hands may have held prey to mouth

ORNITHOMIMUS SKELETON

Long toes

Extended foot bones added to length of leg

LIKE OSTRICHES
The ornithomimosaurs are also known as "ostrich dinosaurs" because of their resemblance to modern ostriches. They had toothless beaks and long, flexible necks. The legs were very long and slender – well designed for fast running.

Long, flexible neck

Crests were made of thin ridges of bone

Strong and slender back legs

Grasping, clawed fingers

DILOPHOSAURUS SKULL

Bird-like foot

STAURIKOSAURUS

STAURIKOSAURUS ("Southern Cross lizard") was a primitive, bipedal dinosaur. It had the typical theropod body shape – long, slim tail, long, powerful hind legs, and short arms. The back was held horizontally, with the tail used for balance. The lower jaw had a joint that allowed the tooth-bearing part to move independently of the back part of the jaw.

LONG AND LIGHT
This lightly built hunter was relatively long in size, but would have been no heavier than a nine-year-old child – around 30 kg (66 lb). It ran swiftly on two legs.

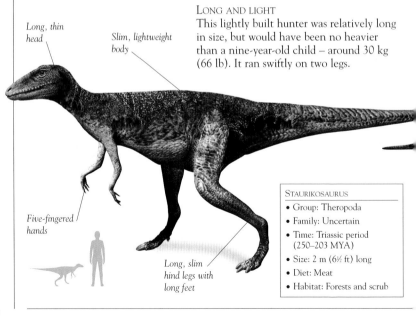

Long, thin head

Slim, lightweight body

Five-fingered hands

Long, slim hind legs with long feet

STAURIKOSAURUS
- Group: Theropoda
- Family: Uncertain
- Time: Triassic period (250–203 MYA)
- Size: 2 m (6½ ft) long
- Diet: Meat
- Habitat: Forests and scrub

EORAPTOR

THE RECENTLY DISCOVERED *Eoraptor*
("dawn raptor") is now regarded as one
of the earliest dinosaurs. It was a very small,
lightly built, bipedal carnivore with hollow
bones. The head was long and slim, with many
small, sharp teeth. The arms were far shorter
than the legs, and had five-fingered hands.
Due to its primitive nature, *Eoraptor* appears
to lack the specialized features of any of the
major groups of dinosaurs.

MINIATURE PREDATOR
Eoraptor would have appeared like
a miniature-sized theropod of later
periods. This small but ferocious
hunter lived in Argentina 228
million years ago and weighed only
about 11 kg (24 lb).

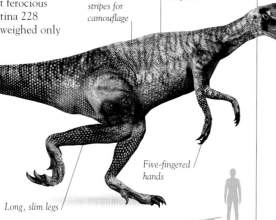

May have had
stripes for
camouflage

Scaly skin

Five-fingered
hands

Long, slim legs

EORAPTOR
- Group: Theropoda
- Family: Uncertain
- Time: Triassic period
  (250–203 MYA)
- Size: 1 m (3¼ ft)
- Diet: Meat
- Habitat: Forests

COELOPHYSIS

COELOPHYSIS ("hollow face") was a lightly built dinosaur with open skull bones (hence its name). Its body was long and slim, and the head was pointed, with many small, serrated teeth. The bones of young *Coelophysis* have been found in the stomach of fossilized adults – suggesting this dinosaur was a cannibal.

COELOPHYSIS
- Group: Theropoda
- Family: Coelophysidae
- Time: Triassic period (250–203 MYA)
- Size: 2.8 m (9 ft) long
- Diet: Lizards, fish
- Habitat: Desert plains

GHOST RANCH, NEW MEXICO
Coelophysis is one of the best-known dinosaurs as many of its fossils have been found at this site.

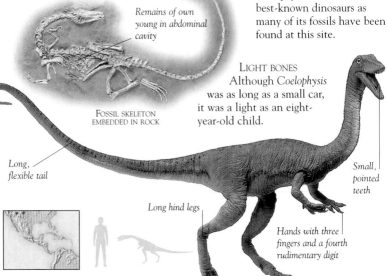

Remains of own young in abdominal cavity

FOSSIL SKELETON
EMBEDDED IN ROCK

LIGHT BONES
Although *Coelophysis* was as long as a small car, it was a light as an eight-year-old child.

Long, flexible tail

Long hind legs

Small, pointed teeth

Hands with three fingers and a fourth rudimentary digit

DILOPHOSAURUS

DILOPHOSAURUS ("two-ridged lizard") was named after the pair of bony crests that adorned its head. These were so fragile that they were probably used only for display, and not in fights. Not all specimens have the crest – they may have been evident only in males, which used them to attract a mate. *Dilophosaurus* had a large head, with a slender neck, body, and tail. It seems to have been closely related to *Coelophysis*.

DILOPHOSAURUS
- Group: Theropoda
- Family: Coelophysidae
- Time: Jurassic period (203–135 MYA)
- Size: 6 m (20 ft)
- Diet: Small animals, fishes
- Habitat: Riverbanks

Flexible tail

Bony, semicircular crests

Long, slim, powerful hind legs

DANGEROUS DISPLAY
The male *Dilophosaurus* may have scared rivals away by standing and nodding its head up and down to appear bigger (and more dangerous) than it actually was.

Three long, forward-facing, clawed toes

177

CERATOSAURUS

CERATOSAURUS ("horned lizard") was named after the short horn above its nose. This dinosaur's other striking feature was the line of bony plates that ran down its back – the only theropod known to have had them. It had strong, yet short, arms, with four fingers on each hand. Three of the fingers were clawed. *Ceratosaurus's* teeth were long and blade-like. It had a deep and flexible tail.

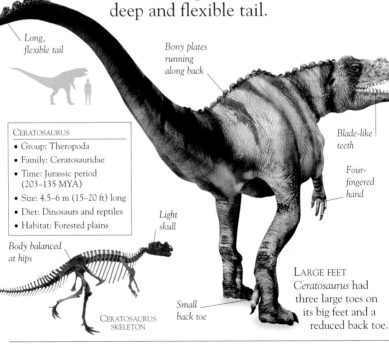

Long, flexible tail

Bony plates running along back

Blade-like teeth

Four-fingered hand

CERATOSAURUS

- Group: Theropoda
- Family: Ceratosauridae
- Time: Jurassic period (203–135 MYA)
- Size: 4.5–6 m (15–20 ft) long
- Diet: Dinosaurs and reptiles
- Habitat: Forested plains

Light skull

Body balanced at hips

Small back toe

CERATOSAURUS SKELETON

LARGE FEET
Ceratosaurus had three large toes on its big feet and a reduced back toe.

ABELISAURUS

THIS LARGE THEROPOD, named after its discoverer, Roberto Abel, is known only from a single skull. Its big head had a rounded snout, and its teeth were small for a carnivorous dinosaur of its size. Its skull is peculiar in that it has a huge opening at the side just above the jaws, which is much larger than in other dinosaurs.

CARNOTAURUS'S COUSIN
Abelisaurus was a primitive dinosaur related to another theropod known as *Carnotaurus*. Since there are no other bones except for the skull available, palaeontologists have had to imagine the rest of *Abelisaurus*'s body based on that of other, better-known abelisaurids.

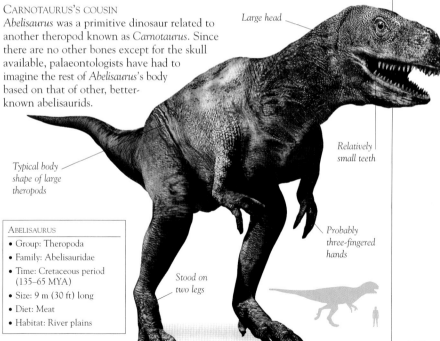

Large head

Relatively small teeth

Typical body shape of large theropods

Probably three-fingered hands

Stood on two legs

ABELISAURUS
- Group: Theropoda
- Family: Abelisauridae
- Time: Cretaceous period (135–65 MYA)
- Size: 9 m (30 ft) long
- Diet: Meat
- Habitat: River plains

179

BIG MEAT-EATERS

OF ALL THE THEROPODS, the ferocious, large carnivores are probably the most famous. These fast runners had massive heads with enormous serrated and curved teeth. *Tyrannosaurus* was one of the largest and fiercest carnivores of the Cretaceous. *Allosaurus* was the top predator of the Jurassic.

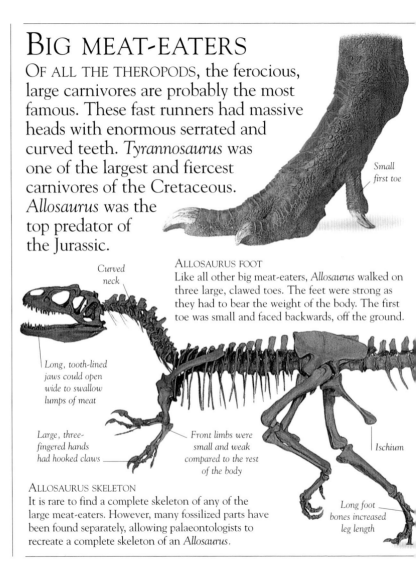

Small first toe

Curved neck

ALLOSAURUS FOOT
Like all other big meat-eaters, *Allosaurus* walked on three large, clawed toes. The feet were strong as they had to bear the weight of the body. The first toe was small and faced backwards, off the ground.

Long, tooth-lined jaws could open wide to swallow lumps of meat

Large, three-fingered hands had hooked claws

Front limbs were small and weak compared to the rest of the body

Ischium

ALLOSAURUS SKELETON
It is rare to find a complete skeleton of any of the large meat-eaters. However, many fossilized parts have been found separately, allowing palaeontologists to recreate a complete skeleton of an *Allosaurus*.

Long foot bones increased leg length

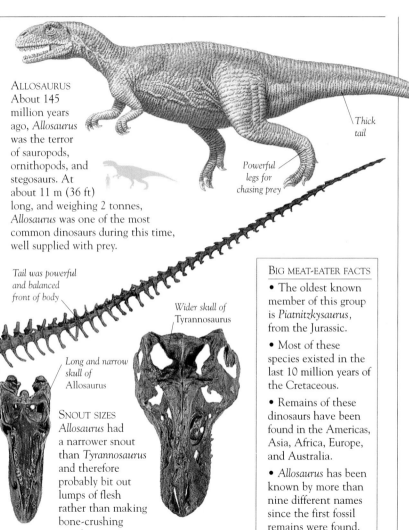

ALLOSAURUS
About 145 million years ago, *Allosaurus* was the terror of sauropods, ornithopods, and stegosaurs. At about 11 m (36 ft) long, and weighing 2 tonnes, *Allosaurus* was one of the most common dinosaurs during this time, well supplied with prey.

Thick tail

Powerful legs for chasing prey

Tail was powerful and balanced front of body

Wider skull of Tyrannosaurus

Long and narrow skull of Allosaurus

SNOUT SIZES
Allosaurus had a narrower snout than *Tyrannosaurus* and therefore probably bit out lumps of flesh rather than making bone-crushing attacks on prey.

BIG MEAT-EATER FACTS

• The oldest known member of this group is *Piatnitzkysaurus*, from the Jurassic.

• Most of these species existed in the last 10 million years of the Cretaceous.

• Remains of these dinosaurs have been found in the Americas, Asia, Africa, Europe, and Australia.

• *Allosaurus* has been known by more than nine different names since the first fossil remains were found.

CARNOTAURUS

THE MOST DISTINCTIVE features of *Carnotaurus* ("meat-eating bull") were the triangular horns over its eyes. Otherwise, it looked very like other large theropods. It had long legs and a lightly built body covered in scales and studs. Its forearms were incredibly small. Its three fingers were short and stubby, and the thumbs bore a small spike. Its tail was long, thick, and flexible.

Very short forearms

Tail held out for balance

Spiked thumb

Slim, powerful legs

Large weight bearing toes

MYSTERY HORNS
Scientists are unsure why *Carnotaurus* had horns on its head. They were too short to kill and in all likelihood this dinosaur hunted its prey by butting it head-first, or scavenged on dead dinosaurs. The horns may have been used by males to attract a mate and ward off rivals.

PIATNITZKYSAURUS

THIS DINOSAUR seems to have been a tetanuran ("stiff-tailed") theropod. It had a very similar body to *Allosaurus*, but its arms were longer. A pair of bony crests ran from between the eyes to the end of the snout. The arms were relatively small, with three clawed fingers on each hand. The body was bulky, and the tail was long and stiff. "Piatnitzky's lizard" was named in honour of the discoverer, José Bonaparte's best friend.

IDENTITY CRISIS
Two partial skeletons of *Piatnitzkysaurus* have been excavated to date in Argentina, and its exact classification is still being debated by palaeontologists.

Short muscular neck

Paired bony crests on snout

Long, powerful tail

Short, strong arms

PIATNITZKYSAURUS

- Group: Theropoda
- Family: Tetanurae
- Time: Jurassic period (203–135 MYA)
- Size: 4.3 m (14 ft) long
- Diet: Herbivorous dinosaurs
- Habitat: Woodland

MEGALOSAURUS

THE FIRST DINOSAUR to be scientifically named and identified, *Megalosaurus* ("great lizard") was a large, bulky, carnivorous theropod. It had a massive head carried on a short, muscular neck. *Megalosaurus* walked with its toes pointing inwards and its tail swaying.

Long, thick tail

Short but strong arms

MEGALOSAURUS
- Group: Theropoda
- Family: Megalosauridae
- Time: Jurassic period (203–135 MYA)
- Size: 9 m (30 ft) long
- Diet: Large herbivorous dinosaurs
- Habitat: Forests

Sharp, serrated teeth

Cracks due to fossilization

FOSSIL TOOTH
This jawbone belonged to *Megalosaurus*. Many fossils have been wrongly identified as *Megalosaurus* remains, but very few real *Megalosaurus* fossils have been found.

LOWER JAW

XUANHANOSAURUS

THIS LITTLE KNOWN theropod ("Xuan lizard") was named after Xuanhan in Sichuan Province, China, where its fossils were found. At present, it is known only from vertebrae and bones from the shoulder, arm, and hand. Its arms were well developed and strong, despite their short length, and the hands were small with strong claws. This *Megalosaurus*-like dinosaur may have had a large head, long and powerful hind legs, clawed feet with three forward-facing toes, and a long, stiff tail.

*Tail stretched
for balance*

*Three clawed
fingers on
each hand*

STEADY WALKER

Xuanhanosaurus's fossils were discovered by the Chinese palaeontologist Dong Zhiming in 1984. He suggested that, although *Xuanhanosaurus* was bipedal, it walked on all-fours for at least some of the time. It kept its long and stiff tail outstretched for balance.

XUANHANOSAURUS
• Group: Theropoda
• Family: Uncertain
• Time: Jurassic period (203–135 MYA)
• Size: 6 m (20 ft) long
• Diet: Meat
• Habitat: Forests

GASOSAURUS

THIS THEROPOD was named "gas lizard" in honour of the Dashanpu gas company, which was working in the quarry in Sichuan, China, where the remains were excavated.

GASOSAURUS
- Group: Theropoda
- Family: Tetanurae
- Time: Jurassic period (203–135 MYA)
- Size: 4 m (13 ft)
- Diet: Large herbivorous dinosaurs
- Habitat: Woodland

Little is known about *Gasosaurus*, and its classification is uncertain – it may be a primitive big meat-eater. *Gasosaurus* had a typical theropod body shape of a large head, powerful legs with three claws, and a long, stiff tail.

Bulky body

Stiffened tail

Large jaws with sharp teeth

LITTLE-KNOWN
Only parts of the arm, thigh, and hip bones of this dinosaur have been found.

Relatively long arms

Three forward-facing clawed toes

Heavily built hind legs

ALLOSAURUS

ALLOSAURUS ("different lizard") was the most abundant, and probably the largest, predator in the Late Jurassic. It had a massive head, short neck, and bulky body, and its three-fingered forelimbs were strong, with large claws. *Allosaurus* had distinctive bony bumps over the eyes.

Teeth 5–10 cm (2½–5 in) long

FOSSIL SKULL
The massive skull was lightened by large gaps known as fenestrae.

OTHNIEL C. MARSH
The greatest dinosaur palaeontologist of the 19th century, Othniel C. Marsh, named this dinosaur *Allosaurus*.

Tail held outstretched for balance

Saw-like teeth

ALLOSAURUS
- Group: Theropoda
- Family: Allosauridae
- Time: Jurassic period (203–135 MYA)
- Size: 12 m (39 ft) long
- Diet: Herbivorous dinosaurs, rotting flesh
- Habitat: Plains

187

GIGANOTOSAURUS

GIGANOTOSAURUS ("giant southern lizard") is the largest flesh-eating dinosaur yet discovered. Its skull was longer than an average man, and held long, serrated teeth. Its hands had three fingers, and it had a slim, pointed tail. Although larger than *Tyrannosaurus*, it was a lighter dinosaur. It also seems to have hunted in a different fashion – by slashing at its prey rather than charging and biting it head on. Despite its huge size, some scientists think that, like other large theropods, it may have been capable of running quite fast.

LAND OF GIANTS
This gigantic hunter from Argentina may have preyed on one of the largest-ever sauropods, *Argentinosaurus*, or eaten the flesh of dead ones. It had a relative in *Carcharodontosaurus* – another giant meat-eater that lived in Africa.

GIGANOTOSAURUS
- Group: Theropoda
- Family: Carcharodontosauridae
- Time: Cretaceous period (135–65 MYA)
- Size: 12.5 m (41 ft)
- Diet: Meat
- Habitat: Warm swamps

Three clawed fingers

Large eyes

Head twice
the size of
Allosaurus

Tail probably
swayed from
side to side

Small
shoulder

189

HOLLOW-TAIL LIZARDS

THE JURASSIC LANDSCAPE teemed with small predators, but very few left fossil remains. Among the best-known of these are *Compsognathus* and *Ornitholestes* – both fast runners, preying on smaller animals. They formed a new group – the coelurosaurs or "hollow-tail lizards", which later gave rise to tyrannosaurs, ornithopods, and the ancestors of birds.

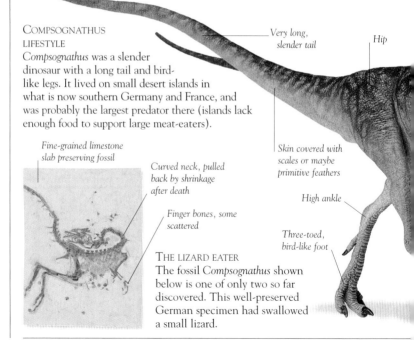

COMPSOGNATHUS
LIFESTYLE
Compsognathus was a slender dinosaur with a long tail and bird-like legs. It lived on small desert islands in what is now southern Germany and France, and was probably the largest predator there (islands lack enough food to support large meat-eaters).

Very long, slender tail

Hip

Skin covered with scales or maybe primitive feathers

High ankle

Three-toed, bird-like foot

Fine-grained limestone slab preserving fossil

Curved neck, pulled back by shrinkage after death

Finger bones, some scattered

THE LIZARD EATER
The fossil *Compsognathus* shown below is one of only two so far discovered. This well-preserved German specimen had swallowed a small lizard.

Large orbit

ORNITHOLESTES

Long, whip-
like tail

Deep
lower jaw

Long hand

Long, low
head

Long,
flexible neck

BIRD HUNTER

Ornitholestes, from Late Jurassic
Wyoming, USA, was much like
Compsognathus, but larger in size and
with longer, more grasping hands. It
may have hunted lizards and early
birds, but it could also have tackled
prey larger than little *Compsognathus*.

Slim
bones

Large gaps

ELEGANT JAW

Compsognathus ("elegant jaw") got
its name from the delicate bones
in its long head. Its lightly built
skull consisted of slim bony struts
with large gaps between them.

Might have had
only two fingers
on each hand

COMPSOGNATHUS
- Group: Theropoda
- Family: Compsognathidae
- Time: Jurassic period
  (203–135 MYA)
- Size: Up to 1.4 m
  (4½ ft) long
- Diet: Small animals
- Habitat: Desert islands

DINOSAURS AND BIRDS

CAUDIPTERYX

THE DISCOVERY OF this small, feathered dinosaur added further proof to the theory that theropods were the ancestors of birds. *Caudipteryx* ("tail feather") was a theropod with feathers covering its arms, most of its body, and its short tail. Some feathers were downy, while others were like quills.

Pointed beak

Small, short skull

Fan of feathers on tail

DOWN FEATHER

FEATHER FUNCTION
Caudipteryx's short down feathers gave it warmth. Its wing feathers were symmetrical, meaning that it could not fly.

WING FEATHER

Three clawed fingers

Short arms with symmetrical feathers

Bird-like feet with three forward-facing clawed toes

Long, slim legs best-suited to running

CAUDIPTERYX
- Group: Theropoda
- Family: Uncertain
- Time: Cretaceous period (135–65 MYA)
- Size: 90 cm (3 ft) long
- Diet: Plants
- Habitat: Wooded lakesides

OVIRAPTOR

THIS DINOSAUR seems to have been closely related to birds, and was probably feathered. Its most distinctive feature was its short, deep head with a stumpy beak. It had no teeth, but there were two bony projections on the upper palate. Its powerful jaws could have crushed bones.

OVIRAPTOR
- Group: Theropoda
- Family: Oviraptoridae
- Time: Cretaceous period (135–65 MYA)
- Size: 2.5 m (8 ft) long
- Diet: Uncertain
- Habitat: Semi-desert

UNJUSTLY NAMED
The first specimen of *Oviraptor* was found with eggs, which it was thought to have been stealing, and this led to its name "egg thief". Later research proved that the *Oviraptor* was actually sitting on its own nest.

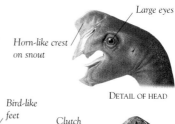

Large eyes

Horn-like crest on snout

DETAIL OF HEAD

Bird-like feet

Clutch of eggs

FOSSILIZED NEST SITE

OVIRAPTOSAURS

OVIRAPTOR WAS given the name "egg stealer" as the first fossil was found lying on a nest of *Protoceratops* eggs. It was thought that it had been killed while trying to steal eggs. We now know, however, that the eggs and nest belonged to the *Oviraptor* itself and it probably died trying to protect them.

FOSSILIZED NEST OF OVIRAPTOR EGGS

TRUE IDENTITY
Proof of the real nature of the "*Protoceratops*" eggs came when one of them was found to contain an *Oviraptor* embryo.

NEST DISCOVERY
Oviraptosaurs resembled large, flightless birds. In 1995, a fossilized *Oviraptor* was found sitting on its nest, as if brooding the eggs like a modern bird. The 18 eggs were laid in a circle in a hollow scooped out of a mound of sand.

Feathers

Toothless beak

Sharp claws

MODEL OF OVIRAPTOR ON NEST

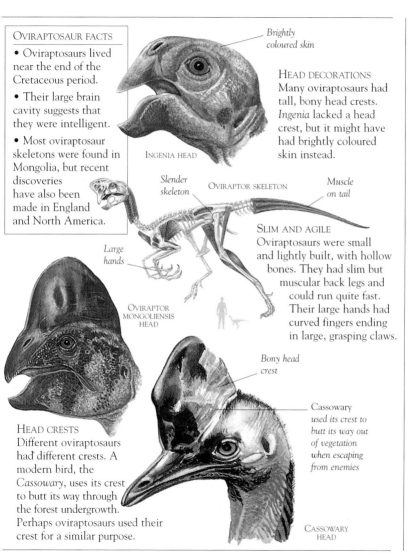

OVIRAPTOSAUR FACTS

- Oviraptosaurs lived near the end of the Cretaceous period.
- Their large brain cavity suggests that they were intelligent.
- Most oviraptosaur skeletons were found in Mongolia, but recent discoveries have also been made in England and North America.

Brightly coloured skin

HEAD DECORATIONS

Many oviraptosaurs had tall, bony head crests. *Ingenia* lacked a head crest, but it might have had brightly coloured skin instead.

INGENIA HEAD

Slender skeleton

OVIRAPTOR SKELETON

Muscle on tail

SLIM AND AGILE

Oviraptosaurs were small and lightly built, with hollow bones. They had slim but muscular back legs and could run quite fast. Their large hands had curved fingers ending in large, grasping claws.

Large hands

OVIRAPTOR MONGOLIENSIS HEAD

Bony head crest

Cassowary used its crest to butt its way out of vegetation when escaping from enemies

HEAD CRESTS

Different oviraptosaurs had different crests. A modern bird, the *Cassowary*, uses its crest to butt its way through the forest undergrowth. Perhaps oviraptosaurs used their crest for a similar purpose.

CASSOWARY HEAD

ARCHAEOPTERYX

ARCHAEOPTERYX
("ancient wing")
was the size of a
modern pigeon.
It was not a strong
flier but its long
slim lower leg bones
suggest that it could
move well on land.
Archaeopteryx is
believed to have
been warm-blooded.

Feathered wings for effective flight

Three clawed digits on elongated hand

Small head with large eyes

ARCHAEOPTERYX
- Group: Theropoda
- Family: Archaeopteridae
- Time: Jurassic period (203–135 MYA)
- Size: 30 cm (1 ft)
- Diet: Insects
- Habitat: Lakeshores or open forests

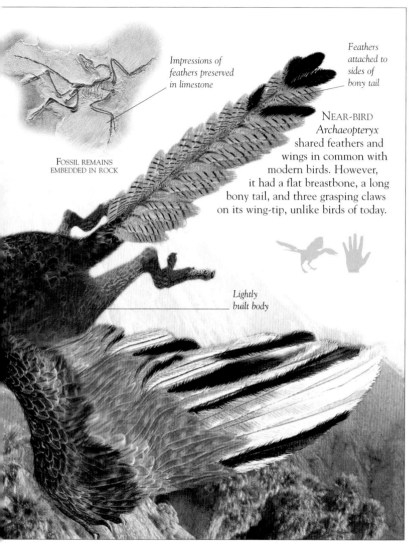

Impressions of
*feathers preserved
in limestone*

**FOSSIL REMAINS
EMBEDDED IN ROCK**

*Feathers
attached to
sides of
bony tail*

NEAR-BIRD
Archaeopteryx
shared feathers and
wings in common with
modern birds. However,
it had a flat breastbone, a long
bony tail, and three grasping claws
on its wing-tip, unlike birds of today.

*Lightly
built body*

197

VELOCIRAPTOR

MANY WELL-PRESERVED skeletons of *Velociraptor*
("fast thief") have been found, making it the
best-known member of its family. This predator
probably hunted in packs. Its hands bore three
clawed fingers and the second toe of its foot
ended in a sickle-shaped
slashing claw.

*Stiff tail held
outstretched for
balance*

*Slim legs with
long shins for
speed*

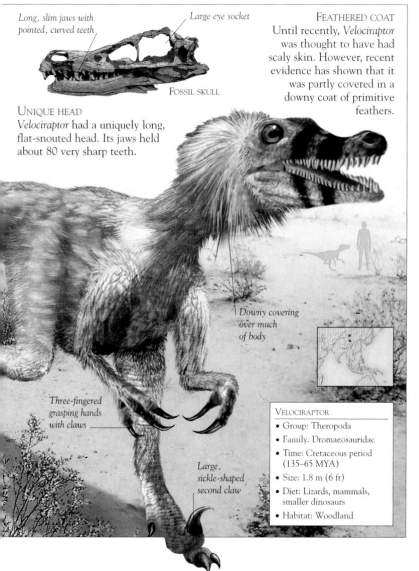

Long, slim jaws with pointed, curved teeth

Large eye socket

FOSSIL SKULL

UNIQUE HEAD
Velociraptor had a uniquely long, flat-snouted head. Its jaws held about 80 very sharp teeth.

FEATHERED COAT
Until recently, *Velociraptor* was thought to have had scaly skin. However, recent evidence has shown that it was partly covered in a downy coat of primitive feathers.

Downy covering over much of body

Three-fingered grasping hands with claws

Large, sickle-shaped second claw

VELOCIRAPTOR
- Group: Theropoda
- Family. Dromaeosauridae
- Time: Cretaceous period (135–65 MYA)
- Size: 1.8 m (6 ft)
- Diet: Lizards, mammals, smaller dinosaurs
- Habitat: Woodland

199

DROMAEOSAURUS

DROMAEOSAURUS ("running lizard") was the first sickle-clawed dinosaur to be discovered. It was difficult to reconstruct as very few bones were found and its true classification was only possible after another sickle-clawed dinosaur, *Deinonychus*, was described. *Dromaeosaurus* was smaller than *Deinonychus*, but otherwise very similar. Its body was slender, with long limbs and a large head. Its sharp claws would have been used for slashing prey.

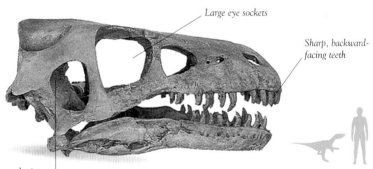

Large eye sockets

Sharp, backward-facing teeth

Large braincase indicating high intelligence

FEROCIOUS HUNTER
Dromaeosaurus belonged to the group of "running lizards" or dromaeosaurids, which were small and aggressive hunting dinosaurs. They had curved claws on their hands and feet and their jaws bristled with huge blade-like teeth.

DROMAEOSAURUS

- Group: Theropoda
- Family: Dromaeosauridae
- Time: Cretaceous period (135–65 MYA)
- Size: 1.8 m (5½ ft) long
- Diet: Herbivorous dinosaurs
- Habitat: Forests, plains

DEINONYCHUS

ONE OF THE MOST fearsome predators of the Cretaceous, *Deinonychus* ("terrible claw") was named after the sickle-shaped claws on the second toe of each foot. These were used alternately to slash at prey as the dinosaur stood on one leg. A group of *Deinonychus* skeletons preserved with that of a large *Tenontosaurus* suggests that *Deinonychus* hunted in packs.

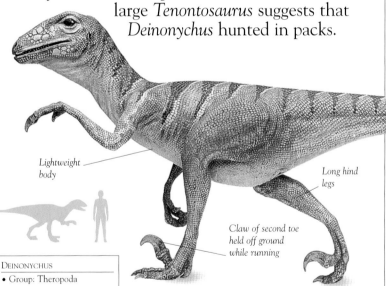

Lightweight body

Long hind legs

Claw of second toe held off ground while running

DEINONYCHUS

- Group: Theropoda
- Family: Dromaeosauridae
- Time: Cretaceous period (135–65 MYA)
- Size: 3–4 m (9¼–13 ft) long
- Diet: Herbivorous dinosaurs
- Habitat: Forests

STRIPES FOR CAMOUFLAGE
Palaeontologists suggest that this fierce hunter had striped skin like a tiger's. This would have helped it to blend into the woodland, where it hunted its prey.

SAURORNITHOIDES

ONLY THE SKULL, a few arm bones, and teeth of *Saurornithoides* ("lizard bird form") have been found to date, and its classification as a dromaeosaur is therefore uncertain. Its long, narrow skull had a relatively large braincase. Its long, powerful arms ended in three-fingered hands capable of grasping prey.

Relatively large braincase

FAST RUNNER
Saurornithoides was very similar to *Troodon*, and like it, was a fast runner. Its remains have been found only in Mongolia.

Jaw containing many sharp teeth

Long, narrow snout

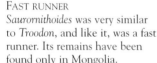

SAURORNITHOIDES
• Group: Theropoda
• Family: Dromaeosauridae
• Time: Cretaceous period (135–65 MYA)
• Size: 2–3.5 m (6½–11 ft) long
• Diet: Meat
• Habitat: Plains

TROODON

TROODON ("wounding tooth") was named after its sharp, saw-like teeth. Its remains are very rare and no complete skeleton has been found to date. *Troodon* was probably very intelligent and an efficient hunter. It had a large curved claw on both second toes, and three long, clawed fingers that could grasp prey.

TROODON

BUSHBABY

NIGHT SIGHT
Troodon had large, forward-facing eyes like today's bushbaby. This may have helped it to see at night.

Large, keen eyes

Slim, lightly built body

FAST RUNNER
Troodon could run very fast on its long back legs. It probably preyed on insects, small mammals, lizards, and baby dinosaurs.

TROODON
- Group: Theropoda
- Family: Troodontidae
- Time: Cretaceous period (135–65 MYA)
- Size: 2 m (6½ ft) long
- Diet: Meat, carrion
- Habitat: Plains

Three-fingered hands

203

ORNITHOMIMOSAURS

WITH THEIR toothless beaks and slender feet, these dinosaurs looked like giant, featherless birds. But they also possessed the dinosaur features of clawed hands and a long tail. Ornithomimosaurs were long-necked and large – up to 5 m (16 ft) long – and among the fastest dinosaurs, racing on slim, powerful rear legs.

ORNITHOMIMOSAUR FACTS

• Ornithomimosaur means "bird-mimic reptile".

• Ornithomimosaurs may have run as fast as 70 km/h (43 mph).

• Predators: carnosaurs and dromaeosaurs

DROMICEIOMIMUS
This dinosaur had ten neck vertebrae, which made a flexible stem for its large-eyed head. It used its slender arms and three-fingered hands for grasping or holding prey.

Knee joint

Ankle joint far up leg

Fingers were thin with long, sharp claws

Only the toes touched the ground

Large eye sockets

Long foot bones

LIKE AN OSTRICH
Struthiomimus had a running style similar to an ostrich. But unlike an ostrich, it had long, mobile arms with clawed fingers to grasp prey. Its long tail was an important balancer at high speed.

Ostrich speed – up to 80 km/h (50 mph)

Struthiomimus speed – less than 50 km/h (30 mph)

Three locked foot bones

FOOT AND LEG
As in all other ornithomimosaurs, the feet and legs of *Dromiceiomimus* were built to give fast acceleration. Only the toes touched the ground – the foot bones were locked into a single, bird-like extension of the leg.

Long, flexible neck

Sharp claws

Mobile wrist

GALLIMIMUS
The largest ornithomimosaur was *Gallimimus*. It had a long and narrow, snouted head with large eyes for good sight. Its weak jaws were covered by a sharp, horny beak.

ORNITHOMIMUS

THE "BIRD MIMIC", or
Ornithomimus, is typical of its
kind. It had slim arms and
long, slim legs. Its stiff tail
made up more than half of its
length. Its small head had a
toothless beak, and was held
upright by an S-shaped bend
in the long, flexible neck. The
brain cavity of *Ornithomimus*
was relatively large.

Impression of toes

FOSSIL FOOTPRINTS
Ornithomimus had feet
with three sharply clawed
toes. It could deliver a
terrible kick to a predator,
such as tyrannosaur.

*Large eyes
on side of
head*

*Long bones
in feet*

*Three clawed
fingers on
each hand*

FAST RUNNER
Ornithomimus ran at
high speed with its
body held horizontal
and its tail outstretched
for better balance.

ORNITHOMIMUS

- Group: Theropoda
- Family: Ornithomimidae
- Time: Cretaceous period
  (135–65 MYA)
- Size: 3.5 m (11 ft) long
- Diet: Omnivorous
- Habitat: Swamps, forests

STRUTHIOMIMUS

FOR MANY YEARS *Struthiomimus* ("ostrich mimic") was thought to be the same dinosaur as *Ornithomimus*. The two dinosaurs are remarkably similar – the main difference is that *Struthiomimus* had longer arms with stronger fingers. In addition, its thumbs did not oppose the fingers and it could not grasp so well.

"OSTRICH DINOSAUR"
Struthiomimus, like all the other "bird-mimics", had a small head with a toothless beak. Its legs, with long shins, feet, and toes, were adapted for sprinting fast across the countryside. Its long tail stiffly jutted out from behind.

STRUTHIOMIMUS
- Group: Theropoda
- Family: Ornithomimidae
- Time: Cretaceous period (135–65 MYA)
- Size: 3.5 m (11 ft) long
- Diet: Omnivorous
- Habitat: Open country, riverbanks

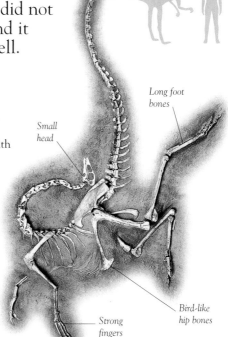

Long foot bones

Small head

Strong fingers

Bird-like hip bones

GALLIMIMUS

GALLIMIMUS ("chicken mimic") is one of the best-known ornithomimids or "bird-mimic" dinosaurs. It had a short body with a long, stiff tail stretched out for balance. Its slim legs were built for running at high speed. The skull ended in a long, toothless beak. *Gallimimus* was probably quite intelligent as its braincase was relatively large.

Large eye socket

Toothless beak

FOSSIL SKULL

RUN LIKE AN OSTRICH
Gallimimus probably ran like an ostrich, making long strides with its powerful hind legs. It had long arms in place of wings.

GALLIMIMUS

- Group: Theropoda
- Family: Ornithomimidae
- Time: Cretaceous period (135–65 MYA)
- Size: 6 m (20 ft) long
- Diet: Omnivorous
- Habitat: Desert plains

Slender, flexible neck

Slender feet with three toes

Long, grasping arms

DEINOCHEIRUS

THE ONLY REMAINS discovered of
this little-known dinosaur are
two arms 2.4 m (8 ft) in length,
hence its name "terrible hand".
The arms of this bipedal hunter
are similar to those of *Ornithomimus*,
and are among the longest known in
dinosaurs. Some experts think that the
claws on the hands were too
blunt for use in hunting.

DEINOCHEIRUS
- Group: Theropoda
- Family: Deinocheiridae
- Time: Cretaceous period (135–65 MYA)
- Size: 12–15 m (43–52 ft) long
- Diet: Unknown
- Habitat: Desert

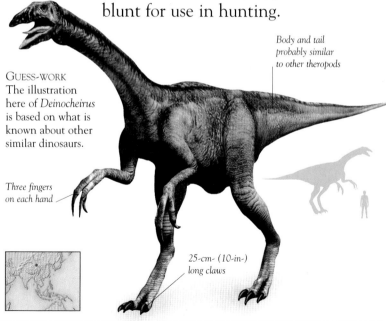

GUESS-WORK
The illustration
here of *Deinocheirus*
is based on what is
known about other
similar dinosaurs.

*Body and tail
probably similar
to other theropods*

*Three fingers
on each hand*

*25-cm- (10-in-)
long claws*

THERIZINOSAURUS

THE RECONSTRUCTION of *Therizinosaurus* ("scythe lizard") is based upon finds of other members of the family. It had very long arms ending in three fingers with claws that were too blunt to use in attack. This bipedal dinosaur was related to *Oviraptor*.

THERIZINOSAURUS
- Group: Theropoda
- Family: Therizinosauridae
- Time: Cretaceous period (135–65 MYA)
- Size: 11 m (36 ft) long
- Diet: Meat, plants or insects
- Habitat: Woodland

Toothless beak

Claws up to 60 cm (2 ft) long

Fine, hairy feathers may have covered the skin

FOSSIL SCYTHE CLAW

BEIPIAOSAURUS

BEIPIAOSAURUS WAS NAMED after Beipiao, the Chinese city where its fossils were discovered. It had a big head, three-clawed hands, and long shins. Evidence shows that feathers covered its arms and legs, further strengthening the theory that some theropods were downy and not scaly.

BEIPIAOSAURUS
- Group: Theropoda
- Family: Therizinosauridae
- Time: Cretaceous period (135–65 MYA)
- Size: 2.2 m (7¼ ft)
- Diet: Plants
- Habitat: Woodland

OLDEST SCYTHE LIZARD
The heavily built *Beipiaosaurus* lived more than 120 million years ago, making it older than other "scythe lizards".

Body covered with feathery filament

Heavy build

SHUVUUIA

THE DISCOVERY OF *Shuvuuia* started a debate as to whether it was a bird, rather than a dinosaur. Named after the Mongolian word for bird ("shuvuu") its skull shows it to have been more closely related to birds than, for example, *Archaeopteryx*. Evidence shows it also had feathers.

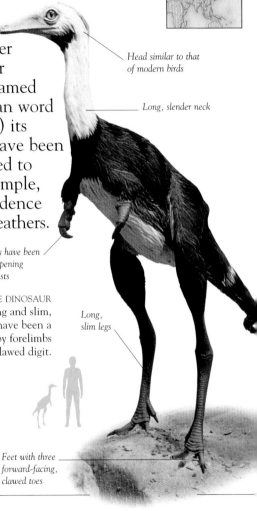

Head similar to that of modern birds

Long, slender neck

Claw may have been used for opening termite nests

BIRD-LIKE DINOSAUR

Shuvuuia's legs were long and slim, suggesting that it may have been a fast runner. Its short, stubby forelimbs ended in a single clawed digit.

Long, slim legs

SHUVUUIA

- Group: Theropoda
- Family: Alvarezsauria
- Time: Cretaceous period (135–65 MYA)
- Size: 1 m (3½ ft) long
- Diet: Insects, small reptiles
- Habitat: Plains

Feet with three forward-facing, clawed toes

SUCHOMIMUS

THIS DINOSAUR, whose name means "crocodile-mimic", was adapted to hunt fish. It had a very long snout and its jaws had sharp, interlocking teeth to grip slippery prey. It probably stood or lay in the water, waiting to snap up fish or hook them with its curved thumb claws.

SUCHOMIMUS
- Group: Theropoda
- Family: Spinosauridae
- Time: Cretaceous period (135–65 MYA)
- Size: 11 m (36 ft) long
- Diet: Fish, possibly meat
- Habitat: Lush forests

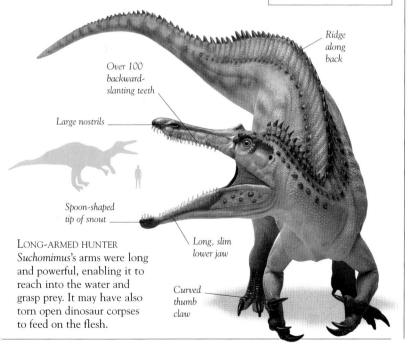

Ridge along back

Over 100 backward-slanting teeth

Large nostrils

Spoon-shaped tip of snout

Long, slim lower jaw

Curved thumb claw

LONG-ARMED HUNTER
Suchomimus's arms were long and powerful, enabling it to reach into the water and grasp prey. It may have also torn open dinosaur corpses to feed on the flesh.

BARYONYX

BARYONYX ("HEAVY CLAW") was named after its huge
thumb claws. It also had an unusual crocodile-shaped
skull, and its jaws were filled with 96 pointed teeth,
twice as many as theropods usually possessed. These
features, along with fish remains found with
the skeleton, suggest that *Baryonyx*
preyed on fishes.

BARYONYX CLAW

*Sharp, curved thumb
claw 30 cm (12 in) long*

*Unusually thick,
powerful arm
bones*

*Sharp claws
on other fingers*

It is possible that *Baryonyx*
used its claws as hooks to spear
fishes out of the water, in the
same way as a bear does.

Fenestrae lightened
weight of skull

Long, narrow
jaws

BARYONYX SKULL

Many small
serrated teeth

Bony ridge
along spine

Relatively
stiff neck

Bony head
crest

BARYONYX
- Group: Theropoda
- Family: Spinosauridae
- Time: Cretaceous period
  (135–65 MYA)
- Size: 10 m (33 ft) long
- Diet: Fish, perhaps meat
- Habitat: Riverbanks

215

SPINOSAURUS

SPINOSAURUS ("spine lizard") was an immense theropod with an impressive sail-like structure running down its back. The function of the sail is not known, but some palaeontologists believe that it served to cool the dinosaur in hot weather.

Tooth socket

FOSSIL TOOTH BATTERY
This fragment from a *Spinosaurus*'s jaw displays empty tooth sockets.

Vertical "sail" supported by spines

Large, straight teeth

Stiff tail

Arms longer than usual for a large theropod

Powerful hind legs

Three long, forward-facing, clawed toes

SPINOSAURUS
- Group: Theropoda
- Family: Spinosauridae
- Time: Cretaceous period (135–65 MYA)
- Size: 15 m (49 ft) long
- Diet: Meat, perhaps fish
- Habitat: Tropical swamps

216

TYRANNOSAURUS

THE "TYRANT LIZARD" was one of the largest land carnivores ever. It was a heavily built theropod with a large head. Despite its fearsome appearance, there is evidence that *Tyrannosaurus* was a scavenger. Its small eyes and arms are not typical of an active hunter.

Tail held stiffly for balance

Pebbled skin texture

15-cm- (6-in-) long, serrated teeth

TYRANNOSAURUS SKELETON
Recent evidence reveal that the dinosaur's body was not held upright, as originally thought, but stood horizontally.

Extremely small hands

STRONG LEGS
Tyrannosaurus had thick, long legs with powerful muscles, for walking long distances.

58 teeth

Tail made up of about 40 vertebrae

SAUROPODOMORPHS

THE PROSAUROPODS and sauropods belong to the sauropodomorph group. Unlike theropods, most members of this group were quadrupedal (walked on four legs) and ate plants. They had long necks and tails, and ranged in length from 2 m (6½ ft) to 40 m (130 ft).

APATOSAURUS
THUMB CLAW

THUMB CLAW
Many sauropodomorphs had big, curved thumb claws. They probably used these dangerous weapons for defence.

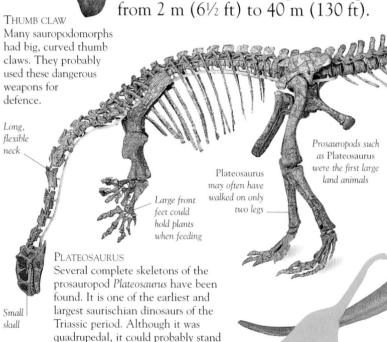

Long, flexible neck

Prosauropods such as Plateosaurus were the first large land animals

Plateosaurus may often have walked on only two legs

Large front feet could hold plants when feeding

PLATEOSAURUS
Several complete skeletons of the prosauropod *Plateosaurus* have been found. It is one of the earliest and largest saurischian dinosaurs of the Triassic period. Although it was quadrupedal, it could probably stand on its hind legs to feed on leaves of higher branches.

Small skull

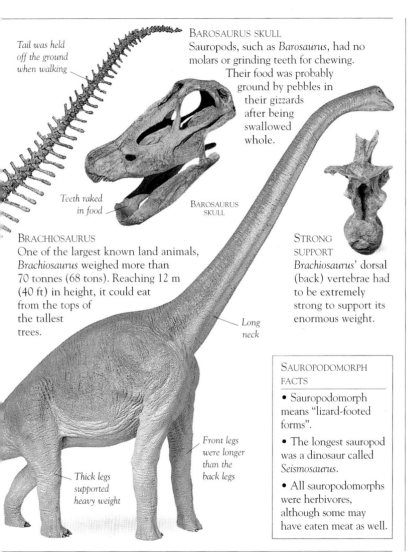

Tail was held off the ground when walking

BAROSAURUS SKULL
Sauropods, such as *Barosaurus*, had no molars or grinding teeth for chewing. Their food was probably ground by pebbles in their gizzards after being swallowed whole.

Teeth raked in food

BAROSAURUS SKULL

BRACHIOSAURUS
One of the largest known land animals, *Brachiosaurus* weighed more than 70 tonnes (68 tons). Reaching 12 m (40 ft) in height, it could eat from the tops of the tallest trees.

Long neck

STRONG SUPPORT
Brachiosaurus' dorsal (back) vertebrae had to be extremely strong to support its enormous weight.

Front legs were longer than the back legs

Thick legs supported heavy weight

SAUROPODOMORPH FACTS

• Sauropodomorph means "lizard-footed forms".

• The longest sauropod was a dinosaur called *Seismosaurus*.

• All sauropodomorphs were herbivores, although some may have eaten meat as well.

PROSAUROPODS

THE PROSAUROPODS are probably
ancestors of the sauropods. Both
had long necks and small heads,
but the prosauropods were
smaller. Most were herbivores,
but some ate meat.

THUMB CLAW
Massospondylus may have
been an omnivore as it had
large, serrated front teeth.
It also had sharp thumb
claws, which may have
been used to attack prey,
as well as for defence.

Teeth

Eye
socket

SMALL SKULL
Riojasaurus, at 10 m (33 ft) in length, was
the largest prosauropod. As with other
prosauropods, its skull was tiny compared
with its massive body, and its jaws
were lined with leaf-shaped
teeth for shredding
plant food.

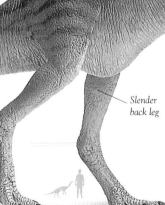

Slender
back leg

ANCHISAURUS
This prosauropod was designed to
walk on all fours, but it may have
occasionally run on two feet.
Anchisaurus had large, sickle-shaped
thumb claws which would have been
dangerous weapons against attackers.

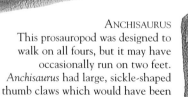

220

PROSAUROPOD FACTS

• The name prosauropod means "before sauropods".

• All prosauropods had small heads, long necks, and long tails.

• *Plateosaurus* was the first large dinosaur.

• Their remains have been found worldwide.

VIEW FROM ABOVE
This view from above of *Anchisaurus* shows that its body was long and slender. It would have held its tail off the ground when walking.

Slim and flexible neck

REACHING HIGH
Plateosaurus was one of the earliest and largest saurischian dinosaurs. It grew to about 8 m (26 ft) in length, and could stand on its hind legs to reach tall trees when feeding.

Lower arm

Thumb claw

Large thumb claw

PULLING CLAW
The digits on the hands of *Plateosaurus* varied greatly in length. The thumb, the largest, ended with a huge, sharp claw.

221

THECODONTOSAURUS

THIS DINOSAUR WAS the first prosauropod to be discovered, and is also one of the most primitive known. Its name ("socket-toothed lizard") was given because its saw-edged teeth looked like those of a monitor lizard, but were embedded in the sockets of the jaw bones. *Thecodontosaurus* had a relatively small head and neck, but a long tail. This dinosaur was the earliest known of the prosauropods.

THECODONTOSAURUS

- Group: Prosauropoda
- Family: Anchisauridae
- Time: Triassic period (250–203 MYA)
- Size: 2.1 m (7 ft) long
- Diet: Plants, possibly omnivorous
- Habitat: Desert plains, dry upland areas

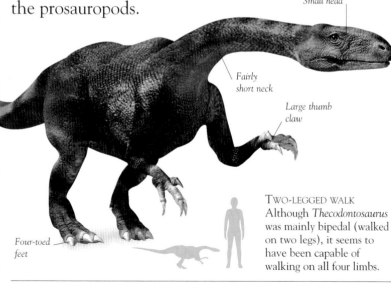

Small head

Fairly short neck

Large thumb claw

Four-toed feet

TWO-LEGGED WALK
Although *Thecodontosaurus* was mainly bipedal (walked on two legs), it seems to have been capable of walking on all four limbs.

EFRAASIA

THIS EARLY PROSAUROPOD was named after its discoverer, E. Fraas. It was lightly built, with a small head, a fairly long neck, a bulky body, and a long tail. Its legs were longer than its arms, and its five-fingered hands had a large thumb claw. It may have walked on all fours, rising onto its hind legs to run.

Nostrils far forward on snout

Flexible tail

Five long digits on hands

Four-toed feet

EFRAASIA

- Group: Prosauropoda
- Family: Anchisauridae
- Time: Triassic period (250–203 MYA)
- Size: 2.4 m (7¼ ft) long
- Diet: Plants
- Habitat: Dry upland plains

ANCHISAURUS

ANCHISAURUS MEANS "near lizard" because this small, early prosauropod was very closely related to its reptilian ancestors. It had a small head with a narrow snout, a long, flexible neck, and a slim body and tail. *Anchisaurus*'s limbs were short and sturdy although its hindlimbs were larger than its forelimbs. Its feet were slender with five clawed toes. The five-fingered hand had a thumb with a large claw that may have been used for defence against attackers.

VERSATILE WALKER
Although *Anchisaurus*'s arms were a third shorter than its legs, it spent most of its time on all fours. However, it may also have run on two legs and could perhaps raise itself up on its hind legs to reach high plants.

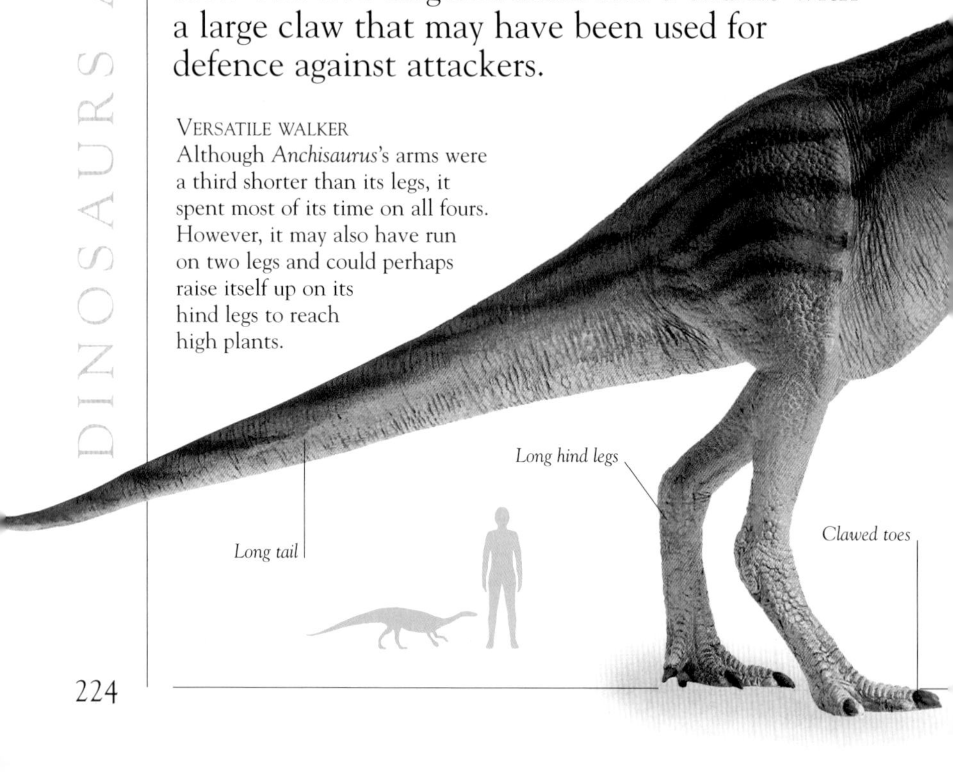

Long hind legs

Clawed toes

Long tail

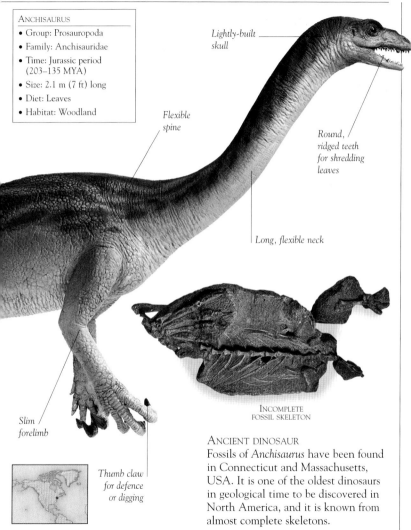

ANCHISAURUS
- Group: Prosauropoda
- Family: Anchisauridae
- Time: Jurassic period (203–135 MYA)
- Size: 2.1 m (7 ft) long
- Diet: Leaves
- Habitat: Woodland

Lightly-built skull

Flexible spine

Round, ridged teeth for shredding leaves

Long, flexible neck

Slim forelimb

Thumb claw for defence or digging

INCOMPLETE FOSSIL SKELETON

ANCIENT DINOSAUR
Fossils of *Anchisaurus* have been found in Connecticut and Massachusetts, USA. It is one of the oldest dinosaurs in geological time to be discovered in North America, and it is known from almost complete skeletons.

225

MASSOSPONDYLUS

MASSOSPONDYLUS ("massive vertebrae") was so named because the first remains found of it were a few large vertebrae. More fossil finds have since been made, suggesting that this prosauropod was one of the most common in southern Africa. *Massospondylus* was four-legged, but could stand on its hind legs to feed from trees.

MASSOSPONDYLUS

- Group: Prosauropoda
- Family: Massospondylidae
- Time: Jurassic period (203–135 MYA)
- Size: 4 m (13 ft) long
- Diet: Plants
- Habitat: Scrubland and desert plains

LONG REACH

This dinosaur had a tiny head on an extremely long neck. It had massive, five-fingered hands that could be used for holding food or for walking.

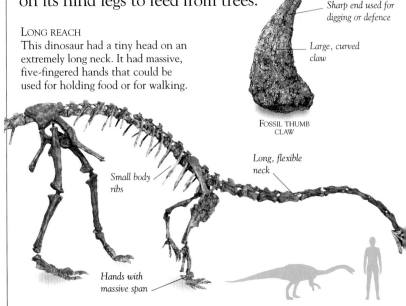

Sharp end used for digging or defence

Large, curved claw

FOSSIL THUMB CLAW

Long, flexible neck

Small body ribs

Hands with massive span

LUFENGOSAURUS

LUFENGOSAURUS ("Lufeng lizard")
was found in China. It was heavy
and stout-limbed. Its small head
held many widely spaced, leaf-shaped
teeth, a typical feature of all
prosauropods. Its lower jaw was
hinged below the level of the
upper teeth, making it
easier for the jaw
muscles to feed on
tough plant food.

*Large, deep
head*

*Bulky,
heavy
body*

*Large hands to
support weight
when walking*

LUFENGOSAURUS

- Group: Prosauropoda
- Family: Melanorosauridae
- Time: Jurassic period
  (203–135 MYA)
- Size: 6 m (20 ft) long
- Diet: Coniferous trees
- Habitat: Desert plains and
  scrubland

SPREADING HANDS AND FEET
Lufengosaurus's broad feet had
four long toes, while the large
hands had long, clawed fingers
and thumbs with massive claws.

PLATEOSAURUS

PLATEOSAURUS WAS ONE of the most common dinosaurs of the Late Triassic Period. The large number of fossil finds suggest that *Plateosaurus* may have lived in herds and migrated in search of food and water. Its small skull was deeper than those of most other prosauropods. *Plateosaurus* had many small, leaf-shaped teeth, and the hinge of the lower jaw was low-slung to give it more flexibility. All these features indicate a diet primarily made up of plants.

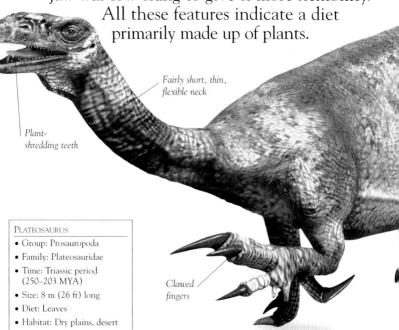

Fairly short, thin, flexible neck

Plant-shredding teeth

PLATEOSAURUS

- Group: Prosauropoda
- Family: Plateosauridae
- Time: Triassic period (250–203 MYA)
- Size: 8 m (26 ft) long
- Diet: Leaves
- Habitat: Dry plains, desert

Clawed fingers

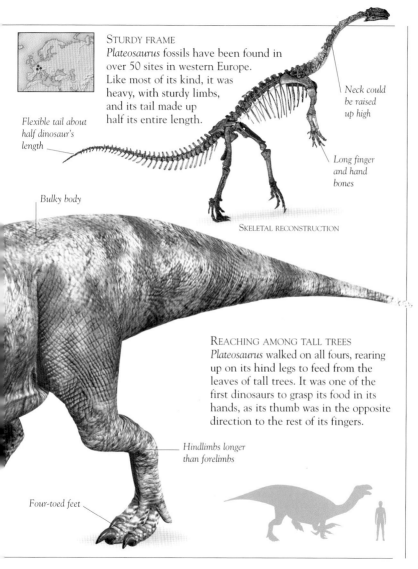

STURDY FRAME

Plateosaurus fossils have been found in over 50 sites in western Europe. Like most of its kind, it was heavy, with sturdy limbs, and its tail made up half its entire length.

Neck could be raised up high

Flexible tail about half dinosaur's length

Long finger and hand bones

Bulky body

SKELETAL RECONSTRUCTION

REACHING AMONG TALL TREES

Plateosaurus walked on all fours, rearing up on its hind legs to feed from the leaves of tall trees. It was one of the first dinosaurs to grasp its food in its hands, as its thumb was in the opposite direction to the rest of its fingers.

Hindlimbs longer than forelimbs

Four-toed feet

SAUROPODS

THE LARGEST-EVER land animals belonged to the sauropod group. These plant-eating dinosaurs were quadrupedal, with long necks, elephant-like legs, and long whip-like tails.

TAIL REINFORCEMENT
Tail bones like the one above were on the underside of *Diplodocus*'s tail. They reinforced and protected the tail when it was pressed against the ground.

FRONT TEETH
Diplodocus had a long skull with peg-like teeth at the front of the jaws. The teeth would have raked in plants such as cycads, ginkgoes, and conifers. *Diplodocus* had no back teeth for chewing, so the food was probably ground in the stomach by gastroliths (stomach stones).

Back of jaws was toothless

Peg-like teeth

APATOSAURUS
This dinosaur was one of the largest sauropods at 23 m (73 ft) long. This reconstruction has *Apatosaurus* dragging its tail, although it almost certainly carried it off the ground. It had a horse-like head with a fist-sized brain, and powerful legs with padded feet.

Tail contained 82 bones

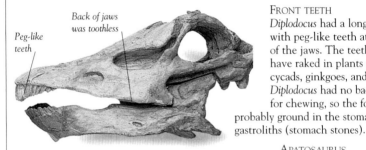

TAIL WEAPON
Barosaurus resembled *Diplodocus*, but had a slightly longer neck and a shorter tail. The narrow tail may have been a defence weapon.

Tail may have been used like a whip against enemies

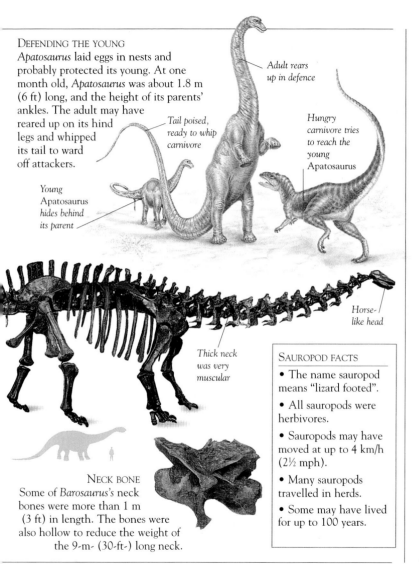

DEFENDING THE YOUNG

Apatosaurus laid eggs in nests and probably protected its young. At one month old, *Apatosaurus* was about 1.8 m (6 ft) long, and the height of its parents' ankles. The adult may have reared up on its hind legs and whipped its tail to ward off attackers.

Tail poised, ready to whip carnivore

Adult rears up in defence

Hungry carnivore tries to reach the young Apatosaurus

Young Apatosaurus hides behind its parent

Thick neck was very muscular

Horse-like head

NECK BONE

Some of *Barosaurus*'s neck bones were more than 1 m (3 ft) in length. The bones were also hollow to reduce the weight of the 9-m- (30-ft-) long neck.

SAUROPOD FACTS

• The name sauropod means "lizard footed".

• All sauropods were herbivores.

• Sauropods may have moved at up to 4 km/h (2½ mph).

• Many sauropods travelled in herds.

• Some may have lived for up to 100 years.

VULCANODON

THIS DINOSAUR WAS NAMED after the volcanic rock in which the first skeleton was found. With the skeleton were seven teeth, which actually came from a predator that may have eaten it. *Vulcanodon* is one of the earliest sauropods known, dating back to the Triassic. It would have roughly been the size of a large crocodile. *Vulcanodon* had blunt claws on its feet and an enlarged claw on each inner toe.

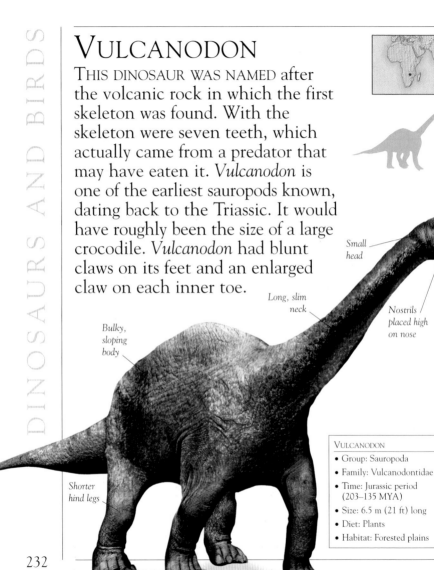

Small head

Long, slim neck

Nostrils placed high on nose

Bulky, sloping body

Shorter hind legs

VULCANODON
- Group: Sauropoda
- Family: Vulcanodontidae
- Time: Jurassic period (203–135 MYA)
- Size: 6.5 m (21 ft) long
- Diet: Plants
- Habitat: Forested plains

BARAPASAURUS

THE NAME *Barapasaurus* means "big-legged lizard". This is one of the earliest and best-known sauropods of the Early Jurassic. All parts of the skeleton, except the skull and feet, have been found. *Barapasaurus* had slim limbs, spoon-shaped, saw-edged teeth, and hollows in the vertebrae of the back. Scientists believe that its head was short and deep.

Relatively short neck

Heavy, bulky body

Long, flexible tail

Elephant-like legs and feet

BARAPASAURUS

- Group: Sauropoda
- Family: Vulcanodontidae
- Time: Jurassic period (203–135 MYA)
- Size: 18 m (59 ft) long
- Diet: Plants
- Habitat: Plains

CETIOSAURUS

THIS DINOSAUR, whose name means "whale lizard", was a large, heavy sauropod with a shorter neck and tail than other sauropods. Its head was blunt, and contained spoon-shaped teeth. *Cetiosaurus* is thought to have roamed across the open countryside in large herds. It had a walking speed of about 15 kph (10 mph).

CETIOSAURUS
- Group: Sauropoda
- Family: Cetiosauridae
- Time: Jurassic period (203–135 MYA)
- Size: 18 m (59 ft) long
- Diet: Plants
- Habitat: Plains

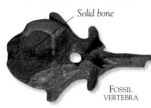

Solid bone

FOSSIL VERTEBRA

SOLID VERTEBRAE
Cetiosaurus was different from other sauropods in that its vertebrae were solid, without hollow spaces to lighten them.

MISTAKEN IDENTITY
This dinosaur was discovered in the early 18th century. Its huge bones were first thought to belong to a whale – hence its name.

Tail held off the ground

Shoulder blade was 1.5m (5ft) long

SHUNOSAURUS

NEARLY COMPLETE skeletons of *Shunosaurus* ("Shuno lizard") have been discovered, meaning it is only the second sauropod to be known entirely. The skull is long and low with small teeth. A surprising feature is the small bony club at the end of its tail, formed by enlarged vertebrae (not seen in the pictured specimen).

SHUNOSAURUS
- Group: Sauropoda
- Family: Possibly Cetiosauridae
- Time: Jurassic period (203–135 MYA)
- Size: 10 m (33 ft) long
- Diet: Plants
- Habitat: Plains

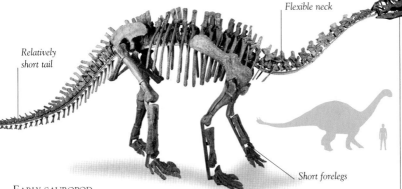

Low head with large nostrils

Flexible neck

Relatively short tail

Short forelegs

EARLY SAUROPOD
Shunosaurus belonged to the Middle Jurassic period. Early sauropods like this showed basic characteristics such as a small head, long neck and tail, deep body, and pillar-like legs – but these were not yet fully developed. Their necks and tails were relatively shorter with fewer and heavier vertebrae.

BAROSAURUS

BAROSAURUS ("heavy lizard") had all the typical features of its family – a long neck and tail, a bulky body, tiny head, and short legs for its huge size. *Barosaurus* probably roamed in herds and relied on its size for defence against the large predators of the time. Its tail had a thin whiplash end and would have hit out with great force, if swung against an attacking dinosaur.

BAROSAURUS
- Group: Sauropoda
- Family: Diplodocidae
- Time: Jurassic period (203–135 MYA)
- Size: 23–27 m (75–89 ft) long
- Diet: Plants
- Habitat: Floodplains

Enormous, bulky body typical of a sauropod

Powerful tail with whiplash end

Elephant-like hind limbs

DINOSAUR HUNTING
This photograph shows the camp at Carnegie Quarry, USA, where three *Barosaurus* skeletons were found in 1922. By the end of the year, 22 skeletons of 10 dinosaur species had been found.

Tiny head at end of incredibly long neck

GIGANTIC NECK
One-third of this dinosaur's length was made up of its thin and long neck. This creature could hold its head at a height of 15 m (49 ft). However, it would have held its neck at shoulder height for most of the time.

Front legs shorter than hind legs

Single-clawed front feet

Elongated vertebra of the back

STRETCHED OUT VERTEBRAE
The neck and back vertebrae of the *Barosaurus* were extremely stretched to create this dinosaur's enormous length.

VERTEBRA

DIPLODOCUS

DIPLODOCUS WAS ONE of the longest dinosaurs. From head to tail, it was longer than a tennis court. Its weight was finely balanced at the hips, and so it may have been able to rise on its hind legs. Its limbs were slim and it had a whiplash tail. *Diplodocus*'s name meaning "double beam" came from twin extensions, called chevrons, under its tail bones.

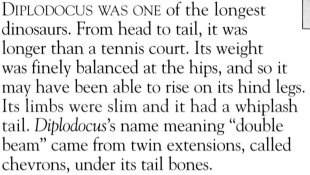

Peg-like teeth at front of jaws

Slim lower jaw

VARIED EATER
The wear on the teeth of *Diplodocus* suggests that it fed both low, from ground-hugging vegetation, and high, from tree branches.

DIPLODOCUS
• Group: Sauropoda
• Family: Diplodocidae
• Time: Jurassic period (203–135 MYA)
• Size: 27 m (87 ft) long
• Diet: Leaves
• Habitat: Plains

APATOSAURUS

THIS SAUROPOD WAS shorter, yet heavier and bulkier than its close relatives. It had a tiny head at the end of a long neck made up of 15 vertebrae. Its back vertebrae were hollow, and its long tail had a whip-like end. The thick hind legs were longer than the front ones. One species of *Apatosaurus*, *A. excelsus*, was the dinosaur originally called *Brontosaurus*.

Neck not as flexible as other sauropods

Tail over half the total length of dinosaur

THICK-LIMBED DINOSAUR *Apatosaurus* may have reared up on its hindlegs to feed or bring its "hands" down on its attacker.

Thick hind legs longer than front legs

APATOSAURUS
- Group: Sauropoda
- Family: Diplodocidae
- Time: Jurassic period (203–135 MYA)
- Size: 21 m (70 ft) long
- Diet: Leaves
- Habitat: Wooded plains

MAMENCHISAURUS

MAMENCHISAURUS had one of the longest necks of any known dinosaur. It was more than half of the animal's total length, and had 19 vertebrae – more than any other dinosaur. Some experts think *Mamenchisaurus* may not have been able to hold its neck much higher than shoulder height.

MAMENCHISAURUS
- Group: Sauropoda
- Family: Mamenchisauridae
- Time: Jurassic period (203–135 MYA)
- Size: 22 m (72 ft) long
- Diet: Leaves and shoots
- Habitat: Deltas and forested areas

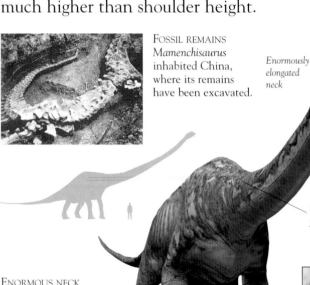

FOSSIL REMAINS
Mamenchisaurus inhabited China, where its remains have been excavated.

Enormously elongated neck

Back sloping from shoulders

ENORMOUS NECK
Mamenchisaurus's neck alone may have measured about 14 m (46 ft).

CAMARASAURUS

CAMARASAURUS ("chambered lizard") was the commonest sauropod of North America. It probably roamed in large herds, stripping tough leaves from shrubby trees at shoulder height. This dinosaur had a relatively large, box-shaped head, and a short neck and tail. *Camarasaurus*'s vertebrae may have contained large holes to lighten the backbone.

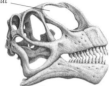

Nasal chambers high on snout

FOSSIL SKULL

BLUNT FACE
Camarasaurus's short, deep skull ended in a blunt muzzle similar to a bulldog.

PILLAR-LIKE LIMBS
The front legs of *Camarasaurus* were relatively long. Its forefeet had one single claw, and the hindfeet three.

Massive, heavy body

Short head

Three claws on hindfeet

CAMARASAURUS
- Group: Sauropoda
- Family: Camarasauridae
- Time: Jurassic period (203–135 MYA)
- Size: 23 m (75 ft) long
- Diet: Tough vegetation
- Habitat: Plains

BRACHIOSAURUS

THE "ARM LIZARD", or *Brachiosaurus*, was one of the tallest and largest sauropods, with extremely long forelimbs compared to its hind limbs. Its stretched-out neck, ending in a small head, gave it enormous height. The nostrils were large and were situated on a bulge on the top of the head. Like other sauropods, it probably travelled in herds, and fed on vegetation from the tops of trees.

Long neck made up of vertebrae 1 m (3 ft) long

Ball-like head of femur

MASSIVE BONES
The femur (thigh bone) of *Brachiosaurus* was over 1.8 m (6 ft) long and massively thick to support the dinosaur's weight. Its legs were pillar-like and each foot had five toes. The first toe of the front foot bore a claw, as did the first three toes of the hind foot.

Nostrils on bulge on top of head

BRACHIOSAURUS
- Group: Sauropoda
- Family: Brachiosauridae
- Time: Jurassic period (203–135 MYA)
- Size: 26 m (85 ft) long
- Diet: Plants
- Habitat: Plains

Chisel-like teeth at front of mouth

Body sloping downwards from shoulder to hip

Pillar-like legs

ARGENTINOSAURUS

ONLY A FEW BONES of *Argentinosaurus* ("Argentina lizard") have been found to date, including some huge vertebrae, which were over 1.5 m (5 ft) wide. Other bones found were the sacrum (the triangular bone between the hip bones), a tibia (shin bone), and a few ribs. As a result, little is known about this dinosaur. However, Argentinosaurus appears to have been the longest dinosaur ever found – the length of three big school buses parked end to end.

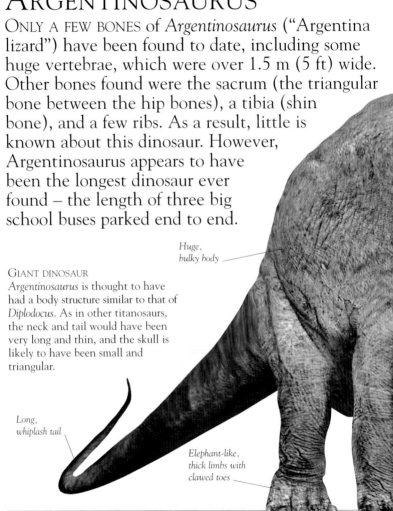

Huge, bulky body

GIANT DINOSAUR
Argentinosaurus is thought to have had a body structure similar to that of *Diplodocus*. As in other titanosaurs, the neck and tail would have been very long and thin, and the skull is likely to have been small and triangular.

Long, whiplash tail

Elephant-like, thick limbs with clawed toes

Long, slim neck

Small, triangular head

ARGENTINOSAURUS

- Group: Sauropoda
- Family: Titanosauridae
- Time: Cretaceous period (135–65 MYA)
- Size: 40 m (130 ft) long
- Diet: Conifers
- Habitat: Forested areas

DISCOVERY IN ARGENTINA

The first bone of *Argentinosaurus* was found on an Argentinian sheep ranch in 1988. The rancher who found it thought the fossils were firewood at first. It took several years to dig the bones out of the ground, and the dinosaur was finally named in 1993.

245

TITANOSAURUS

"TITAN LIZARD"
is known only
from some
lower-back
vertebrae and limb bones.
Its skull has never been found.
However, it probably had the
typical sauropod body shape. Its
vertebrae were not hollow for
weight-saving as they were in
most other sauropods.

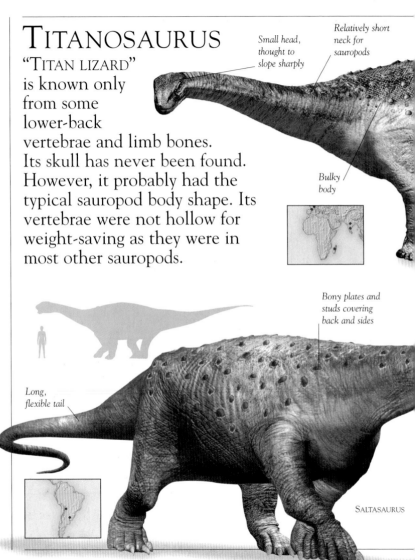

Small head, thought to slope sharply

Relatively short neck for sauropods

Bulky body

Bony plates and studs covering back and sides

Long, flexible tail

SALTASAURUS

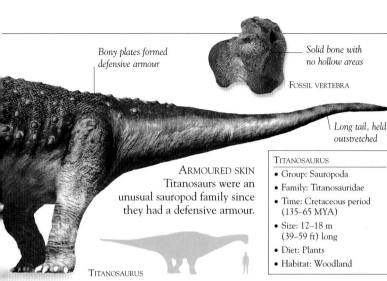

Bony plates formed defensive armour

Solid bone with no hollow areas

FOSSIL VERTEBRA

Long tail, held outstretched

ARMOURED SKIN
Titanosaurs were an unusual sauropod family since they had a defensive armour.

TITANOSAURUS

TITANOSAURUS
- Group: Sauropoda
- Family: Titanosauridae
- Time: Cretaceous period (135–65 MYA)
- Size: 12–18 m (39–59 ft) long
- Diet: Plants
- Habitat: Woodland

Nostrils high on head

Fossilized impressions of bony plates of varying sizes

FOSSIL ARMOUR

SALTASAURUS

SALTASAURUS was named after the province in Argentina where it was first found. Its fossils consisted of a group of partial skeletons surrounded by thousands of bony plates – large and small. This was the first evidence of armoured skin on a sauropod. It may have used its strong tail as a prop when it reared up on its hind legs.

SALTASAURUS
- Group: Sauropoda
- Family: Titanosauridae
- Time: Cretaceous period (135–65 MYA)
- Size: 12 m (39 ft) long
- Diet: Plants
- Habitat: Woodland

ABOUT ORNITHISCHIANS

THERE WERE FIVE main groups of ornithischian. They were all herbivores with hoofed feet and hip-bones arranged like modern birds. Most of them had beaked mouths. Ornithischians were either bipedal or quadrupedal; the bipedal ones held out their tails stiffly to balance their bodies while feeding or running.

CERATOPSIANS

ANKYLOSAURS

ORNITHOPODS

PACHYCEPHALOSAURS

FIVE GROUPS
The five groups of ornithischians were: ceratopsians, with their neck frills; ankylosaurs, with their body armour; pachycephalosaurs, with their domed heads; stegosaurs, with their back plates; and the bird-like ornithopods.

STEGOSAURS

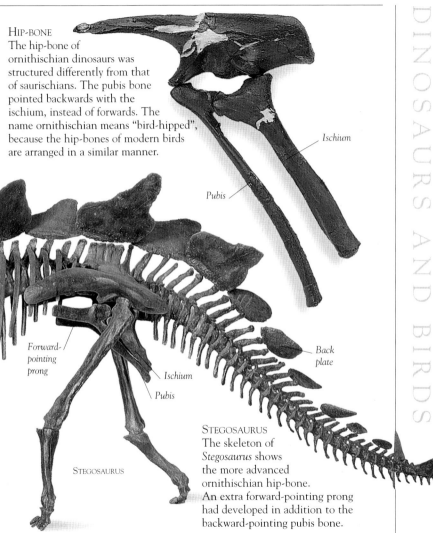

HIP-BONE
The hip-bone of ornithischian dinosaurs was structured differently from that of saurischians. The pubis bone pointed backwards with the ischium, instead of forwards. The name ornithischian means "bird-hipped", because the hip-bones of modern birds are arranged in a similar manner.

Ischium

Pubis

Forward-pointing prong

Ischium

Pubis

Back plate

STEGOSAURUS

STEGOSAURUS
The skeleton of *Stegosaurus* shows the more advanced ornithischian hip-bone. An extra forward-pointing prong had developed in addition to the backward-pointing pubis bone.

ORNITHOPODS

ALL THE ORNITHOPOD dinosaurs were herbivores with horned beaks. Their jaws and leaf-shaped cheek teeth were ideal for chewing vegetation. They were bipedal, although some of them may have foraged for food on all fours. Their feet had three or four toes, and their hands had four or five fingers.

Cheek teeth

Tusk-like teeth

HETERODONTOSAURUS
Heterodontosaurus had three different kinds of teeth. These were the front upper teeth, which bit against the toothless lower beak; the scissor-like cheek teeth; and a pair of upper and lower tusk-like teeth.

GROUP LIVING
Hypsilophodon may have moved in herds for protection against predatory theropods. Moving as a large group, they would have been able to warn each other of any danger, giving them a better chance of survival.

Group members looked from side to side for any danger

Slim, long legs for speed

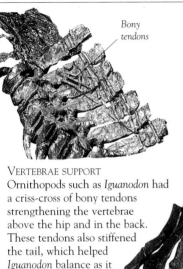

Bony tendons

VERTEBRAE SUPPORT
Ornithopods such as *Iguanodon* had a criss-cross of bony tendons strengthening the vertebrae above the hip and in the back. These tendons also stiffened the tail, which helped *Iguanodon* balance as it walked on its hind legs.

Toes ended in flattened hooves

THREE-TOED FEET
The powerful three-toed feet of *Corythosaurus* were built to carry its heavy weight. *Corythosaurus* weighed approximately 4 tonnes and was about 7.5 m (24 ft) long. It belonged to a group of ornithopods called hadrosaurs.

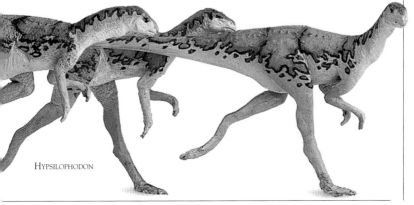

HYPSILOPHODON

HETERODONTOSAURUS

AS ITS NAME ("different-toothed lizard") suggests, the most remarkable feature of this small bipedal dinosaur was its teeth. *Heterodontosaurus* had three kinds: cutting incisors at the front of the upper jaw, two pairs of large tusk-like teeth, and tall chisel-like teeth used for shredding vegetation. The tusks may have been used to frighten or attack enemies, or in fights between competing males.

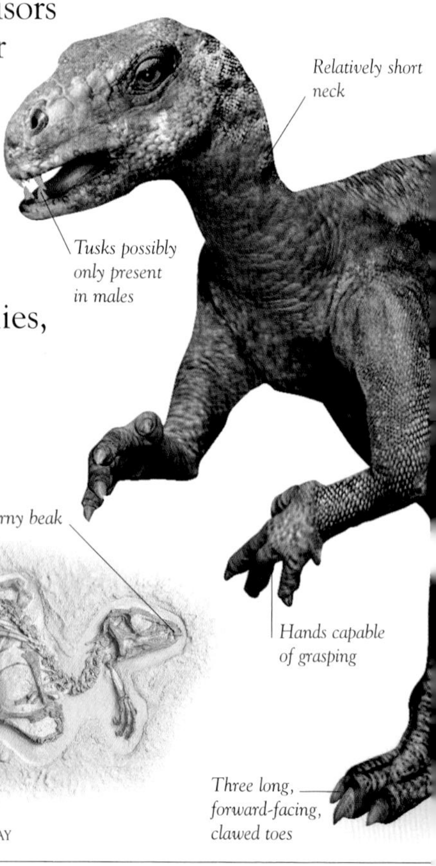

Relatively short neck

Tusks possibly only present in males

Bony rods stiffened back and tail

Horny beak

Hands capable of grasping

Three long, forward-facing, clawed toes

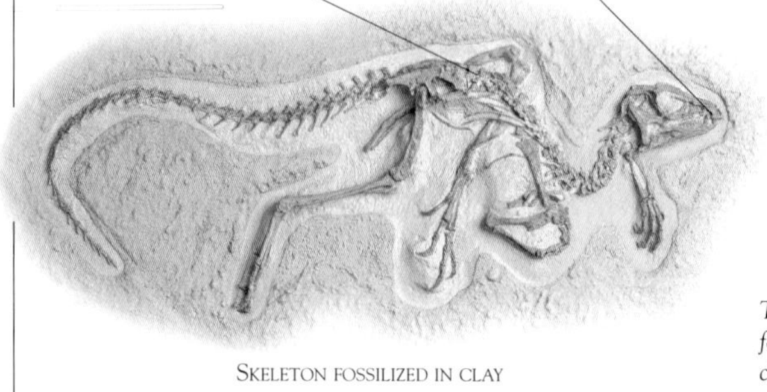

SKELETON FOSSILIZED IN CLAY

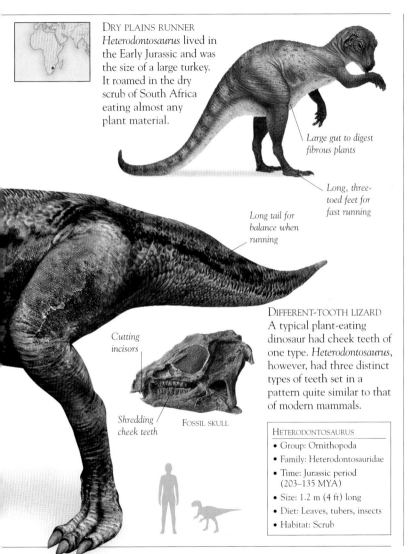

DRY PLAINS RUNNER
Heterodontosaurus lived in the Early Jurassic and was the size of a large turkey. It roamed in the dry scrub of South Africa eating almost any plant material.

Large gut to digest fibrous plants

Long, three-toed feet for fast running

Long tail for balance when running

Cutting incisors

Shredding cheek teeth FOSSIL SKULL

DIFFERENT-TOOTH LIZARD
A typical plant-eating dinosaur had cheek teeth of one type. *Heterodontosaurus*, however, had three distinct types of teeth set in a pattern quite similar to that of modern mammals.

HETERODONTOSAURUS
• Group: Ornithopoda
• Family: Heterodontosauridae
• Time: Jurassic period (203–135 MYA)
• Size: 1.2 m (4 ft) long
• Diet: Leaves, tubers, insects
• Habitat: Scrub

DRYOSAURUS

DRYOSAURUS ("oak lizard") was a lightly built bipedal herbivore, with powerful, slender legs that were much longer than its arms. Its tail was stiffened by bony tendons for better balance. It had a short skull with large eyes. The horny beak at the front of the lower jaw met with a toothless beak on the upper jaw – perfectly suited for cropping tough vegetation.

SWIFT RUNNER

Dryosaurus lived in the woodlands of what is now North America, Africa, and Europe. Its legs and feet were meant for swift running. Although it was two-legged, hatchlings may have walked on all fours.

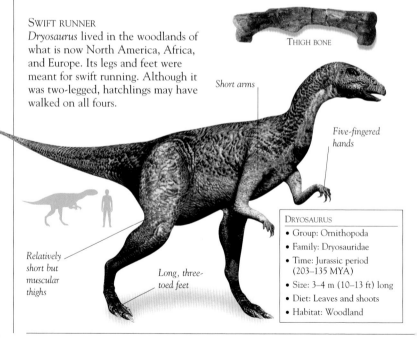

THIGH BONE

Short arms

Five-fingered hands

Relatively short but muscular thighs

Long, three-toed feet

DRYOSAURUS
- Group: Ornithopoda
- Family: Dryosauridae
- Time: Jurassic period (203–135 MYA)
- Size: 3–4 m (10–13 ft) long
- Diet: Leaves and shoots
- Habitat: Woodland

CAMPTOSAURUS

CAMPTOSAURUS ("bent lizard") was
a bulky plant-eater that browsed on
plants and shrubs close to the ground. Its head was
long and low, with a sharp, horny beak at the tip
of the broad snout. Its arms were shorter than its
legs, but a large wrist and hoof-like claws on its
fingers allowed it to walk on its hands.
Camptosaurus probably browsed
on all fours, rising onto its
powerful hind legs to run.

STRONG BACKBONE
Like other ornithopods,
Camptosaurus had criss-cross
tendons growing on the
spines of its vertebrae. This
strengthened the spine
and made it stiff.

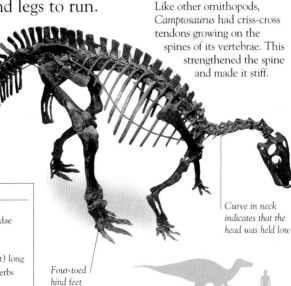

*Tail stiffened
by bony
ligaments*

*Curve in neck
indicates that the
head was held low*

*Four-toed
hind feet*

CAMPTOSAURUS
- Group: Ornithopoda
- Family: Camptosauridae
- Time: Jurassic period
  (203–135 MYA)
- Size: 5–7 m (16–23 ft) long
- Diet: Low-growing herbs
  and shrubs
- Habitat: Open woodland

HYPSILOPHODON

THIS PRIMITIVE ORNITHISCHIAN, whose name means "high-ridge tooth", was named for its grooved cheek teeth, was very efficient at chewing tough Cretaceous vegetation. Its jaws hinged below the level of the teeth giving it a strong bite, and held 28 or 30 teeth that were self-sharpening. The mouth had cheek pouches that could be used for storing food. Its small head had a horny beak and large eyes.

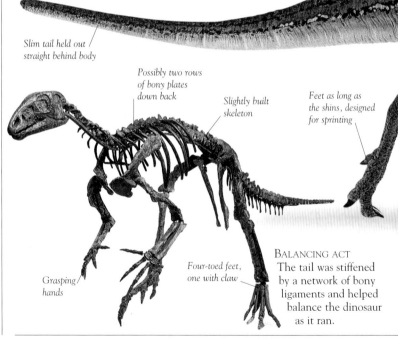

Slim tail held out straight behind body

Possibly two rows of bony plates down back

Slightly built skeleton

Feet as long as the shins, designed for sprinting

Grasping hands

Four-toed feet, one with claw

BALANCING ACT
The tail was stiffened by a network of bony ligaments and helped balance the dinosaur as it ran.

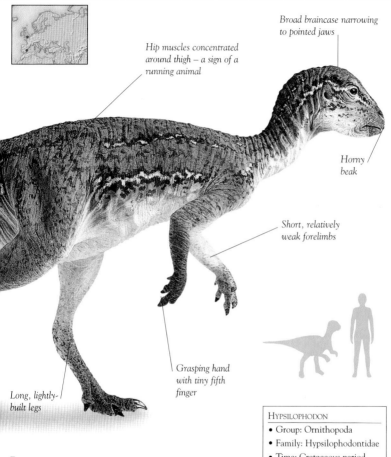

Hip muscles concentrated around thigh – a sign of a running animal

Broad braincase narrowing to pointed jaws

Horny beak

Short, relatively weak forelimbs

Grasping hand with tiny fifth finger

Long, lightly-built legs

BIGGER THAN THOUGHT

Hypsilophodon is known from several skeletons, all sub-adult. This has led to the idea that it was a very small dinosaur. The adult, however, would have been about 3 m (10 ft) long.

HYPSILOPHODON
- Group: Ornithopoda
- Family: Hypsilophodontidae
- Time: Cretaceous period (135–65 MYA)
- Size: 2 m (6½ ft) long
- Diet: Plants
- Habitat: Forests

257

IGUANODON

IGUANODON ("iguana tooth") is one of the best-known dinosaurs. Its fossils have been found in Europe, Asia, and North America. *Iguanodon* was a stoutly built herbivore that walked with its body and tail held horizontally.

IGUANODON
- Group: Ornithopoda
- Family: Iguanodontidae
- Time: Cretaceous period (135–65 MYA)
- Size: 9 m (30 ft) long
- Diet: Plants
- Habitat: Woodland

DEXTEROUS DINOSAUR

Iguanodon was primarily quadrupedal, but also capable of bipedal walking. It had very specialized hands, which could have been used for walking, as a weapon, and to grasp food. The thumb was armed with a vicious spike. The second, third, and fourth fingers were webbed, while the fifth finger could curl and grasp.

Thumb spike 15 cm (½ ft) long

FOSSIL THUMB SPIKE

Horny beak at front of jaw

FOSSIL SKULL

EFFICIENT JAW

Iguanodon could chew food with its batteries of cheek teeth. It had a hinged upper jaw that allowed the teeth in the upper jaw to grind over those in the lower jaw.

OURANOSAURUS

THE MOST REMARKABLE feature of this dinosaur was the row of spines growing out from its backbone – from the shoulders to halfway down its tail. Some experts think they supported a sail that acted as a heat controller; others suggest that it may have been covered by a bison-like hump.

Spines longest just behind shoulder

Height of spines less towards the tail

SKELETAL RECONSTRUCTION

Long hind limbs

Pair of bony bumps formed head crest

Tail held rigid and outstretched

Horny beak

BRAVE ONE
The name *Ouranosaurus*, means "brave lizard".

Hind legs longer than forelimbs

OURANOSAURUS
- Group: Ornithopoda
- Family: Iguanodontidae
- Time: Cretaceous period (135–65 MYA)
- Size: 7 m (23 ft) long
- Diet: Leaves, fruit, and seeds
- Habitat: Tropical plains and forest

Hoof-like nails on three-toed feet

Thumb spike

HADROSAURUS

HADROSAURUS ("STURDY LIZARD") was one of the first dinosaurs ever found in North America. Its skull had a toothless, horny beak used for scraping off vegetation, and hundreds of blunt cheek teeth for chewing. Although its forelimbs were much shorter than its hind legs, *Hadrosaurus* spent most of its time browsing on all fours. It walked with its stiff tail held outstretched for better balance.

Crest of solid bone

NEW TEETH
Hadrosaurus's teeth were continually replaced as they wore down from chewing on tough plant material.

Jaw would have been covered with a horny beak

Low jaw hinge for powerful chewing action

Batteries of grinding cheek teeth

HADROSAURUS
- Group: Ornithopoda
- Family: Hadrosauridae
- Time: Cretaceous period (135–65 MYA)
- Size: 9 m (30 ft) long
- Diet: Leaves and twigs
- Habitat: Swamps and forests

MAIASAURA

THIS DINOSAUR'S NAME means "good earth-mother lizard". It was so named because remains were found close to fossilized nests scooped out of mud, which contained eggs arranged in circular layers. *Maiasaura* migrated and nested each year in large herds.

NEST-SITE RECONSTRUCTION

FEEDING THE YOUNG
Fossil evidence show that the dinosaur parents brought food to their young at the nest site over quite a lengthy period.

DUCK-BILLED DINOSAUR
Maiasaura was a flat-headed, duck-billed dinosaur. It had hollows around its nostrils that may have been skin pouches.

Large eye sockets characterize juvenile

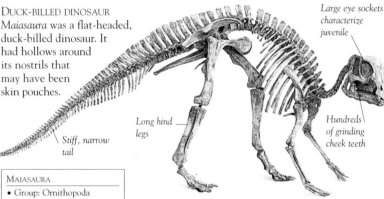

Stiff, narrow tail

Long hind legs

Hundreds of grinding cheek teeth

SKELETON OF JUVENILE

MAIASAURA
- Group: Ornithopoda
- Family: Hadrosauridae
- Time: Cretaceous period (135–65 MYA)
- Size: 9 m (30 ft) long
- Diet: Leaves
- Habitat: Coastal plains

CORYTHOSAURUS

CORYTHOSAURUS ("helmet lizard") was named for the distinctive hollow crest on top of its head. This seems to have been larger in males and may have produced a booming foghorn-like sound used for signalling amongst herds. The angle of the neck, and the broad beak, suggest that *Corythosaurus* fed from low undergrowth.

CORYTHOSAURUS
- Group: Ornithopoda
- Family: Hadrosauridae
- Time: Cretaceous period (135–65 MYA)
- Size: 10 m (33 ft) long
- Diet: Leaves, seeds, pine needles
- Habitat: Forests

FOREST SWAMP DWELLER
Corythosaurus and other hadrosaurs lived among cypresses, pines and ferns in the warm forests of North America. The first flowering plants were beginning to spread during this period.

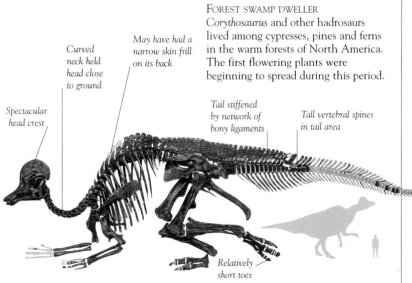

Curved neck held head close to ground

May have had a narrow skin frill on its back

Spectacular head crest

Tail stiffened by network of bony ligaments

Tall vertebral spines in tail area

Relatively short toes

LAMBEOSAURUS

LAMBEOSAURUS WAS named after Lawrence Lambe who discovered it in 1898 in Alberta. It is closely related to *Corythosaurus*, but was unusual in having two head structures: a tall, hollow crest over the snout and a backward-pointing spike behind it. These were probably used for signalling and for recognition.

LAMBEOSAURUS
- Group: Ornithopoda
- Family: Hadrosauridae
- Time: Cretaceous period (135–65 MYA)
- Size: 9 m (30 ft) long
- Diet: Low-growing leaves, fruit, seeds
- Habitat: Woodland

SOCIAL ANIMAL
Like other members of this family, *Lambeosaurus* had a deep, narrow tail, held stiff and immobile. It travelled in large herds, browsing on low-growing vegetation.

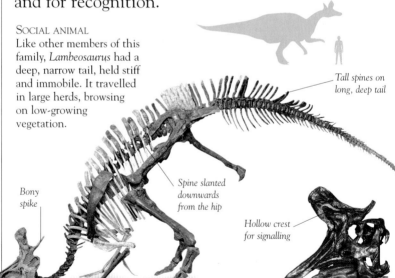

Tall spines on long, deep tail

Bony spike

Spine slanted downwards from the hip

Hollow crest for signalling

FOSSIL SKULL

PARASAUROLOPHUS

THIS DINOSAUR is instantly recognized from its long, back-swept head crest, which was up to 1.8 m (6 ft) long. The crest was longer on males than on females. A frill of skin may have joined the crest to the neck. *Parasaurolophus* had hundreds of strong teeth for chewing tough ferns and plants.

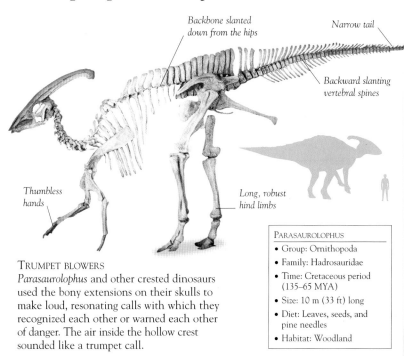

Backbone slanted down from the hips

Narrow tail

Backward slanting vertebral spines

Thumbless hands

Long, robust hind limbs

TRUMPET BLOWERS

Parasaurolophus and other crested dinosaurs used the bony extensions on their skulls to make loud, resonating calls with which they recognized each other or warned each other of danger. The air inside the hollow crest sounded like a trumpet call.

PARASAUROLOPHUS
- Group: Ornithopoda
- Family: Hadrosauridae
- Time: Cretaceous period (135–65 MYA)
- Size: 10 m (33 ft) long
- Diet: Leaves, seeds, and pine needles
- Habitat: Woodland

CERATOPSIANS

HORNS, BONY FRILLS, and a parrot-like beak were the trade-marks of the ceratopsians. They evolved from fleet-footed bipeds into heavy four-footed herbivores. Most ceratopsians can be divided into two groups. One group had short neck frills, the other had long neck frills. The ceratopsians were among the last surviving dinosaurs.

PSITTACOSAURUS
SKULL

Psittacosaurus *may have moved on all fours when foraging*

PSITTACOSAURUS
This dinosaur was a bipedal ancestor of the ceratopsians. It had a parrot-like beak and a very small neck frill, but lacked the horns of other ceratopsians.

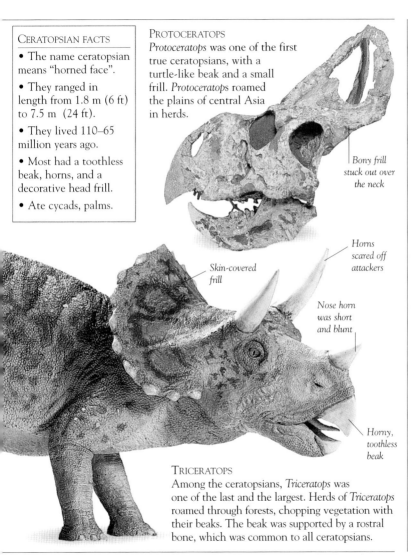

CERATOPSIAN FACTS

• The name ceratopsian means "horned face".

• They ranged in length from 1.8 m (6 ft) to 7.5 m (24 ft).

• They lived 110–65 million years ago.

• Most had a toothless beak, horns, and a decorative head frill.

• Ate cycads, palms.

PROTOCERATOPS

Protoceratops was one of the first true ceratopsians, with a turtle-like beak and a small frill. *Protoceratops* roamed the plains of central Asia in herds.

Bony frill stuck out over the neck

Skin-covered frill

Horns scared off attackers

Nose horn was short and blunt

Horny, toothless beak

TRICERATOPS

Among the ceratopsians, *Triceratops* was one of the last and the largest. Herds of *Triceratops* roamed through forests, chopping vegetation with their beaks. The beak was supported by a rostral bone, which was common to all ceratopsians.

267

SHORT-FRILLED CERATOPSIANS

THE GROUP OF ceratopsians with short frills had long nose horns and short brow horns. *Styracosaurus* had the most dramatic frill. *Brachyceratops* looked after its young, and when a herd was in danger, the males probably used their horned heads to protect the young and the females.

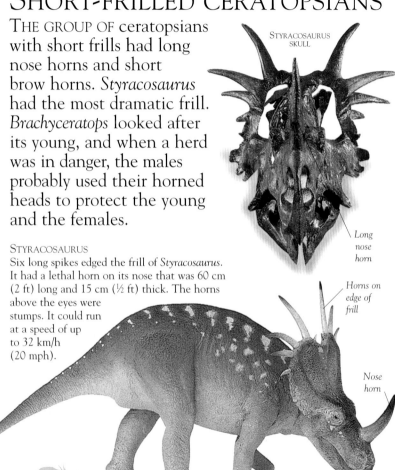

STYRACOSAURUS
SKULL

Long nose horn

Horns on edge of frill

Nose horn

STYRACOSAURUS
Six long spikes edged the frill of *Styracosaurus*. It had a lethal horn on its nose that was 60 cm (2 ft) long and 15 cm (½ ft) thick. The horns above the eyes were stumps. It could run at a speed of up to 32 km/h (20 mph).

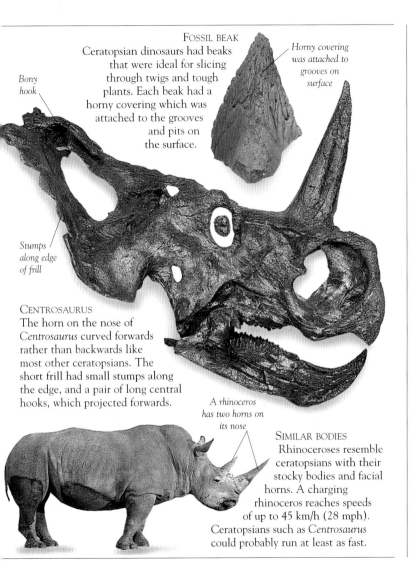

FOSSIL BEAK

Ceratopsian dinosaurs had beaks that were ideal for slicing through twigs and tough plants. Each beak had a horny covering which was attached to the grooves and pits on the surface.

Bony hook

Horny covering was attached to grooves on surface

Stumps along edge of frill

CENTROSAURUS

The horn on the nose of *Centrosaurus* curved forwards rather than backwards like most other ceratopsians. The short frill had small stumps along the edge, and a pair of long central hooks, which projected forwards.

A rhinoceros has two horns on its nose

SIMILAR BODIES

Rhinoceroses resemble ceratopsians with their stocky bodies and facial horns. A charging rhinoceros reaches speeds of up to 45 km/h (28 mph). Ceratopsians such as *Centrosaurus* could probably run at least as fast.

LONG-FRILLED CERATOPSIANS

THE FRILL OF long-frilled Ceratopsians extended back to, or over, the shoulders. Sometimes it had short spikes and usually the bones had large holes to lighten the load.

Horn was made of solid bone

Solid bony frill

Brow horns 1 m (3 ft) long

FOSSIL HORN
This fossil is the core of the brow horn of *Triceratops*. In life it would have been sheathed in horn.

TRICERATOPS SKULL
Triceratops had a solid bony frill, a short nose horn, and two long brow horns. The parrot-like beak and sharp teeth were ideal for its vegetarian diet.

Beak was used to crop vegetation

Sharp teeth cut up leaves

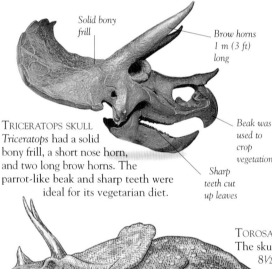

TOROSAURUS
The skull of *Torosaurus* was 8½ ft (2.6 m) long, making its head bigger than that of any other known land animal.

Two large holes in the frill bone reduced its weight

CHASMOSAURUS

The earliest long-frilled ceratopsian was *Chasmosaurus*. To lighten its weight, the frill had two large holes which were probably filled with muscle. Its skeleton was solidly built to bear its 2-tonne weight, and was not designed for speed. As with most ceratopsians, *Chasmosaurus* probably had few predators and used its horns mostly in territorial disputes.

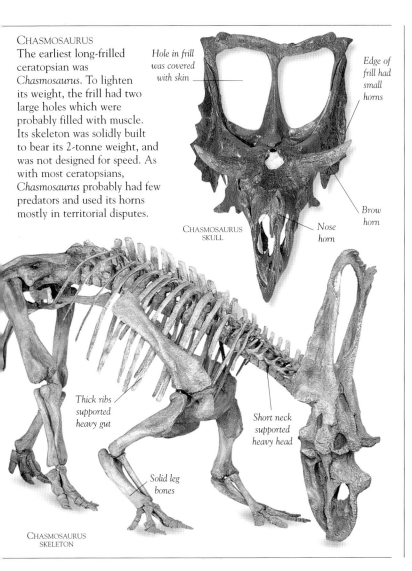

Hole in frill was covered with skin

Edge of frill had small horns

CHASMOSAURUS SKULL

Nose horn

Brow horn

Thick ribs supported heavy gut

Short neck supported heavy head

Solid leg bones

CHASMOSAURUS SKELETON

PSITTACOSAURUS

THIS DINOSAUR GOT its name, "parrot lizard", from its square skull and curved beak – similar to those of modern parrots. It had a pair of horns on its cheeks, believed to have been used for fighting or to attract mates. Members of this family are relatives of the horned dinosaurs and are the most primitive known ceratopsians, or bird-hipped dinosaurs.

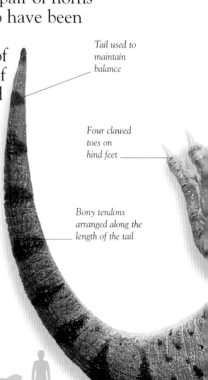

Tail used to maintain balance

Four clawed toes on hind feet

Bony tendons arranged along the length of the tail

TWO-FOOTED RUNNER

Psittacosaurus may have been a bipedal runner since its hind legs were long and thin. The long toes with blunt claws were perhaps used for digging. Its long tail was stiffened by bony tendons along its length.

PSITTACOSAURUS

- Group: Ceratopsia
- Family: Psittacosauridae
- Time: Cretaceous period (135–65 MYA)
- Size: 2 m (6½ ft) long
- Diet: Plants
- Habitat: Desert and scrubland

Cheek horn

Teeth behind toothless beak

PSITTACOSAURUS SKULL

MODERN PARROT HEAD

PARROT-LIKE HEADS
The psittacosaurs'
remarkably deep skulls
superficially resemble
those of parrots.

*Sharp claws suggest
that* Psittacosaurus
*may have been a
good digger*

FOSSILIZED PSITTACOSAURUS
Found in the 1920s, this
was the first psittacosaur to
be discovered. *Psittacosaurus*
skeletons are often found
in desert sandstones,
indicating its arid habitat.

PROTOCERATOPS

PROTOCERATOPS ("before the horned faces") was an early horned dinosaur with a relatively small horn. It had a broad neck frill at the back of its skull, which was larger and taller in males. Its small nasal horn was between the eyes and it had two pairs of teeth in the upper jaw. Tall spines on the top of its tail made it appear humped.

SHEEP OF THE GOBI
Protoceratops is very well-known from the many specimens discovered buried under the sand in Mongolia. Its fossils are so abundant in the Gobi Desert that it has been called "sheep of the Gobi".

PROTOCERATOPS

- Group: Ceratopsia
- Family: Ceratopsidae
- Time: Cretaceous period (135–65 MYA)
- Size: 1.8 m (6 ft) long
- Diet: Plants
- Habitat: Scrubland and desert

Nasal horn between the eyes

Protoceratops *was a four-footed animal*

Hump in tail for display or for fat storage

The Velociraptor's *arm is gripped by the* Protoceratops' *beak*

Protoceratops

Velociraptor

FOSSILIZED BATTLE SCENE
This famous fossil was discovered in the Gobi Desert in 1971. It preserves a *Protoceratops* locked in battle with a *Velociraptor*. Both animals died in the fight.

Large eyes

STAGES OF DEVELOPMENT
The frill on the *Protoceratops*'s head grew with age. Several fossils at different stages of growth have been found to prove this. The females' frills were probably smaller.

Possibly female

Possibly female

| HATCHLING | BABY | JUVENILE | SUB-ADULT | SUB-ADULT | ADULT | ADULT |

CHASMOSAURUS

CHASMOSAURUS ("cleft lizard") was a typical frilled, horned dinosaur. It had a large body with four stocky legs. Its enormous neck frill, which reached over the shoulders, was likely to have been brightly coloured and used to attract females. The bony structure below it was lightened by two large holes covered with skin.

Blunt brow horn on either side

Small nose horn

TOP VIEW OF SKULL

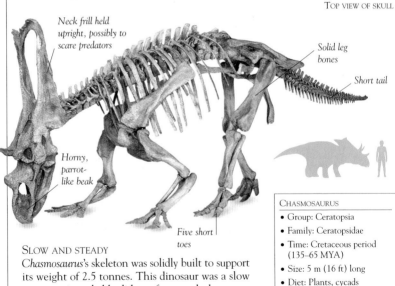

Neck frill held upright, possibly to scare predators

Solid leg bones

Short tail

Horny, parrot-like beak

Five short toes

SLOW AND STEADY

Chasmosaurus's skeleton was solidly built to support its weight of 2.5 tonnes. This dinosaur was a slow mover as it probably did not face much danger from predators.

CHASMOSAURUS
- Group: Ceratopsia
- Family: Ceratopsidae
- Time: Cretaceous period (135–65 MYA)
- Size: 5 m (16 ft) long
- Diet: Plants, cycads
- Habitat: Woodland

CENTROSAURUS

CENTROSAURUS ("pointed lizard") was a commonly found horned dinosaur of the late Cretaceous. Its most distinctive feature was the long rhino-like horn on its snout. It also had two small brow horns and a neck frill standing up behind the head. This had a wavy edge and was frilled with spines. *Centrosaurus* had a massive body, quite a short tail, and sturdy legs.

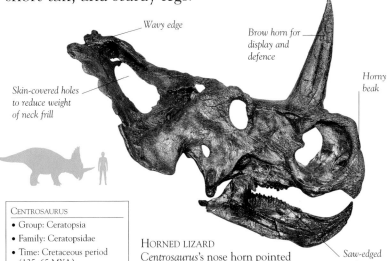

Wavy edge

Brow horn for display and defence

Horny beak

Skin-covered holes to reduce weight of neck frill

Saw-edged teeth

CENTROSAURUS
- Group: Ceratopsia
- Family: Ceratopsidae
- Time: Cretaceous period (135–65 MYA)
- Size: 6 m (20 ft) long
- Diet: Low-lying plants
- Habitat: Woodland

HORNED LIZARD
Centrosaurus's nose horn pointed forwards rather than backwards as on most ceratopsians. Its horny beak was ideal for cutting through twigs and tough vegetation.

STYRACOSAURUS

ONE OF THE MOST spectacular of the horned lizards, *Styracosaurus* ("spiked lizard") had six long spikes on the back edge of its neck frill, and smaller spikes around them. There was a large horn on the snout that pointed upwards. All four feet had five fingers or toes with claw-like hooves.

STYRACOSAURUS
- Group: Ceratopsia
- Family: Ceratopsidae
- Time: Cretaceous period (135–65 MYA)
- Size: 5 m (17 ft) long
- Diet: Ferns and palm-like plants
- Habitat: Open woodland

Holes in neck frill
to reduce weight

Six long spikes
around frill

DECEPTIVELY LARGE *Styracosaurus*'s enormous head gear made it look bigger and more fierce than it actually was. Bright colours may have also frightened away attackers.

FOSSIL SKULL

Defensive
horn on
snout

PENTACERATOPS

PENTACERATOPS ("five-horn face") had a straight horn on the snout and two large, curved brow horns. Two small "horns", or rather outgrowths of the cheekbones, made up the total of five. Its most unusual feature was its huge head – over 3 m (10 ft) long– with its spectacular frill.

SKULL FRAGMENT

DRESSED TO IMPRESS
Male *Pentaceratops* may have used their colourful frills to impress females, much as a peacock spreads its colourful tail to attract a peahen. No one knows how the frill was patterned, but perhaps it sported eyespots.

Triangular, bony projections

Heavily built body with thick hide

Straight nose horn

PENTACERATOPS
- Group: Ceratopsia
- Family: Ceratopsidae
- Time: Cretaceous period (135–65 MYA)
- Size: 5–8 m (16–26 ft) long
- Diet: Plants
- Habitat: Wooded plains

Cheek horn

Short legs

Curved beak made of horn

TRICERATOPS

PROBABLY THE BEST-KNOWN of the horned dinosaurs, *Triceratops* ("three-horned face") lived in North America, at the end of the Cretaceous. Many of the fossil skulls found are scarred, suggesting that *Triceratops* may have fought with rival males by locking its horns.

Bony studs around margin of frill ———

THREE-HORNED FACE
A short, thick nose horn, and two longer brow horns adorned the face. There were studs around the neck frill.

TRICERATOPS
- Group: Ceratopsia
- Family: Ceratopsidae
- Time: Cretaceous period (135–65 MYA)
- Size: 9 m (30 ft) long
- Diet: Plants
- Habitat: Woodland

Strong hip bone

Short nose horn

RECONSTRUCTION OF SKELETON

Head joined to neck by ball and socket joint

Heavy frill of solid bone

Brow horns much longer than nose horn

Solid neck frill

Horny beak

TRICERATOPS SKULL
The skulls of *Triceratops* have survived fossilization very well since they are so solid.

PACHYCEPHALOSAURS

THE THICK, DOMED skulls of pachycephalosaurs earned them the name "bone-headed dinosaurs". Rival males used to bash their heads together, their brains protected by the thick bone. Pachycephalosaurs probably had a good sense of smell, which would have allowed them to detect nearby predators and escape from them.

HORN CLUSTER
Stygimoloch had a cluster of horns behind its dome. But the horns were probably just for show, and had no practical use.

LOTS OF NODULES
Prenocephale's head had a well-developed solid dome and small nodules on the back of the skull.

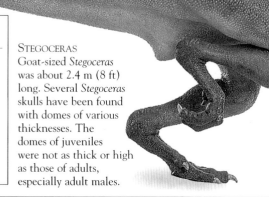

PACHYCEPHALOSAUR FACTS

• The name pachycephalosaur means "thick-headed lizard".

• They ranged in length from 90 cm (3 ft) to 4.6 m (15 ft).

• Diet included fruits, leaves, and insects.

STEGOCERAS
Goat-sized *Stegoceras* was about 2.4 m (8 ft) long. Several *Stegoceras* skulls have been found with domes of various thicknesses. The domes of juveniles were not as thick or high as those of adults, especially adult males.

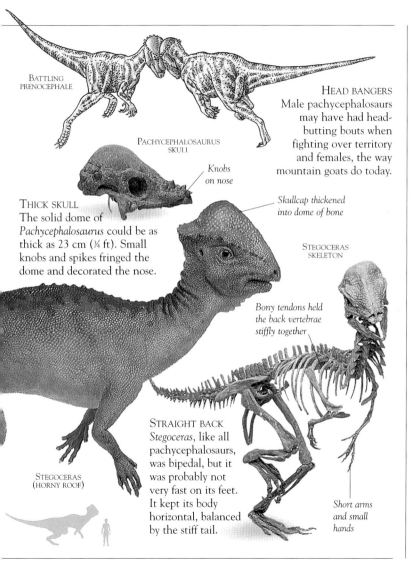

BATTLING PRENOCEPHALE

PACHYCEPHALOSAURUS SKULL

Knobs on nose

HEAD BANGERS
Male pachycephalosaurs may have had head-butting bouts when fighting over territory and females, the way mountain goats do today.

THICK SKULL
The solid dome of *Pachycephalosaurus* could be as thick as 23 cm (¾ ft). Small knobs and spikes fringed the dome and decorated the nose.

Skullcap thickened into dome of bone

STEGOCERAS SKELETON

Bony tendons held the back vertebrae stiffly together

STRAIGHT BACK
Stegoceras, like all pachycephalosaurs, was bipedal, but it was probably not very fast on its feet. It kept its body horizontal, balanced by the stiff tail.

STEGOCERAS (HORNY ROOF)

Short arms and small hands

283

STEGOCERAS

Bony ridge over eye and round back of head

Skullcap thickened into dome of bone

A FAST RUNNER, *Stegoceras* (meaning "roof horn") had a body made for head-butting. When charging, it held its head in a straight line with its neck, body, and tail. Its skullcap was a thick dome of solid bone. Two types of skull have been found – ones with flat domes, and others with rounded ones. *Stegoceras* had small, saw-like teeth for shredding plants.

FOSSIL SKULL

Domed skull

Neck designed to be held flat when charging

Large chamber at base of tail had unknown function

Long, slim arms

Three long, forward-facing, clawed toes

STEGOCERAS
- Group: Pachycephalosauria
- Family: Pachycephalosauridae
- Time: Cretaceous period (135–65 MYA)
- Length: 2 m (6½ ft)
- Weight: 54 kg (120 lb)
- Diet: Leaves, fruits
- Habitat: Upland forests

PACHYCEPHALOSAURUS

NAMED "THICK-HEADED LIZARD", *Pachycephalosaurus*'s skull had a dome of solid bone 25 cm (10 in) thick. It probably used its head as a ram to defend itself or guard its territory. *Pachycephalosaurus* was the last of its kind to exist before dinosaurs died out at the end of the Cretaceous.

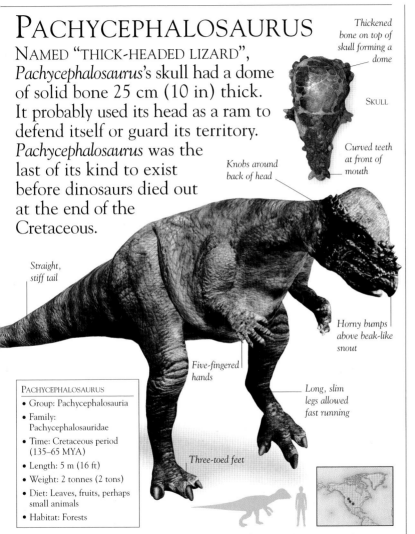

Thickened bone on top of skull forming a dome

Skull

Curved teeth at front of mouth

Knobs around back of head

Straight, stiff tail

Horny bumps above beak-like snout

Five-fingered hands

Long, slim legs allowed fast running

Three-toed feet

PACHYCEPHALOSAURUS

- Group: Pachycephalosauria
- Family: Pachycephalosauridae
- Time: Cretaceous period (135–65 MYA)
- Length: 5 m (16 ft)
- Weight: 2 tonnes (2 tons)
- Diet: Leaves, fruits, perhaps small animals
- Habitat: Forests

THYREOPHORANS

THYREOPHORANS or "shield barriers" is the name given to a large family of quadrupedal, low-walking dinosaurs that were covered in protective armour. This armour came in the form of spikes, plates, and sticking-out bones. This family includes the plated dinosaurs, such as *Stegosaurus*, and those with body armour and tail clubs, including *Ankylosaurus* and *Euoplocephalus*.

FOSSILIZED SAUROPELTA HIDE

Continuous mass of plates

Bony studs along shoulder and back

Parallel row of spikes along tail

EMAUSAURUS

SCELIDOSAURIDS

The first of the thyreophorans to evolve, Scelidosaurids were also the first dinosaurs to develop armour in the form of a hard, leather jacket. Such a dinosaur was *Emausaurus*, with cone shaped plates in the skin of the back and sides, and flat plates on its tail.

ANKYLOSAURIDS

The most developed of the thyreophorans, were the ankylosaurids, which had bands of studs, horns, and spikes on the entire back, neck, and parts of the tail. *Sauropelta* had armour (shown left) like chain mail, with rows of bony cones set among studs.

Small head ending in horny beak

THYREOPHORAN FACTS

• Thyreophorans lived from the mid-Jurassic until the end of the Cretaceous.

• "Thyreophoran" was coined as a word in 1915 and covered the horned dinosaurs as well as the armoured forms. It was not accepted as an official classification until the 1980s.

Twin spikes along back

Soft, unprotected lower side

STEGOSAURIDS

These are the most commonly known of the thyreophoran family. They are characterized as having protection in the form of rows of spikes, like that of *Stegosaurus*. Another feature distinctive to these dinosaurs is their short front legs. This reconstruction of *Tuojiangosaurus* clearly shows the difference in length of the front and back legs.

Short forelegs helped animal to browse

TUOJIANGOSAURUS

SCUTELLOSAURUS

SCUTELLOSAURUS OR "little shield lizard" had a long body and slim limbs. Over 300 low, bony studs covered its back, flanks, and the base of its tail to form a defensive armour. *Scutellosaurus* probably ran away from predators on its hind legs, holding its tail stiffly out behind it to counterbalance the weight of its armour.

SCUTELLOSAURUS
- Group: Thyreophora
- Family: Scutellosauridae
- Time: Jurassic period (203–135 MYA)
- Size: 1.2 m (4 ft) long
- Diet: Leaves
- Habitat: Woodland

Row of large studs down the middle of the back

HEAVY FOR ITS SIZE
Scutellosaurus was the smallest armoured dinosaur known. Its bony armour made its body heavy from the front, so it probably ambled on all fours.

Long, slim hind legs

Serrated, leaf-like teeth

Very long tail for bipedal balance

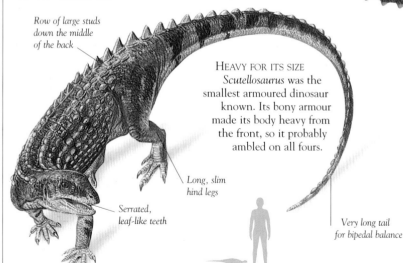

SCELIDOSAURUS

THIS SMALL, HEAVY, armoured dinosaur seems to be one of the earliest and most primitive ornithischians. It had impressive defensive armour: its back was covered with bony plates and a double row of bony spikes. Additional rows of studs ran along its sides, and there was a pair of triple-spiked bony plates behind the neck.

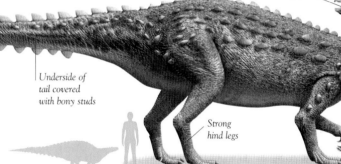

Triple-spiked bony plates on neck

Horny beak for nipping at plants

Underside of tail covered with bony studs

Strong hind legs

SCELIDOSAURUS
- Group: Thyreophora
- Family: Scelidosauridae
- Time: Jurassic period (203–135 MYA)
- Size: 3.5 m (11 ft) long
- Diet: Plants
- Habitat: Woodland

Longer feet than later thyreophorans

FOSSIL FOOT

LONG FEET
Scelidosaurus had longer feet than its later relatives. Although its forelimbs were much shorter than its hind limbs, it seems to have walked on all fours.

STEGOSAURS

THE MOST NOTICEABLE features of the stegosaurs were the large plates, or spines, along an arched back. These plates may have regulated body temperature, and they may have also given protection, or even attracted a mate. Stegosaurs had small heads, and tiny brains no larger than a golf ball. The head was carried close to the ground for eating short, leafy plants and fruits.

Eye socket

STEGOSAURUS SKULL
The skull of *Stegosaurus* was long and narrow. It had a toothless beak and small cheek teeth for chewing vegetation.

Spines had a sharp end

PLATES AND SPINES
From above you can see the staggered plates along the top of *Stegosaurus*'s body. This view also shows the tail spines pointing backwards and outwards – protection against attack from behind for when *Stegosaurus* was escaping.

TAIL END
Stegosaurus is the most commonly known of all stegosaurs. It had long, horny spines on the end of its tail. With a quick swing of the tail, these spines could inflict a crippling stab to a predator, such as *Allosaurus*.

Sideways-pointing spines

Staggered plates

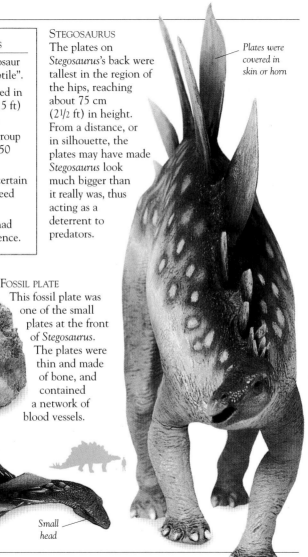

STEGOSAURUS

The plates on *Stegosaurus*'s back were tallest in the region of the hips, reaching about 75 cm (2 1/2 ft) in height. From a distance, or in silhouette, the plates may have made *Stegosaurus* look much bigger than it really was, thus acting as a deterrent to predators.

Plates were covered in skin or horn

FOSSIL PLATE

This fossil plate was one of the small plates at the front of *Stegosaurus*. The plates were thin and made of bone, and contained a network of blood vessels.

Small head

DINOSAURS AND BIRDS

291

TUOJIANGOSAURUS

TUOJIANGOSAURUS ("Tuojiang lizard") had 15 pairs of pointed spines running down its neck, shoulders, and back, and two pairs of long spikes at the end of its tail. Unlike *Stegosaurus*, it did not have broad plates over its hips and lower back. It was similar to *Kentrosaurus*.

TUOJIANGOSAURUS

- Group: Stegosauria
- Family: Stegosauridae
- Time: Jurassic period (203–135 MYA)
- Size: 7 m (23 ft) long
- Diet: Low-lying vegetation
- Habitat: Forests

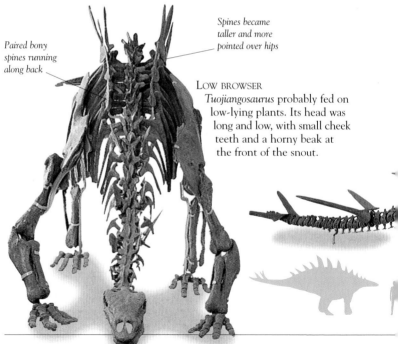

Paired bony spines running along back

Spines became taller and more pointed over hips

LOW BROWSER
Tuojiangosaurus probably fed on low-lying plants. Its head was long and low, with small cheek teeth and a horny beak at the front of the snout.

KENTROSAURUS

THIS EAST AFRICAN dinosaur lived during the time of *Stegosaurus*. It was smaller than its more famous relative, but as well protected. *Kentrosaurus* ("spiked lizard") had paired rectangular plates running down from the neck to half of the back. Sharp spikes ran down in pairs from the hips to the tip of the tail. A pair of longer spikes also jutted out from the shoulders.

KENTROSAURUS
- Group: Stegosauria
- Family: Stegosauridae
- Time: Jurassic period (203–135 MYA)
- Size: 5 m (16 ft) long
- Diet: Low-lying vegetation
- Habitat: Forests

Paired bony plates running down neck and upper back

Small, sloping head

Large body cavity

Relatively long, sturdily built hind legs

Forelegs much shorter than hind legs for low browsing

TINY HEAD
The skull of *Kentrosaurus*, housed a tiny brain, and is known only from fragments of bone. It was probably long and slender with a toothless, horny beak.

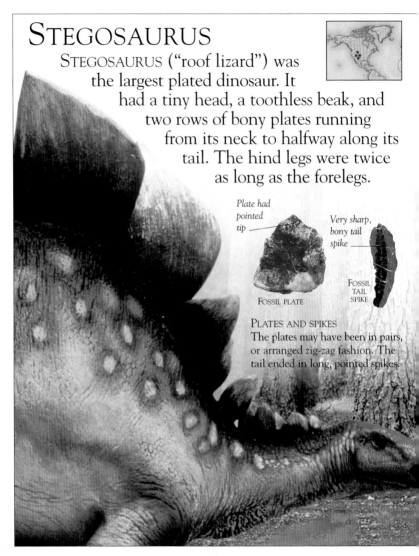

STEGOSAURUS

STEGOSAURUS ("roof lizard") was the largest plated dinosaur. It had a tiny head, a toothless beak, and two rows of bony plates running from its neck to halfway along its tail. The hind legs were twice as long as the forelegs.

Plate had pointed tip

FOSSIL PLATE

Very sharp, bony tail spike

FOSSIL TAIL SPIKE

PLATES AND SPIKES
The plates may have been in pairs, or arranged zig-zag fashion. The tail ended in long, pointed spikes.

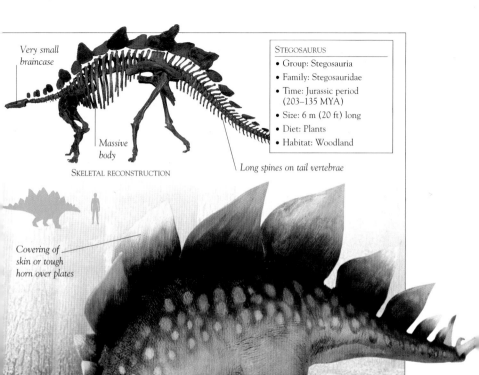

Very small braincase

SKELETAL RECONSTRUCTION

Massive body

Long spines on tail vertebrae

STEGOSAURUS
- Group: Stegosauria
- Family: Stegosauridae
- Time: Jurassic period (203–135 MYA)
- Size: 6 m (20 ft) long
- Diet: Plants
- Habitat: Woodland

Covering of skin or tough horn over plates

ANKYLOSAURS

PROTECTED BY SPIKES and bony plates, the stocky ankylosaurs were the armoured "tanks" of the dinosaur world. Slow on their feet, they relied on their armour for defence against predators. There were two main groups of ankylosaur – the ankylosaurids and the nodosaurids.

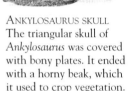

ANKYLOSAURUS SKULL
The triangular skull of *Ankylosaurus* was covered with bony plates. It ended with a horny beak, which it used to crop vegetation.

ANKYLOSAURIDS
Many ankylosaurids had spines on their sides as well as bony body scutes (plates). Their most notable feature was a heavy tail club, which they used as a formidable weapon.

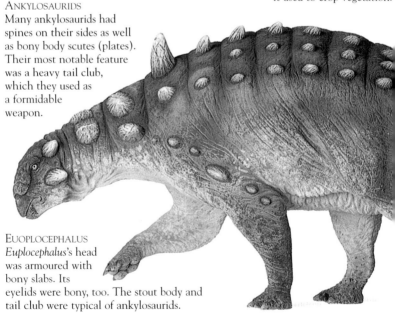

EUOPLOCEPHALUS
Euoplocephalus's head was armoured with bony slabs. Its eyelids were bony, too. The stout body and tail club were typical of ankylosaurids.

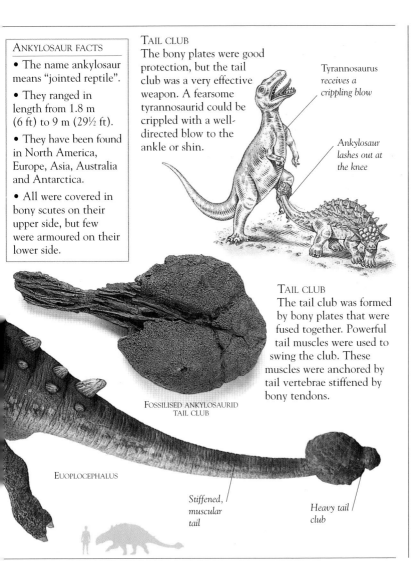

ANKYLOSAUR FACTS

• The name ankylosaur means "jointed reptile".

• They ranged in length from 1.8 m (6 ft) to 9 m (29½ ft).

• They have been found in North America, Europe, Asia, Australia and Antarctica.

• All were covered in bony scutes on their upper side, but few were armoured on their lower side.

TAIL CLUB

The bony plates were good protection, but the tail club was a very effective weapon. A fearsome tyrannosaurid could be crippled with a well-directed blow to the ankle or shin.

Tyrannosaurus receives a crippling blow

Ankylosaur lashes out at the knee

FOSSILISED ANKYLOSAURID TAIL CLUB

TAIL CLUB

The tail club was formed by bony plates that were fused together. Powerful tail muscles were used to swing the club. These muscles were anchored by tail vertebrae stiffened by bony tendons.

EUOPLOCEPHALUS

Stiffened, muscular tail

Heavy tail club

ACANTHOPHOLIS

ACANTHOPHOLIS ("spiny scales")
is a little-known nodosaur (a type
of ankylosaur) with a low-slung,
bulky body. A typical nodosaur
had armour of rows of oval plates
(scutes) set into the skin. It also had
long, bony spikes jutting out of its neck
and shoulder area along the spine.
Further spikes ran along each side down
to the end of the tail.

ACANTHOPHOLIS
- Group: Ankylosauria
- Family: Nodosauridae
- Time: Cretaceous period
  (135–65 MYA)
- Size: 4 m (13 ft)
- Diet: Low-lying vegetation
- Habitat: Woodland

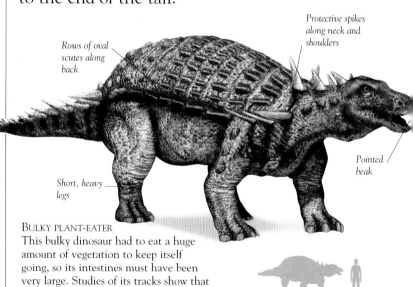

Rows of oval
scutes along
back

Protective spikes
along neck and
shoulders

Short, heavy
legs

Pointed
beak

BULKY PLANT-EATER
This bulky dinosaur had to eat a huge
amount of vegetation to keep itself
going, so its intestines must have been
very large. Studies of its tracks show that
it could run at a moderate pace.

MINMI

THIS THICKLY ARMOURED dinosaur had rows of small, bony plates on its back and triangular spikes over the hips. There were also large plates over its neck and shoulders. Unlike other ankylosaurs, *Minmi* had horizontal plates of bone running along each side of the vertebrae. Its box-shaped head had a narrow snout ending in a horny beak. Four small horns jutted out from the back of its face.

MINMI
- Group: Ankylosauria
- Family: Nodosauridae
- Time: Cretaceous period (135–65 MYA)
- Size: 3 m (9¾ ft)
- Diet: Low-lying vegetation
- Habitat: Scrubby and wooded plains

SOUTHERN HEMISPHERE DINOSAUR
Named after the Minmi Crossing in Australia, this creature was the first armoured dinosaur to be found south of the equator. It was smaller than most ankylosaurs, but heavily built and well armoured.

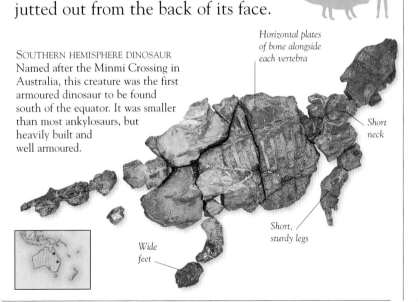

Horizontal plates of bone alongside each vertebra

Short neck

Short, sturdy legs

Wide feet

GASTONIA

GASTONIA WAS named after fossil hunter, Robert Gaston. This herbivore's defensive armour was impressive: it had four horns on its head, and bony rings covering the neck; rows of spikes covered its back and flanks, and fused, bony armoured plates protected the hips. The tail, which could lash from side to side, had rows of triangular blades along each side.

GASTONIA
- Group: Ankylosauria
- Family: Polacanthidae
- Time: Cretaceous period (135–65 MYA)
- Size: 5 m (16 ft) long
- Diet: Plants
- Habitat: Woodland

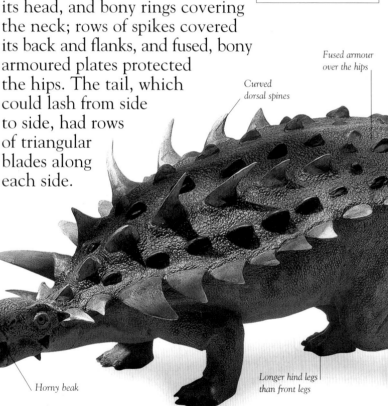

Fused armour over the hips

Curved dorsal spines

Horny beak

Longer hind legs than front legs

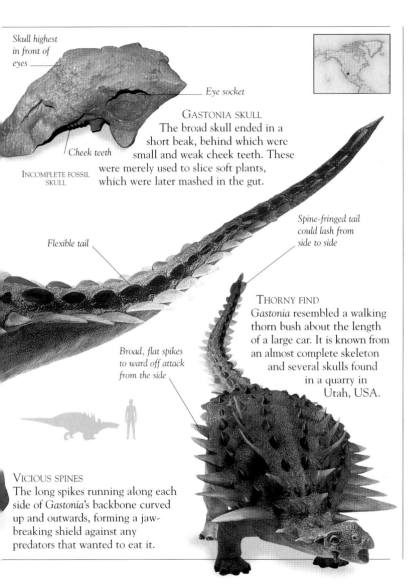

Skull highest
in front of
eyes

Eye socket

GASTONIA SKULL
The broad skull ended in a
short beak, behind which were
small and weak cheek teeth. These
were merely used to slice soft plants,
which were later mashed in the gut.

Cheek teeth

INCOMPLETE FOSSIL
SKULL

Spine-fringed tail
could lash from
side to side

Flexible tail

THORNY FIND
Gastonia resembled a walking
thorn bush about the length
of a large car. It is known from
an almost complete skeleton
and several skulls found
in a quarry in
Utah, USA.

Broad, flat spikes
to ward off attack
from the side

VICIOUS SPINES
The long spikes running along each
side of *Gastonia*'s backbone curved
up and outwards, forming a jaw-
breaking shield against any
predators that wanted to eat it.

301

PANOPLOSAURUS

PANOPLOSAURUS WAS A typical nodosaurid ankylosaur. It did not have the bony club at the end of its tail – instead all of its armour was concentrated around its shoulders. Huge spikes stuck out sideways and forwards, and these would have been used for defence or for sparring with other nodosaurids.

PANOPLOSAURUS
- Group: Ankylosauria
- Family: Nodosauridae
- Time: Cretaceous period (135-65 MYA)
- Size: 5 m (17 ft) long
- Diet: Certain low-growing plants
- Habitat: Woodland

PICKY EATER
Panoplosaurus and the other nodosaurid ankylosaurs had narrow mouths and only ate particular plants. The ankylosaurid ankylosaurs – those with the tail clubs – had broad mouths and were less selective.

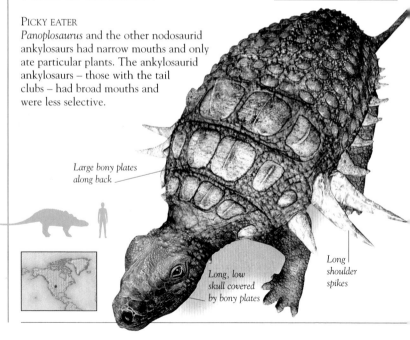

Large bony plates along back

Long, low skull covered by bony plates

Long shoulder spikes

ANKYLOSAURUS

ANKYLOSAURUS ("fused lizard") had thick bands of armour-plating on its body, neck, and head. Its skin was thick and leathery, and was studded with hundreds of oval bony plates and rows of spikes. Two long spikes emerged from its head and its cheekbones formed another pair of spikes on its face.

ANKYLOSAURUS
- Group: Ankylosauria
- Family: Ankylosauridae
- Time: Cretaceous period (135–65 MYA)
- Size: 7.5–10.5 m (25–35 ft) long
- Diet: Large herbivorous dinosaurs
- Habitat: Woodland

FOSSIL TAIL CLUB

LIVING TANK
Ankylosaurus has aptly been described as a living tank. Its tail was armed with a bony club, which could be swung with great force.

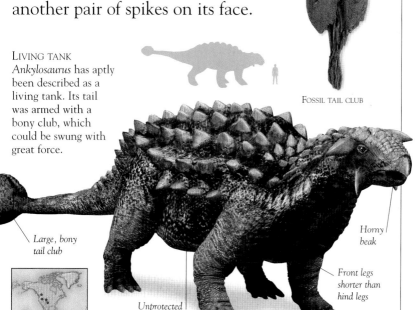

Large, bony tail club

Unprotected underbelly

Horny beak

Front legs shorter than hind legs

EDMONTONIA

THIS ANKYLOSAUR (whose name means "from Edmonton") had a bulky body, short, thick legs, wide feet, and a short neck. Two collars of flat, bony plates protected its neck, while a third collar lay between the shoulders, which were particularly well-armoured. Its back and tail were covered with rows of bony plates (scutes) and spikes. *Edmontonia's* long, pear-shaped head was covered in scales to protect the brain case. The head ended in a toothless beak and its weak jaw had small cheek teeth.

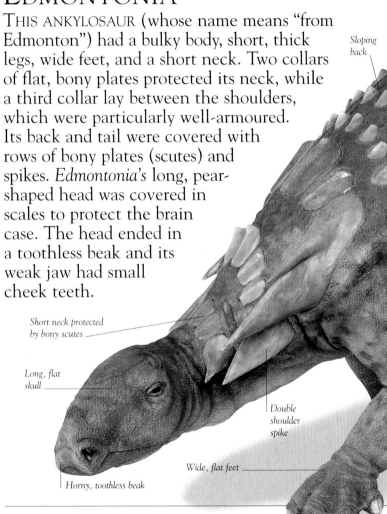

Sloping back

Short neck protected by bony scutes

Long, flat skull

Double shoulder spike

Wide, flat feet

Horny, toothless beak

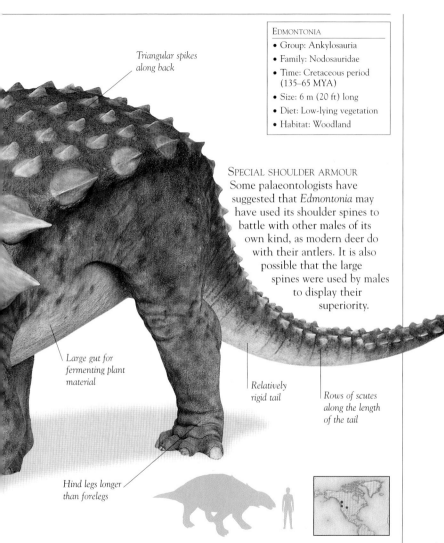

Triangular spikes
along back

EDMONTONIA
- Group: Ankylosauria
- Family: Nodosauridae
- Time: Cretaceous period
  (135–65 MYA)
- Size: 6 m (20 ft) long
- Diet: Low-lying vegetation
- Habitat: Woodland

SPECIAL SHOULDER ARMOUR
Some palaeontologists have
suggested that *Edmontonia* may
have used its shoulder spines to
battle with other males of its
own kind, as modern deer do
with their antlers. It is also
possible that the large
spines were used by males
to display their
superiority.

Large gut for
fermenting plant
material

Relatively
rigid tail

Rows of scutes
along the length
of the tail

Hind legs longer
than forelegs

EUOPLOCEPHALUS

BUILT LIKE a military tank, *Euoplocephalus* ("well-armoured head") was one of the most common Late Cretaceous ankylosaurids. Fused plates covered the back and neck, and triangular horns protected the shoulders, tail, and the face. Thick legs bore the weight of its bulky body as it ambled across the woodland in search of plant food.

EUOPLOCEPHALUS
- Group: Ankylosauria
- Family: Ankylosauridae
- Time: Cretaceous period (135–65 MYA)
- Size: 6 m (20 ft) long
- Diet: Plants
- Habitat: Woodland

Strong hips fused to backbone

CLUBBED TAIL
A large ball of fused bone at the end of the tail acted as a club that could be swung at attacking predators. This was probably the dinosaur's main weapon. The flexible, muscular tail base swung the club from side to side.

Fused bony tail plates

TAIL CLUB

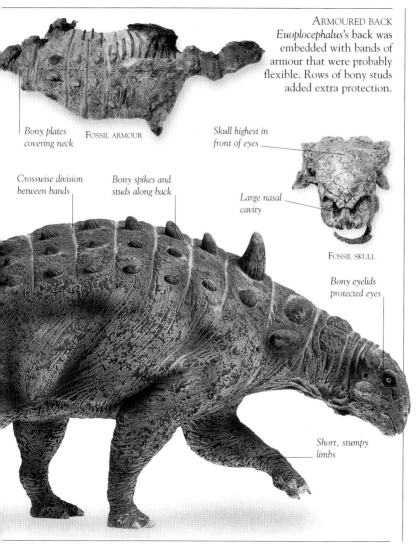

ARMOURED BACK
Euoplocephalus's back was embedded with bands of armour that were probably flexible. Rows of bony studs added extra protection.

Bony plates covering neck

FOSSIL ARMOUR

Skull highest in front of eyes

Large nasal cavity

FOSSIL SKULL

Crosswise division between bands

Bony spikes and studs along back

Bony eyelids protected eyes

Short, stumpy limbs

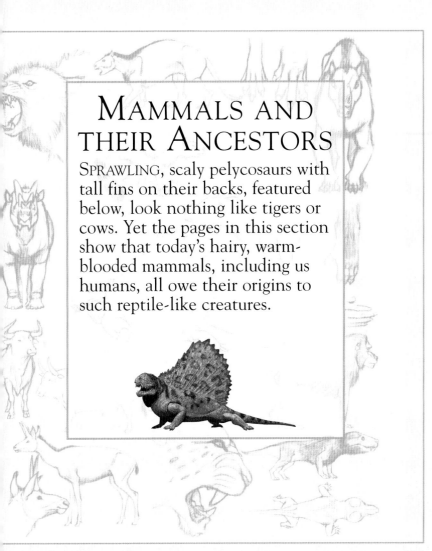

MAMMALS AND THEIR ANCESTORS

SPRAWLING, scaly pelycosaurs with tall fins on their backs, featured below, look nothing like tigers or cows. Yet the pages in this section show that today's hairy, warm-blooded mammals, including us humans, all owe their origins to such reptile-like creatures.

EARLY SYNAPSIDS

Synapsids ("with arch") include the mammal-like "reptiles" and their descendants. They had a large hole low in the skull behind each eye, and muscles near the jaws passed through this hole. Early synapsids known as pelycosaurs died out towards the end of the Permian period.

The body was kept warm by the blood that flowed through its sail

SAIL-BACKED KILLER
Dimetrodon was one of the first big land animals to attack and kill creatures its own size. It could grow up to 3.5m (11½ ft) in length.

Canine teeth with serrated blades

DIMETRODON
SKULL

TYPES OF TEETH
Dimetrodon's pointed upper canine teeth were used to pierce flesh. Front teeth served for biting and gripping, and back teeth aided in chewing.

DIMETRODON

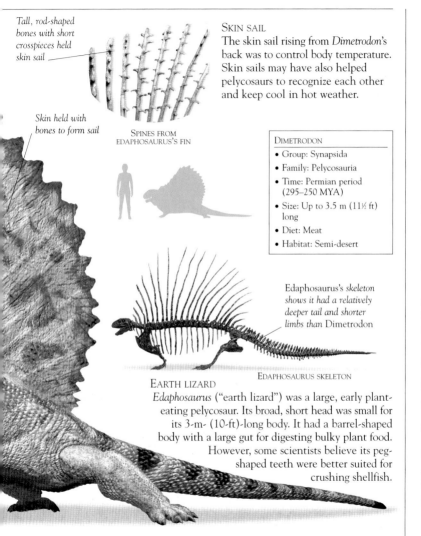

Tall, rod-shaped bones with short crosspieces held skin sail

Skin held with bones to form sail

SPINES FROM EDAPHOSAURUS'S FIN

SKIN SAIL

The skin sail rising from *Dimetrodon's* back was to control body temperature. Skin sails may have also helped pelycosaurs to recognize each other and keep cool in hot weather.

DIMETRODON

- Group: Synapsida
- Family: Pelycosauria
- Time: Permian period (295–250 MYA)
- Size: Up to 3.5 m (11½ ft) long
- Diet: Meat
- Habitat: Semi-desert

Edaphosaurus's *skeleton shows it had a relatively deeper tail and shorter limbs than* Dimetrodon

EDAPHOSAURUS SKELETON

EARTH LIZARD

Edaphosaurus ("earth lizard") was a large, early plant-eating pelycosaur. Its broad, short head was small for its 3-m- (10-ft)-long body. It had a barrel-shaped body with a large gut for digesting bulky plant food. However, some scientists believe its peg-shaped teeth were better suited for crushing shellfish.

TERRIBLE HEADS

DINOCEPHALIAN ("terrible head") therapsids were synapsids whose elaborately horned heads were massive compared with their bodies. They were diverse and abundant, but they did not survive beyond the Permian, and left no descendants. There were both carnivorous and herbivorous dinocephalians.

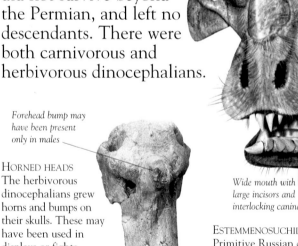

Horns of some Estemmenosuchids had many branches

Wide mouth with large incisors and interlocking canines

Forehead bump may have been present only in males

HORNED HEADS
The herbivorous dinocephalians grew horns and bumps on their skulls. These may have been used in displays or fights between males during the breeding season.

TOP VIEW OF
STRUTHIOCEPHALUS SKULL

ESTEMMENOSUCHIDS
Primitive Russian dinocephalians called estemmenosuchids were famous for the massive bony protuberances that grew from their cheeks and upper skulls. These may have been covered in horn.

ESTEMMENOSUCHUS

- Group: Therapsida
- Family: Estemmenosuchidae
- Time: Permian period (295–250 MYA)
- Size: 3 m (10 ft) long
- Diet: Horsetails and ferns
- Habitat: Lakeside forest

The top of the head was up to 10 cm (⅓ ft) thick

HEAD BANGERS
Some dinocephalians such as *Moschops* had thickened skull bones suggesting that they head-butted each other in fights for dominance.

MOSCHOPS SKELETON

Large canines gave a sabre-toothed appearance

Upper arms had powerful muscles

ESTEMMENOSUCHUS

TITANOPHONEUS
The well-preserved skeleton of this carnivore shows that it had a large, elongated skull with interlocking teeth, used to kill big animal prey.

313

TWO DOG TEETH

DICYNODONTS ("two dog teeth") were short-tailed synapsids with beaked jaws who lived from the Early Permian to the Late Triassic. The unusual dicynodont jaw, combined with their stout, barrel-shaped bodies, suggests that they were herbivores, and ate fibrous plants, such as horsetails and ferns.

SINOKANNEMEYERIA
- Group: Therapsida
- Family: Kannemeyeriidae
- Time: Triassic period (250–203 MYA)
- Size: 3 m (10 ft) long
- Diet: Fibrous plants
- Habitat: Woodland near lakes and rivers

SINOKANNEMEYERIA
This was a large, long-snouted, Chinese dicynodont with downward-pointing tusks that grew from bulbous projections on its upper jaw. It did not have powerful skull muscles for cropping plants like other dicynodonts and fed by tearing plants with the front of its snout.

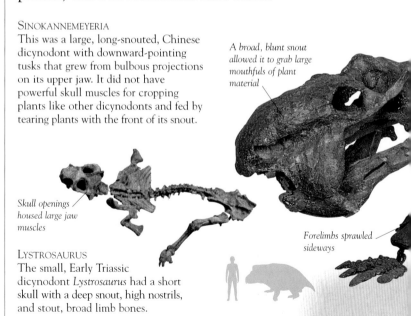

A broad, blunt snout allowed it to grab large mouthfuls of plant material

Skull openings housed large jaw muscles

LYSTROSAURUS
The small, Early Triassic dicynodont *Lystrosaurus* had a short skull with a deep snout, high nostrils, and stout, broad limb bones.

Forelimbs sprawled sideways

The feet were short and broad

PLACERIAS

THE LAST DICYNODONTS

By the Late Triassic, dicynodonts had become rare. The few surviving species, such as *Placerias*, were large beasts – more than 3 m (10 ft) long – and all found in the Americas.

BURROW DWELLERS

Some small dicynodonts such as *Cistecephalus* of Late Permian South Africa may have dug burrows.

Wedge-shaped skull with broad roof as found in burrowers

CISTECEPHALUS SKULL

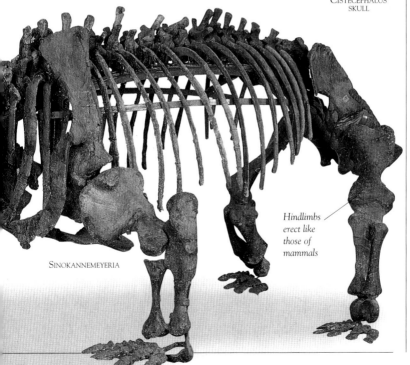

SINOKANNEMEYERIA

Hindlimbs erect like those of mammals

DOG TEETH

CYNODONTS ("dog teeth") were small to medium-sized carnivorous synapsids. A bony palate that separated the nasal passages from the mouth made this group the most likely ancestors of mammals. They lived worldwide for 80 million years, before dying out in the Mid Jurassic – no other group of therapsids lasted as long.

Strong, upright hind limbs helped in fast running

TRIDENT TOOTH

A low-slung, sharp-toothed carnivore, *Thrinaxodon* ("trident tooth") lived in Early Triassic South Africa and Antarctica. *Thrinaxodon* lived in burrows, and ate small creatures. Clues in its remains show that this creature was more mammal-like than its synapsid ancestors.

THRINAXODON

- Group: Therapsida
- Family: Galesauridae
- Time: Triassic period (250–203 MYA)
- Size: 50 cm (1½ ft) long
- Diet: Small animals
- Habitat: Open woodland

DOG JAW

CYNOGNATHUS SKULL

Cynognathus ("dog jaw") was one of most dangerous of Early Triassic carnivores. It had formidable jaws capable of biting savagely.

Dentary bone

Two part body division into chest and lower back

SKULL OF THE EARLY SYNAPSID DIMETRODON

Dentary bone

SKULL OF THE CYNODONT THRINAXODON

EVOLUTION OF THE JAW
Cynodont jaws illustrate key changes in the evolution from synapsid to mammal. In time, jaw bones shrank so that the entire lower jaw consisted of the large dentary bone. Other changes produced the mammals' unique chewing bite.

THRINAXODON

oad back teeth
th ridged crowns
chewing

THREE KNOB TEETH
Not all cynodonts were carnivores. Tritylodonts ("three knob teeth") like *Bienotherium* had jaws designed for eating plants.

Incisors for gnawing tough plants and back teeth for chewing them

BIENOTHERIUM SKULL

THE FIRST MAMMALS

MAMMALS ARE warm-blooded, backboned animals whose females have glands that produce milk to feed their young. All mammals evolved from the therapsids. The first mammals were probably Triassic shrew-like animals that shared the same types of jawbones and middle ear bones as living mammals.

TINY MAMMAL ANCESTOR
This tiny mammal from the Jurassic *Morganucodon* ("Morgan's tooth") is usually grouped with the triconodonts. These extinct early mammals were named after the three cusps (points) on the surface of each tooth.

JEHOLODENS
The first complete skeleton of a triconodont to be discovered was that of *Jeholodens*, which was found in China.

Morganucodon
stood upright

Sharp claws helped subdue prey or dig holes in which to hide from enemies

JEHOLODENS

MORGANUCODON
- Group: Prototheria
- Family: Morganucodontidae
- Time: Jurassic period (203–135 MYA)
- Size: 10 cm (⅓ ft) long
- Diet: Insects and worms
- Habitat: Forest

Reptile-like posture of early mammals

MODERN DUCK-BILLED PLATYPUS

AN ANCIENT LINE

The duck-billed platypus is one of the egg-laying monotremes – the group of living mammals with the oldest fossil record. The earliest-known monotreme fossils date from 100 million years ago in Australia.

Even early mammals were covered with hair

LOWER JAWBONE OF TAENIOLABIS

RAT-LIKE MAMMALS

Taeniolabis is an example of the multituberculates, a major line of rodent-like, plant-eating mammals with many-cusped teeth.

Sensitive whiskers allowed Morganucodon to feel its way in the dark

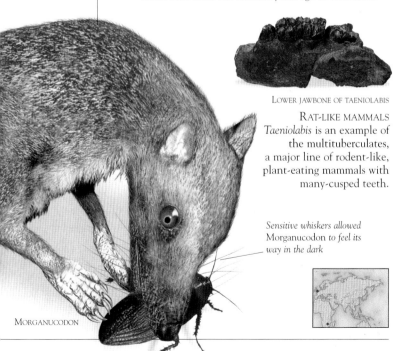

MORGANUCODON

AUSTRALIAN POUCHED MAMMALS

MANY OF THE earliest mammals had a pouch in their skin in which they carried their developing babies. Most mammals later evolved a womb inside their body for the babies and slowly lost their pouch. Marsupials such as kangaroos and koalas, kept this pouch, and have modern descendants in Australia.

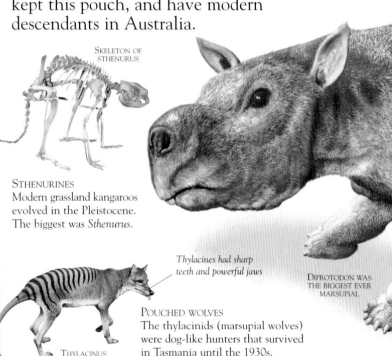

SKELETON OF
STHENURUS

STHENURINES
Modern grassland kangaroos evolved in the Pleistocene. The biggest was *Sthenurus*.

*Thylacines had sharp
teeth and powerful jaws*

DIPROTODON WAS
THE BIGGEST EVER
MARSUPIAL

POUCHED WOLVES
The thylacinids (marsupial wolves) were dog-like hunters that survived in Tasmania until the 1930s.

THYLACINUS

DIPROTODON

- Group: Marsupialia
- Family: Diprotodontidae
- Time: Pleistocene-Holocene epochs (1.75 MYA -present)
- Size: 3 m (10 ft) long
- Diet: Shrubs and bushes
- Habitat: Scrubland, open woodland

Worn out teeth show that thylacoleonids were predators

THYLACOLEO SKULL

MARSUPIAL LIONS

One of the most remarkable marsupial groups are the thylacoleonids, also called "marsupial lions" because of their cat-like skull and teeth.

Diprotodontids had hippopotamus-like bodies

DIPROTODON

From the Oligocene to the Pleistocene, Australia was populated by heavy-bodied herbivores called diprotodontids. The most famous is *Diprotodon*, a rhinoceros-sized herbivore. Diprotodontids died out as the tropical forests of Australia were replaced by grasslands.

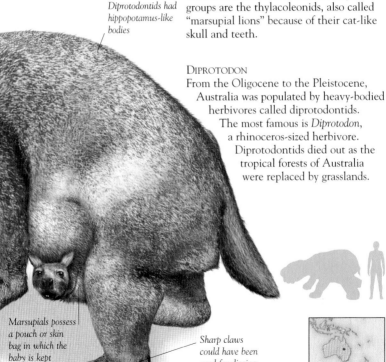

Marsupials possess a pouch or skin bag in which the baby is kept

Sharp claws could have been used for digging

AMERICAN MARSUPIALS

AMERICAN POUCHED mammals evolved in the Late Cretaceous and included dog- and bear-like forms, and a species that resembled sabre-toothed cats. Opossums, the most successful American marsupials moved into other continents and survive today.

Thylacosmilus may have had a coat like a lion's

ALPHADON

THYLACOSMILUS
One of the most remarkable marsupials was *Thylacosmilus*, which superficially resembled sabre-toothed cats. However, the details of its skeleton reveal that it was more like a giant opossum.

AMERICAN OPOSSUMS
Alphadon is one of the earliest known opossums from North America.

Long, powerful hind legs

LYCOPSIS
SKELETON

Feet with five clawed toes

THE DIDELPHOIDS
A major group of predatory American marsupials was known as the Didelphoids. They included the *Lycopsis* and *Thylacosmilus*.

Large, deep
skull

THYLACOSMILUS
- Group: Marsupialia
- Family: Thylacosmilidae
- Time: Paleocene-Pliocene
  epochs (65-1.75 MYA)
- Size: 1.3 m (4 ft) long
- Diet: Slow, hoofed mammals
- Habitat: Plains

Powerful
shoulders

ARGYROLAGUS

Stabbing
sabre teeth

Large protective
collar grew
downwards
from the chin

POUCHED HOPPERS
The argyrolagids were
mouse-sized American
marsupials with very
long hind limbs and
small forelimbs.

THYLACOSMILUS SKULL
The fossil skull of the
Thylacosmilus shows its
enormous sabre teeth, the
roots of which arched
upwards, above the eyes.

FOSSIL SKULL

323

STRANGE-JOINTED MAMMALS

A GROUP of mammals called the xenarthrans are among the most primitive placental mammals (animals whose babies develop inside the womb). The name means "strange joints" and refers to the extra joints these mammals have between their vertebrae. Xenarthrans evolved in South America; some also migrated into North America. Sloths, anteaters, and armadillos are their living descendants.

Ground sloths had a stout tail probably used as a prop when they stood on their back legs

Glossotherium had robust hips and limbs

MEGATHERIUM
Ground sloths grew to be as large as elephants. Rather than climbing on branches to eat leaves, they reached up with their arms to pull branches down toward their mouths. The biggest were *Eremotherium* and *Megatherium*.

GLOSSOTHERIUM
A medium-sized sloth called *Glossotherium* lived in the wooded grasslands and forests of the two Americas.

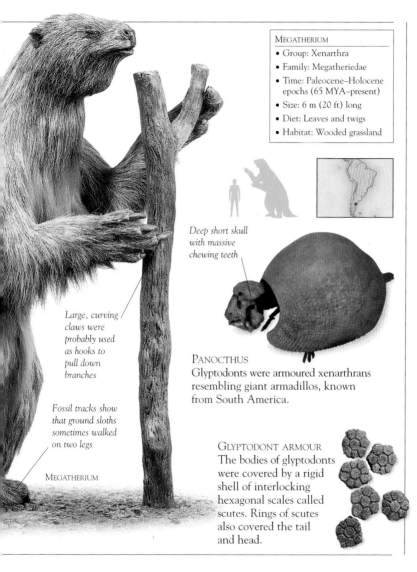

MEGATHERIUM
- Group: Xenarthra
- Family: Megatheriedae
- Time: Paleocene–Holocene epochs (65 MYA–present)
- Size: 6 m (20 ft) long
- Diet: Leaves and twigs
- Habitat: Wooded grassland

Deep short skull with massive chewing teeth

Large, curving claws were probably used as hooks to pull down branches

Fossil tracks show that ground sloths sometimes walked on two legs

MEGATHERIUM

PANOCTHUS
Glyptodonts were armoured xenarthrans resembling giant armadillos, known from South America.

GLYPTODONT ARMOUR
The bodies of glyptodonts were covered by a rigid shell of interlocking hexagonal scales called scutes. Rings of scutes also covered the tail and head.

325

PLACENTAL PIONEERS

PLACENTALS (the group of mammals whose young develop inside their bodies) arose in the Late Cretaceous, when the dinosaurs were becoming extinct. The earliest were small, nocturnal omnivores that resembled living shrews. Nearly all living mammals are classed as placentals, except for the monotremes, which lay eggs, and the marsupials, whose young are carried in a pouch.

CORYPHODON

Brain about three-quarters the size of the brain of a living shrew

ZALAMBDALESTES
One of the best-known early placentals was *Zalambdalestes* from Mongolia. It was a long-snouted mammal resembling the living elephant-shrew.

ZALAMBDALESTES
- Group: Eutheria
- Family: Zalambdalestidae
- Time: Cretaceous period (135–65 MYA)
- Size: 20 cm (⅔ ft) long
- Diet: Insects, small animals
- Habitat: Scrubland, desert

Below its long snout, Zalambdalestes had long incisor teeth

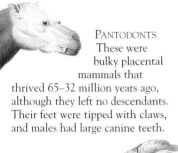

PANTODONTS
These were bulky placental mammals that thrived 65–32 million years ago, although they left no descendants. Their feet were tipped with claws, and males had large canine teeth.

TILLODONTS
This group of placentals had clawed feet and large gnawing teeth, and probably fed on roots and tubers.

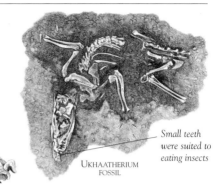

TROGOSUS
SKULL

Small teeth were suited to eating insects

UKHAATHERIUM
FOSSIL

UKHAATHERIUM AND RELATIVES
The asioryctitheres were Mongolian Cretaceous placentals that superficially resembled living shrews. However, features in their skull and hip bones show that they were not actually related to shrews.

EARLY CARNIVORES

CARNIVORES – cats, hyenas, dogs, bears, and their relatives – are one of the most successful groups of mammals. Their key feature is their specialized shearing teeth, called carnassials. This group has a fossil record from the early Palaeocene. The earliest carnivores – the miacoids – first appeared in North America.

Miacoids had smaller brains for their body size than modern carnivores

Flexible and powerful limbs

VULPAVUS
SKELETON

LIFE IN THE TREES
The limb skeletons of miacoids, such as *Vulpavus*, show that they had highly mobile limbs like those of modern, tree-dwelling carnivores.

MIACIS
One of the best-known miacoids was *Miacis* of the dog-branch group of carnivores. It was an agile climber and probably ate small animals, as well as eggs and fruit.

Large incisors
for tearing
flesh

HYAENODON SKULL

May have used
tail as a
balancing aid

CREODONTS
Hyaenodon was a wolf-like
animal, which had slicing teeth
at the back of the jaws. It is
part of a group called the
creodonts, which resembled
modern civets, cats, or dogs.

Early carnivores
such as Miacis have
five toes

Claws that can be pulled back
into sheaths, are unique to
primitive carnivores

MIACIS
- Group: Carnivora
- Family: Canidae
- Time: Paleocene–Pliocene
  epochs (65–1.75 MYA)
- Size: 30 cm (1 ft) long
- Diet: Small mammals,
  reptiles, birds
- Habitat: Tropical forests

CATS AND OTHER FELIFORMS

FELIFORMS, including cats, emerged during the Eocene epoch (53–33.7 million years ago). While some feliforms became large predators in open environments, others continued as forest-dwellers. Civets and genets, properly called viverrids, are primitive feliforms that have remained largely unchanged.

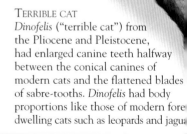

EARLY HYENA SKULL

HYENAS
Although hyenas resemble dogs more than cats, they belong to the cat-group of carnivores.

SKULL OF SABRE-TOOTHED CAT

ENLARGED CANINES
As cats evolved, they enlarged their canines for biting, but reduced their molars. The sabre-toothed cats enlarged their canines to an extreme.

TERRIBLE CAT
Dinofelis ("terrible cat") from the Pliocene and Pleistocene, had enlarged canine teeth halfway between the conical canines of modern cats and the flattened blades of sabre-tooths. *Dinofelis* had body proportions like those of modern fore-dwelling cats such as leopards and jagu

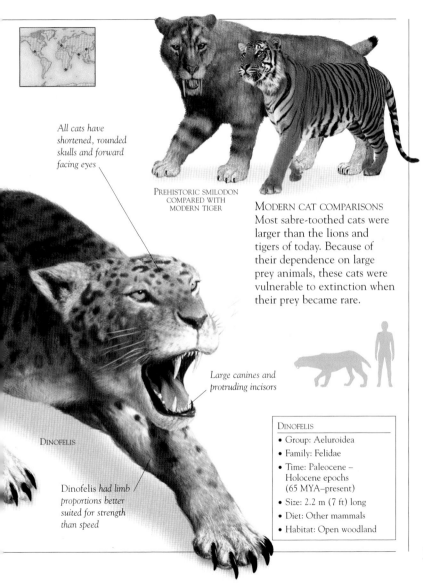

All cats have shortened, rounded skulls and forward facing eyes

PREHISTORIC SMILODON COMPARED WITH MODERN TIGER

MODERN CAT COMPARISONS
Most sabre-toothed cats were larger than the lions and tigers of today. Because of their dependence on large prey animals, these cats were vulnerable to extinction when their prey became rare.

Large canines and protruding incisors

DINOFELIS

Dinofelis had limb proportions better suited for strength than speed

DINOFELIS

- Group: Aeluroidea
- Family: Felidae
- Time: Paleocene – Holocene epochs (65 MYA–present)
- Size: 2.2 m (7 ft) long
- Diet: Other mammals
- Habitat: Open woodland

331

SABRE-TOOTHED CATS

THE MACHAIRODONTINES, or sabre-toothed cats, were prehistoric members of the cat family, known for their massive canine teeth. They diversified into American, African, European, and Asian species, ranging in size from that of a modern puma to that of a lion. The last sabre-toothed cat died out as recently as 10,000 years ago. The most famous member of the family is *Smilodon*.

Smilodon *had powerful arms and shoulders, and a strong and flexible neck*

HUNTING AND SCAVENGING TOGETHER

More carnivores lived alongside one another in the Pleistocene than today, so competition was probably more severe. Fossils of many cats show injuries from hunting and fighting. Perhaps *Smilodons* lived in social groups, as the injured would have then been able to scavenge from kills made by other group members.

In the largest cats, the upper canines were more than 25 cm (1 ft) long

SMILODON

- Group: Carnivora
- Family: Felidae
- Time: Pleistocene–Holocene epochs (1.75 MYA–present)
- Size: 1.7–2.5 m (5–8 ft) long
- Diet: Large mammals
- Habitat: Grasslands

DOGS AND OTHER CANIFORMS

CANIFORMS, A GROUP THAT includes dogs, bears, and seals, evolved in the Eocene. Dogs were the earliest caniforms to appear. New types of caniforms, such as weasels, raccoons, and bears, evolved late in the Eocene. Many became omnivores, others became herbivores, and some took to life in the water.

DIRE WOLF
Canis dirus ("dire wolf") was a large wolf from Pleistocene North America. Its fossils are best known from tar pits in California, where over 1,600 wolves are preserved. Compared with modern wolves, dire wolves had larger skulls and teeth, but shorter legs.

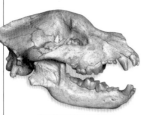

Canis dirus had a wider head, stronger jaws, and larger teeth than living wolves and was better at chewing bones

OSTEOBORUS SKULL

HYENA-LIKE DOGS
Borophagines were a group of dogs that lived from the Oligocene to the Pleistocene. They are best known for *Osteoborus*, a wolf-sized dog that had hyena-like habits. Other Borophagines may have resembled raccoons or coyotes.

THALASSOLEON
MEXICANUS SKULL

SEALS AND SEALIONS

Seals, sealions, and walruses evolved from bear-like ancestors. By the late Miocene, seals had spread across the world, while walruses and sealions such as *Thalassoleon* had evolved in the northern hemisphere.

SKELETON OF
URSUS SPELAEUS

The tail is an important social signal in living dogs, and probably was in all prehistoric dogs as well

BEARS

The eight living species of bear belong to a group called the ursines. *Ursus spelaeus*, of the Pleistocene, went on to become a cave bear.

Hands and feet were specialized for running

CANIS DIRUS

- Group: Carnivora
- Family: Canidae
- Time: Pleistocene–Holocene epochs (1.75 MYA–present)
- Size: 2 m (6½ ft) long
- Diet: Mammals, carrion
- Habitat: Grassland, woodland

ISLAND GIANTS AND DWARFS

AROUND 1.75 MILLION YEARS AGO, rising sea levels in the Mediterranean led to some areas being cut off from the mainland. Unusual mammals inhabited these islands until as recently as 8,000 years ago. Hippos, deer, and elephants here were remarkable for being dwarfs, while others, such as lizards, owls, and dormice, became giants. They became extinct due to hunting and competing with farmed animals.

GIANT DORMICE

Leithia, a giant dormouse from Malta and Sicily, was closely related to living forest dormice. However, it was a giant in comparison with living dormice, reaching about 40 cm (1⅓ ft) in total length – about as large as a squirrel.

Dwarf elephants lived off plant food that grew close to the ground

Like its living relatives, Leithia probably had dark markings around the eyes

DWARF ELEPHANTS

Palaeoloxodon falconeri was a miniature elephant with a shoulder height of 90 cm (3 ft). The small islands meant reduced quantities of food. Thus smaller individuals were more likely to survive than large ones.

DWARF ELEPHANT

- Group: Proboscidae
- Family: Elephantidae
- Time: Pleistocene – Holocene epochs (1.75 MYA–present)
- Size: 90 cm (3 ft) tall
- Diet: Leaves, grasses, fruit
- Habitat: Forests

Like other elephants, dwarf forms had tusks that they probably used in fights and as tools

TERRIBLE HORNS

DINOCERATANS, the "terrible horned" mammals, were rhinoceros-like hoofed creatures famous for their paired horns and tusk-like canine teeth. The earliest dinoceratan, *Prodinoceras*, first appeared in Asia during the Palaeocene, but nearly all later types are from North America.

UINTAH BEAST

The largest and best-known dinoceratan, *Uintatherium*, was as big as a White Rhino. It was named in 1872 after the Uintah Indians, a tribe that, like *Uintatherium*, lived in Utah.

Paired horns

Uintatherium had a barrel-shaped body

CAST OF THE SKULL OF UINTATHERIUM

HORNS, BUMPS, AND TUSKS

The various shapes on the long skulls of dinoceratans such as *Uintatherium* and *Eobasileus* were probably display structures used to attract a mate.

The advanced dinoceratans had column-like legs

UINTATHERIUM

Pair of horns at the back of the head was always the biggest

The horns were blunt and may have been covered in skin

Like elephants, dinoceratans had very short finger and toe bones

The enlarged flanges on the lower jaw may have helped protect the tusk-like canines

---

UINTATHERIUM
- Group: Dinocerata
- Family: Uintatheriidae
- Time: Paleocene–Pliocene epochs (65–1.75 MYA)
- Size: 3.5 m (11 ft) long
- Diet: Leaves, fruits, waterplants
- Habitat: Forests

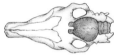

MODERN HORSE SKULL

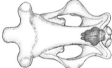

MEGACEROPS SKULL

UINTATHERIUM SKULL

BIG SKULL, SMALL BRAIN
Compared to later hoofed mammals, dinoceratans had small brains. While the skull of *Uintatherium* or *Eobasileus* may have been nearly 1 m (3 ft) long, the space in the skull for the brain was only about 10 cm (⅓ ft) long.

PRIMITIVE HOOFED MAMMALS

CONDYLARTHS, a recently defined group, consisted of related hoofed mammals from the early Tertiary. They ranged from the size of a rat to the size of a large sheep. Some condylarths had claws, although others had developed blunt hooves. Their teeth show that they were plant-eaters, and some had enlarged molars to pulp plant material.

PHENACODUS
The most famous condylarth is *Phenacodus*, which experts mistakenly thought was an ancestor of the horse. Like horses, it had a skeleton suited to a life of running in the open.

DIDOLODUS

Long limbs were quite flexible

DIDOLODONTIDS
These South American mammals are similar in anatomy to litopterns – horse and camel-like creatures found also there.

AARDVARK PROTOTYPE
Ectoconus was from North America and perhaps Asia. Its body shape has been compared with that of the aardvark, a modern ant-eater.

Dappled coat for camouflage

RAT-LIKE HOOFED MAMMALS
Some condylarths were tiny. *Hyopsodus*, the best-known of the hyopsodontid group, was a rat-sized animal.

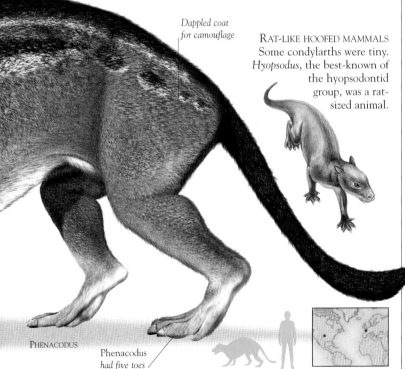

PHENACODUS

Phenacodus had five toes

SOUTH AMERICAN HOOFED MAMMALS

IN THE TERTIARY AND EARLY quaternary, South America was home to a range of unusual hoofed mammals – the meridiungulates. Some of these animals resembled hoofed mammals from elsewhere, such as horses and camels. These similarities probably came about due to similar lifestyles.

Macrauchenia had a small shoulder hump

It could probably kick powerfully with its hind limbs

Short trunk, like that of a modern tapir

Macrauchenia's long neck resembled that of a camel

Jaws were lined with 44 large chewing teeth

SKELETON OF MACRAUCHENIA
Macrauchenia was discovered by Charles Darwin and named and described by Sir Richard Owen, two of the most important scientists of Victorian times. Darwin wrote that the skeleton appeared to be from a large llama.

BIG LLAMA
The litopterns were a group of meridiungulates that resembled camels and horses. One of the best-known ones was *Macrauchenia* ("big llama"). It had nostrils placed high up on its head. Some experts think this shows that it had a short trunk, but others dispute this.

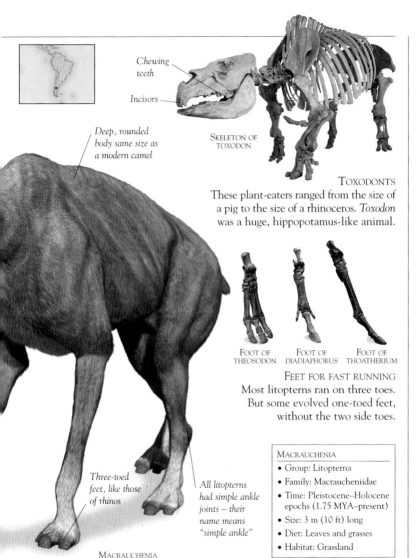

Chewing teeth

Incisors

SKELETON OF TOXODON

Deep, rounded body same size as a modern camel

TOXODONTS

These plant-eaters ranged from the size of a pig to the size of a rhinoceros. *Toxodon* was a huge, hippopotamus-like animal.

FOOT OF THEOSODON

FOOT OF DIADIAPHORUS

FOOT OF THOATHERIUM

FEET FOR FAST RUNNING

Most litopterns ran on three toes. But some evolved one-toed feet, without the two side toes.

Three-toed feet, like those of rhinos

All litopterns had simple ankle joints – their name means "simple ankle"

MACRAUCHENIA

MACRAUCHENIA
- Group: Litopterna
- Family: Macraucheniidae
- Time: Pleistocene–Holocene epochs (1.75 MYA–present)
- Size: 3 m (10 ft) long
- Diet: Leaves and grasses
- Habitat: Grassland

HOOFED PREDATORS

EARLY IN THEIR evolution, hoofed
mammals, or Acreodi, were very different
from their plant-eating descendants. Like sheep or
cows, they had hoofed toes. But instead of molars
shaped for munching vegetation, they had massive
teeth designed for slicing meat or
crushing bones. Acreodi looked
and behaved very much
like wolves, hyenas,
and bears.

*Long,
narrow
jaw with
teeth like
a bear's*

GIGANTIC OMNIVORE
Andrewsarchus lived in Eocene
Mongolia more than 40 million
years ago, and was the biggest
known carnivorous land mammal.
It probably grew up to 6 m (19 ft) long. Its jaws
were equipped with massive canines and molars.

*Toes tipped with short
hooves instead of long
sharp claws*

ANDREWSARCHUS

- Group: Acreodi
- Family: Mesonychidae
- Time: Paleocene – Pliocene epochs (65–1.75 MYA)
- Size: Up to 6 m (19 ft) long
- Diet: Meat, plants, insects
- Habitat: Scrub, open woodland

Long, lean body shaped like a wolf's

Strong limbs to support its great weight

MESONYX

May have had a long tail

ANDREWSARCHUS

AGILE HUNTER
Mesonyx was a member of the mesonychids, the best-known family of the Acreodi. This wolf-like predator was a fast runner, and it probably hunted hoofed plant-eaters. Its large jaw muscles gave it a powerful bite.

Long, low, narrow jaws like those of mesonychids

WHALE ANCESTORS
Although the acreodi became extinct, a very successful and longer-lived group of mammals evolved – the whales. The skull of early whales like *Archaeocetes* resemble that of certain Acreodi.

ARCHAEOCETES
SKULL

345

URANOTHERES

ONE OF THE most peculiar groups of mammals is the Uranotheria, a collection of herbivorous, hoofed mammals that includes elephants, seacows, and hyraxes. Although these animals are very different, they share features not seen in other mammals. The first elephants, for example, were dog-sized animals probably similar to hyraxes. Another group of uranotheres, the tethytheres, took to life in water and evolved into the first seacows.

Males had larger and more pointed horns than females

ARSINOITHERIUM
- Group: Uranotheria
- Family: Arsinotheriidae
- Time: Paleocene–Pliocene epochs (65–1.75 MYA)
- Size: 3.5 m (12 ft) long
- Diet: Tough vegetation
- Habitat: Woodland, wooded grassland

Teeth had tall crowns and could have been used to chew very tough plants

Shoulders were
massive and
powerfully muscled

Tusk-like
front teeth

KVABEBIHYRAX

HYRAXES

Modern hyraxes are small African
mammals that look like guinea pigs.
Fossil hyraxes, however, were quite
different and came in a huge range
of shapes and sizes. *Kvabebihyrax*,
shown here, was like a hippo and
may have been amphibious.

Foot had five blunt
toes, each tipped with
a small hoof

ARSINOITHERES

These rhinoceros-like uranotheres
lived in Asia, Europe, and Africa
from the Palaeocene until the
Oligocene (65–23.5 million
years ago). The best-known
arsinoithere is *Arsinoitherium* – a
large, heavy animal with two massive horns on its skull.
The largest individuals of *Arsinoitherium* (probably old
males) were about the size of small elephants. Unlike
rhinoceros horns, arsinoithere horns were hollow.

ARSINOITHERIUM

BRONTOTHERES AND CHALICOTHERES

THESE TWO GROUPS of animals were odd-toed hoofed mammals, or perissodactyls. Brontotheres were large, rhino-like animals with horns, while Chalicotheres were horse-like perissodactyls with curved claws.

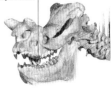

Weak teeth suggest that brontotheres mostly ate soft leaves

SKULL OF BRONTOPS

BRONTOTHERE HORNS

As brontotheres evolved, their horns became larger. Males had larger horns than females, suggesting that they were used for display and for fighting with rival males.

Injuries found on skulls suggest that brontotheres used their horns to fight

Horns were covered in skin

BRONTOPS

- Group: Perissodactyla
- Family: Brontotheriidae
- Time: Paleocene – Pliocene epochs (65–1.75 MYA)
- Size: 5 m (17 ft) long
- Diet: Leaves
- Habitat: Open woodland

Long neck to reach up to branches

Powerful front legs were longer than the back legs

MOROPUS SKELETON

The hip bones were broad, probably to help support the weight of the body

A CLAWED "HOOFED MAMMAL"
Moropus was a chalicothere from North America. Like all chalicotheres, it had massive, powerful front legs and curving claws on its hands. Chalicotheres may have dug roots and tubers out of the ground, and also browsed on leaves.

Brontothere tails probably ended in a tuft of hairs

BRONTOPS

LAST OF THE BRONTOTHERES
Embololotherium and its relatives were related to *Brontops*, and were among the last and largest of the brontotheres. *Embololotherium* was equipped with a large, forked nose horn.

RHINOCEROSES

TODAY THERE ARE five surviving species of rhinoceros – plant-eaters with horns on their snout. Fossil rhinoceroses were diverse and evolved many different lifestyles and body shapes. Perhaps the most primitive rhinoceroses were the hornless hyracodontids, or running rhinoceroses. Another family, the amynodontids, included amphibious rhinoceroses with short mobile trunks, like the trunks of modern-day tapirs.

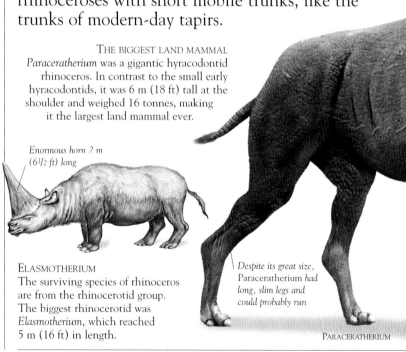

THE BIGGEST LAND MAMMAL
Paraceratherium was a gigantic hyracodontid rhinoceros. In contrast to the small early hyracodontids, it was 6 m (18 ft) tall at the shoulder and weighed 16 tonnes, making it the largest land mammal ever.

Enormous horn 2 m (6¹/₂ ft) long

ELASMOTHERIUM
The surviving species of rhinoceros are from the rhinocerotid group. The biggest rhinocerotid was *Elasmotherium*, which reached 5 m (16 ft) in length.

Despite its great size, Paraceratherium had long, slim legs and could probably run

PARACERATHERIUM

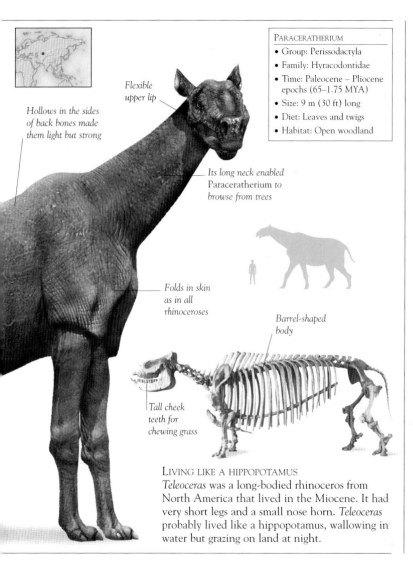

Hollows in the sides
of back bones made
them light but strong

Flexible
upper lip

PARACERATHERIUM
- Group: Perissodactyla
- Family: Hyracodontidae
- Time: Paleocene – Pliocene epochs (65–1.75 MYA)
- Size: 9 m (30 ft) long
- Diet: Leaves and twigs
- Habitat: Open woodland

Its long neck enabled
Paraceratherium *to*
browse from trees

Folds in skin
as in all
rhinoceroses

Barrel-shaped
body

Tall cheek
teeth for
chewing grass

LIVING LIKE A HIPPOPOTAMUS

Teleoceras was a long-bodied rhinoceros from North America that lived in the Miocene. It had very short legs and a small nose horn. *Teleoceras* probably lived like a hippopotamus, wallowing in water but grazing on land at night.

HORSES

HORSES WERE PROBABLY the best suited animals to life on the open grasslands. They appeared in the Eocene and about eight species of them survive today. Successive groups of horse species evolved different features and body sizes to suit their environments. *Hipparion* lived in the Northern Hemisphere grasslands during the Miocene.

Long, squarish muzzle with large nostrils

Life in open grassland favoured the evolution of large body size and long limbs in horses

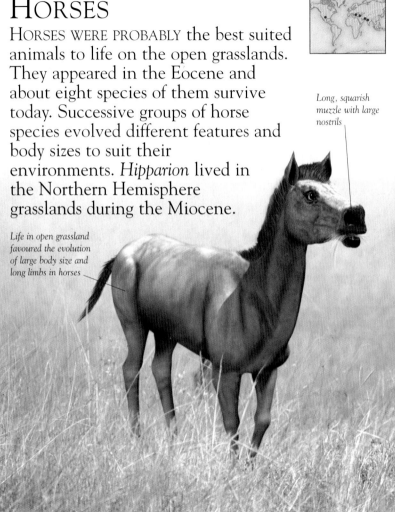

HIPPARION

- Group: Perissodactyla
- Family: Equidae
- Time: Paleocene – Pliocene epochs (65–1.75 MYA)
- Size: 1.5 m (5 ft) long
- Diet: Grass, open woodland
- Habitat: Plains

TEETH FOR GRASS-EATING

Advanced horses, such as *Hipparion*, had large, high-crowned molar teeth with complicated chewing surfaces made up of loops of enamel. Their premolars became large and squarish and came to look like the molars. These powerful teeth may have evolved when horses accidentally chewed sand, and allowed advanced horses to eat rough grasses.

THREE-TOED FEET

Like modern horses, *Hipparion* was a grassland animal. Earlier horses were probably inhabitants of forests. Unlike modern horses, which only have one toe on each foot, *Hipparion* had three-toed feet.

Moderately long tail

MAMMALS AND ANCESTORS

353

ELEPHANTS

THE EARLIEST KNOWN elephant was *Phosphatherium* from the Palaeocene, which was just 60 cm (2 ft) tall at the shoulder. Later elephants increased in size and evolved column-like legs, and tusks in their upper jaws. Nearly all fossil elephants had a trunk.

PHIOMIA
This primitive elephant lived in northern Africa during the Oligocene. *Phiomia* was only about as big as a modern horse.

Phiomia *probably had a short trunk*

MOERITHERIUM
One of the most primitive known elephants is *Moeritherium*. Its skull indicates that it had an enlarged upper lip, but experts do not know whether this was a true trunk.

Moeritherium's *neck was longer than that of more advanced elephants*

Primitive elephants had not yet developed column-like legs

Gomphotherium *was about as big as an Asian elephant*

SHOVEL-TUSKERS

Like most primitive elephants, *Phiomia* had tusks in both its upper and lower jaws. Its long lower jaw had flattened tusks, which could have been used to shovel water plants or cut branches or bark from trees.

GOMPHOTHERIUM

A successful group of elephants called gomphotheres spread around the world in the Miocene and Pliocene. Species such as *Gomphotherium* were the ancestors of mammoths and of modern-day elephants.

SKULL OF
PHIOMIA

Deinotherium *was 4 m (13 ft) tall at the shoulder*

Trunk shorter than living elephants

DEINOTHERES

These strange elephants had no tusks in their skulls and two down-curved tusks in their lower jaws. These tusks may have been used to dig up roots.

The enlarged upper lip and nose may have formed a very short trunk

MOERITHERIUM

MOERITHERIUM
- Group: Proboscidea
- Family: Moeritheriidae
- Time: Paleocene – Pliocene epochs (65–1.75 MYA)
- Size: 3 m (10 ft) long
- Diet: Water plants
- Habitat: Lakes, rivers, riverside forests

PLATYBELODON

PLATYBELODON WAS A "shovel-tusker" from the gomphothere group. It had a long, scoop-like tip to its lower jaw, formed by the tusk and jaw bone. Once thought to have lived in marshes, evidence now suggests that it lived in grasslands and forests and cropped tough vegetation from trees.

FLEXIBLE TRUNK

Old reconstructions of *Platybelodon* show it with a short, wide trunk that would not have been very flexible. This was based on evidence from the more primitive *Phiomia*, which had a short trunk. However, *Platybelodon* had the same type of nasal openings as modern elephants and it is now established that the animal had a long, flexible trunk.

> **PLATYBELODON**
> - Group: Proboscidea
> - Family: Gomphotheriidae
> - Time: Paleocene – Pliocene epochs (65–1.75 MYA)
> - Size: 3 m (10 ft) at shoulder
> - Diet: Leaves, grasses, bark
> - Habitat: Grasslands, forests

LOWER JAW

The wear marks on *Platybelodon*'s lower jaw show that vegetation was pulled across the tips of the tusks. *Platybelodon* may have used the tusks to slice through the wood.

Larger ears than more primitive elephants

CAMELS

CAMELS AND THEIR relatives evolved in the Eocene and include nearly 100 fossil species. Although modern camels inhabit deserts, they were once grassland and woodland herbivores. Camels swallow their food and later regurgitate it to be chewed a second time. They also produce less urine, thus retaining more water and being better adapted to dry environments.

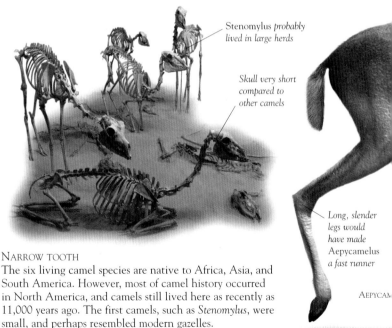

Stenomylus *probably lived in large herds*

Skull very short compared to other camels

Long, slender legs would have made Aepycamelus a fast runner

AEPYCAM

NARROW TOOTH

The six living camel species are native to Africa, Asia, and South America. However, most of camel history occurred in North America, and camels still lived here as recently as 11,000 years ago. The first camels, such as *Stenomylus*, were small, and perhaps resembled modern gazelles.

AEPYCAMELUS

- Group: Artiodactyla
- Family: Camelidae
- Time: Paleocene – Pliocene epochs (65–1.75 MYA)
- Size: 2 m (7 ft) at shoulder
- Diet: Tree leaves
- Habitat: Open woodland, grassland with trees

Teeth and skull suggest a closer relation to living llamas than to modern camels

Pointed front teeth were small

GIANT GIRAFFE CAMEL
Aepycamelus ("high camel") was a large camel with tremendously long leg and neck bones. It was probably a browsing herbivore that, like modern giraffes, fed from trees. Eight *Aepycamelus* species are known.

Advanced camels such as Oxydactylus had two toes only, while more primitive species had four toes

Front and back legs of camels are more equal in size than in other hoofed mammals

Like living camels, fossil species may have had dense, woolly fur

FOSSIL OXYDACTYLUS FOOT

CAMEL FEET AND WALKING
Advanced camels have unique feet. Unlike other artiodactyls, they do not walk on the tips of their toes, but on the whole toe. Soft toe pads help them walk on rocks or sand with ease.

MAMMOTHS

THE EIGHT SPECIES of mammoth were all true elephants, closely related to present day elephants. Mammoth genetic material, or DNA, was found in 1994 and it is almost identical to that of living elephants. The woolly mammoth is perhaps the most famous fossil animal from the Pleistocene.

Shoulder hump

Both male and female woolly mammoths had long tusks, which they used for combat and display, and for gathering food

WOOLLY MAMMOTH

WOOLLY MAMMOTH

These mammoths lived in herds and fed on grasses and other small plants, which they plucked with the two "fingers" on the tips of their trunks. Several woolly mammoths have been found preserved in the frozen ground of Siberia. Their fur, skin, muscles, and even their stomach contents are still intact.

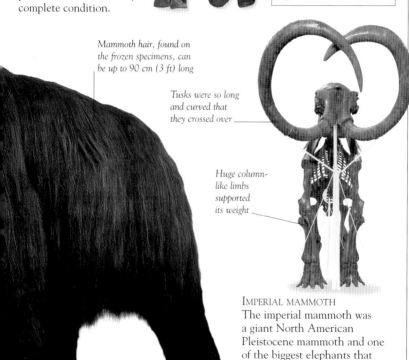

Domed skull not
yet developed

DIMA THE MAMMOTH
Dima was the name
given to a frozen
male baby woolly
mammoth, recovered in
1977 in Russia, and
preserved in a remarkably
complete condition.

WOOLLY MAMMOTH
• Group: Proboscidea
• Family: Elephantidae
• Time: Pleistocene–
  Holocene epochs
  (1.75 MYA–present)
• Size: 3.3 m (11 ft) long
• Diet: Grasses and plants
• Habitat: Woodland,
  grassland

Mammoth hair, found on
the frozen specimens, can
be up to 90 cm (3 ft) long

Tusks were so long
and curved that
they crossed over

Huge column-
like limbs
supported
its weight

IMPERIAL MAMMOTH
The imperial mammoth was
a giant North American
Pleistocene mammoth and one
of the biggest elephants that
ever lived. Its huge curving tusks
could be as long as 4.3 m (14 ft).

PIGS, HIPPOS, AND PECCARIES

THE LARGEST AND MOST successful group of hoofed mammals are the artiodactyls, or even-toed hoofed mammals. Their distinctive ankle and foot bones allow them to run fast. Most forms have two or four toes, hence the group's name. One of the groups within the artiodactyls is the suiforms, which includes pigs, hippos, and peccaries.

HIPPOPOTAMUSES
The first hippos appeared in the Late Miocene. Two kinds survive today – the large, amphibious *Hippopotamus* and the small, land-living *Hexaprotodon*. The recently extinct *Hippopotamus lemerlei* was a pygmy hippo from Madagascar.

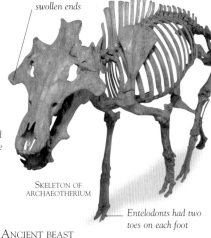

Large cheek bones with swollen ends

Eyes located on top of the head

SKELETON OF ARCHAEOTHERIUM

Enteledonts had two toes on each foot

Amphibious hippos have elongated snouts and lower jaws

SKULL OF HIPPOPOTAMUS LEMERLEI

ANCIENT BEAST
Enteledonts were pig- to bison-sized suiforms known from Europe, Asia, and North America. They had long legs and deep bodies. Their huge skulls have bony bumps on the cheeks and lower jaws, crushing teeth, and huge, curving, canine teeth. *Archaeotherium* was a successful pig-sized enteledont.

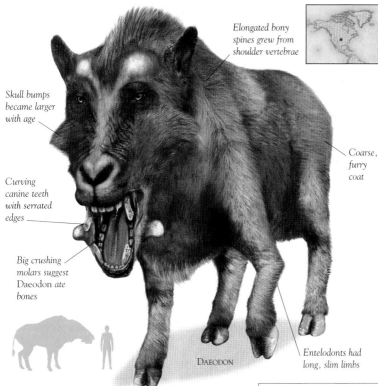

Elongated bony
spines grew from
shoulder vertebrae

Skull bumps
became larger
with age

Curving
canine teeth
with serrated
edges

Big crushing
molars suggest
Daeodon ate
bones

Coarse,
furry
coat

Entelodonts had
long, slim limbs

DAEODON

THE "KILLER BUFFALO" PIG
Daeodon is one of the biggest, best known, and
last of the entelodonts. Like others of its group,
it had tall shoulders, a deep body, and long legs.
The bumps on its skull and jaws were probably
used for fighting – some fossil specimens have
wounds that appear to have resulted from such
battles. The teeth and muscle scars of *Daeodon*
suggest that it was an omnivore, easily able to
break bones and eat animal carcasses.

DAEODON
- Group: Artiodactyla
- Family: Entelodontidae
- Time: Paleocene–Pliocene
  epochs (65–1.75 MYA)
- Size: 3 m (10 ft) long
- Diet: Vegetation, carrion,
  smaller animals
- Habitat: Grassland, open
  woodland

DEER AND KIN

SEVERAL NEW GROUPS of small, forest-dwelling herbivores first appeared 24–5 million years ago. The spread of grasslands allowed some of them to move out of the forest, becoming larger and more widespread. The most successful of these were the deer family.

Antlers may have spanned 3.7 m (12 ft) in large males

GIANT ANTLERS
The largest-ever antlers belonged to *Megaloceros*, that was still living 9,000 years ago.

PROTOCERAS

Dappled coat may have helped Cranioceras to hide in dense foliage

SYNTHETOCERAS

Horns look impressive from front view

SYNDYOCERAS

All weight was carried by the middle two toes

EARLY HORNS
Male protoceratids ("early horns") that lived 55 to just 2 million years ago, displayed some of the most spectacular horns ever evolved.

THREE-HORNED DEER RELATIVE

Cranioceras was a palaeomerycid – one of a group of deer-like hoofed mammals that lived from the Oligocene to the Pliocene (33.7–1.75 million years ago). Many, but not all, palaeomerycids had bony horns that grew backwards, forwards, or upwards from above their eyes. In the group that includes *Cranioceras*, a third horn grew upwards and back from the rear of the skull.

Long rear ossicones

Third horn at the back of the head

GIRAFFOKERYX

GIRAFFIDS

Giraffokeryx was a primitive giraffid (cud-chewing hoofed animal) that lived in Asia, Europe, and Africa, around 5 million years ago. It had two pairs of pointed, furry, horn-like structures called ossicones.

Limbs were not as long or slim as those of grassland-dwelling relatives

Horns may have been used for fighting rival males

CRANIOCERAS
- Group: Artiodactyla
- Family: Dromomerycidae
- Time: Oligocene–Pliocene epochs (33.7–1.75 MYA)
- Size: 1 m (3 ft) tall at shoulder
- Diet: Leaves
- Habitat: Subtropical woodland

CATTLE, SHEEP, AND GOATS

CATTLE AND THEIR RELATIVES are the most plentiful of the large, hoofed, grazing animals alive today. Wild and domestic cattle, sheep, goats, antelopes, and musk oxen are grouped together as bovoids. All these animals probably evolved more than 20 million years ago from small, hornless, deer-like ancestors.

Sharp, strong horns

Cattle do not shed their horns like deer

OVIS CANADENSIS SKULL

Jaws have high-crowned teeth, which evolved for chewing

EARLY SHEEP AND GOATS

Goats and sheep, including mountain sheep like *Ovis canadensis*, shared a common ancestor with other bovoids. This animal existed over 20 million years ago. Its descendants gave rise first to antelopes, then to sheep and goats, and finally to cattle.

ANCESTRAL OX

Bos primigenius, also known as aurochs, was the ancestor of most domesticated cattle. It roamed the forests of Europe, Asia, and Africa. The last wild aurochs was killed in Poland in 1627. Prehistoric cattle are now extinct, but wild cattle such as bison, buffaloes, and yak still survive.

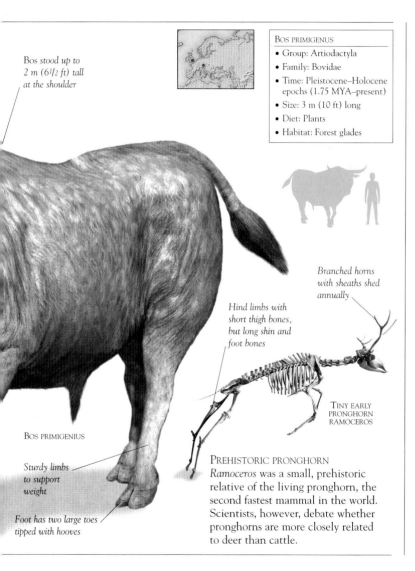

Bos stood up to
2 m (6¹/2 ft) tall
at the shoulder

BOS PRIMIGENUS
- Group: Artiodactyla
- Family: Bovidae
- Time: Pleistocene–Holocene epochs (1.75 MYA–present)
- Size: 3 m (10 ft) long
- Diet: Plants
- Habitat: Forest glades

Branched horns
with sheaths shed
annually

Hind limbs with
short thigh bones,
but long shin and
foot bones

TINY EARLY
PRONGHORN
RAMOCEROS

BOS PRIMIGENIUS

Sturdy limbs
to support
weight

Foot has two large toes
tipped with hooves

PREHISTORIC PRONGHORN
Ramoceros was a small, prehistoric
relative of the living pronghorn, the
second fastest mammal in the world.
Scientists, however, debate whether
pronghorns are more closely related
to deer than cattle.

EARLY WHALES

THE EARLIEST whales were very different from living whales – some had hind limbs and could probably move on land. Their skeletons show that they had started to swim with an up and down motion of the tail. By the end of the Eocene, fully aquatic whales like *Basilosaurus* had evolved.

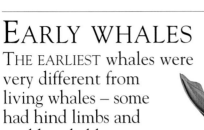

Long tail flukes provided the main swimming thrust

Tiny, three-toed hind limbs would have projected from sides

Long skull, with nostrils close to the tip of snout

AMBULOCETUS

FIRST WHALES
Ambulocetus, an early whale, looked something like a cross between a wolf and a seal and had a long crocodile-like head. The first known whale, *Pakicetus*, comes from the Middle Eocene of Pakistan, a site rich in whale fossils.

ECHOLOCATION AT WORK
Whales gain a mental picture of their surroundings by a unique method called echolocation. They project noises through a structure on the forehead called the melon. Echoes of the noises are then transmitted from external objects to the whale's ears via a fatty pad in its lower jaw.

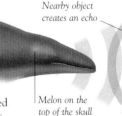

Nearby object creates an echo

Melon on the top of the skull

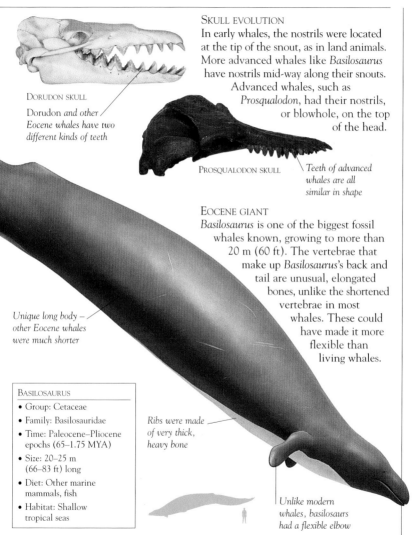

DORUDON SKULL

Dorudon and other Eocene whales have two different kinds of teeth

SKULL EVOLUTION

In early whales, the nostrils were located at the tip of the snout, as in land animals. More advanced whales like *Basilosaurus* have nostrils mid-way along their snouts. Advanced whales, such as *Prosqualodon*, had their nostrils, or blowhole, on the top of the head.

PROSQUALODON SKULL

Teeth of advanced whales are all similar in shape

EOCENE GIANT

Basilosaurus is one of the biggest fossil whales known, growing to more than 20 m (60 ft). The vertebrae that make up *Basilosaurus*'s back and tail are unusual, elongated bones, unlike the shortened vertebrae in most whales. These could have made it more flexible than living whales.

Unique long body – other Eocene whales were much shorter

BASILOSAURUS
- Group: Cetaceae
- Family: Basilosauridae
- Time: Paleocene–Pliocene epochs (65–1.75 MYA)
- Size: 20–25 m (66–83 ft) long
- Diet: Other marine mammals, fish
- Habitat: Shallow tropical seas

Ribs were made of very thick, heavy bone

Unlike modern whales, basilosaurs had a flexible elbow

INSECTIVORES AND BATS

MOLES, HEDGEHOGS, SHREWS, and other insectivores first appeared in the Eocene and share distinctive snout muscles and skull bones. Like pterosaurs and birds, bats evolved true flapping flight and have modified forelimbs, in which the fingers support skin membranes that reach the ankles.

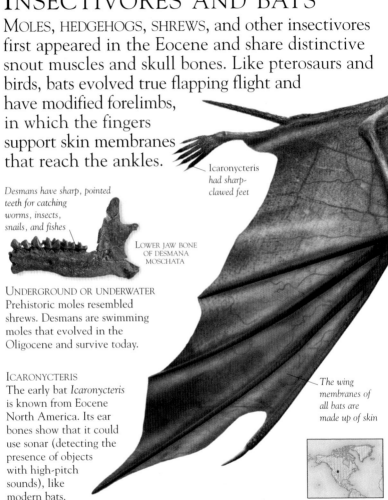

Icaronycteris had sharp-clawed feet

Desmans have sharp, pointed teeth for catching worms, insects, snails, and fishes

LOWER JAW BONE OF DESMANA MOSCHATA

UNDERGROUND OR UNDERWATER
Prehistoric moles resembled shrews. Desmans are swimming moles that evolved in the Oligocene and survive today.

ICARONYCTERIS
The early bat *Icaronycteris* is known from Eocene North America. Its ear bones show that it could use sonar (detecting the presence of objects with high-pitch sounds), like modern bats.

The wing membranes of all bats are made up of skin

Bats have large ears
for acute hearing

Icaronycteris
had more teeth
than modern
insect-eating bats

VARIED DIET

Before the
Eocene, the bat
group split into
two main groups:
the insect-eating
small bats and the fruit-eating
large bats. Fish-eating bats evolved in the
Miocene and survive today. Vampire bats
feed on the blood of animals, while
horseshoe bats feed on pollen.

LIVING
HORSESHOE BAT

Unlike modern bats,
early forms such as
Icaronycteris had
claws on their second
fingers as well as on
their thumbs

Long, thin fingers
support wing
membranes

MACROCRANION FOSSIL

SPINY AND HAIRY HEDGEHOGS

Hedgehogs have a rich fossil record and numerous
types are known. Some were tiny while others, like
Deinogalerix, were 1 m (3 ft) long. *Macrocranion* was
an Eocene hedgehog with a long tail and no spines.

ICARONYCTERIS

- Group: Chiroptera
- Family: Uncertain
- Time: Paleocene–Pliocene
  epochs (65–1.75 MYA)
- Size: 40 cm (1¼ ft) wingspan
- Diet: Flying insects
- Habitat: Forests, caves,
  riverbanks

MONKEYS

MONKEYS ARE PART OF a group of
primates called the anthropoidea.
There are two main types
of monkey: the Old World
monkeys from Asia and
Africa, which are called
the catarrhines, and the
New World monkeys, which
evolved in South America,
and are called the platyrrhines.

*The New World
includes North and
South America*

*The Old World includes
Africa, Europe, and Asia*

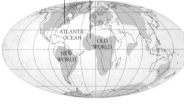

ATLANTIC
OCEAN

OLD
WORLD

NEW
WORLD

AMERICAN INVASION

In the past experts have
wondered about the origins of
the New World monkeys.
However, new fossils show that
platyrrhines have an African
ancestor that crossed over to
South America at a time when
the Atlantic Ocean was not as
wide as it is today.

THEROPITHECUS OSWALDI

Old World monkeys
invaded grassland habitats
to exploit new sources of
food. Various species of
Theropithecus, a seed-eating
grassland monkey, evolved in
the Pliocene and lived across
Europe, Africa, and Asia.
Theropithecus oswaldi was the
largest among them.

*Opposable thumb used
for delicate handling
of objects*

Unlike New World monkeys Old World monkeys cannot use the tail to grasp things

PARACOLOBUS SKELETON

MONKEY EMPIRE

Old World monkeys, many of them agile tree-climbers, replaced apes during the Miocene. One group, the colobids, migrated out of Africa and evolved in Asia into the leaf-eating langurs and proboscis monkeys. *Mesopithecus* and *Paracolobus* were early colobids.

UPPER SKULL OF TREMACEBUS

NEW WORLD FOREST-DWELLERS

New World monkeys did not take to grassland life and have remained animals of the forest. *Tremacebus* from the late Oligocene of Patagonia, was like the living owl monkey.

THEROPITHECUS

- Group: Anthropoidea
- Family: Cercopithecidae
- Time: Paleocene – Holocene epochs (65 MYA – present)
- Size: 1–2 m (3–6 ft) long
- Diet: Grasses, seeds, fruits, insects, and worms
- Habitat: Grasslands

PRIMITIVE PRIMATES

THE PRIMATES GROUP includes
primitive forms, such as lemurs,
and advanced forms such as
apes and humans. Primate-like
mammals appeared early in the
Palaeocene and evolved through
the Eocene. Lemurs, tree shrews,
and lorises are the only survivors
of the more primitive primates.

*The long skull was
unlike that of later
primates*

*Megaladapis had
a dog-like head*

Huge molar teeth

LEMURS LARGE AND SMALL
Prehistoric lemurs were
more diverse than they are
today. *Megaladapis* was as
large as the living orang-utan.
It died out only 600 years ago.

*Koala-like
build*

MEGALADAPIS
EDWARDIS
SKELETON

PLESIADAPIS
The plesiadapids were an early primate group.
Best-known among them was *Plesiadapis*, which
had grasping fingers and toes, and a long tail. It
probably looked like a cross between a lemur
and a squirrel and chewed on wood, using its
large incisors to feed on grubs and sap.

Long finger

LONG FINGER EVOLUTION

Aye-ayes are a group of primates from Madagascar that may be more primitive than lemurs. The aye-aye has a remarkable long third finger, which it uses to extract grubs out of wood.

LIVING AYE-AYE

Like squirrels, Plesiadapis could have used its tail for balance

Long fingers that could grip

NOTHARCTUS

One of North America's last native primates was *Notharctus*. It was the first North American fossil primate to be recognized in the 1870s.

PLESIADAPIS
• Group: Primates
• Family: Plesiadapidae
• Time: Paleocene–Pliocene epochs (65–1.75 MYA)
• Size: 80 cm (2½ ft) long
• Diet: Insects, fruits
• Habitat: Subtropical forests

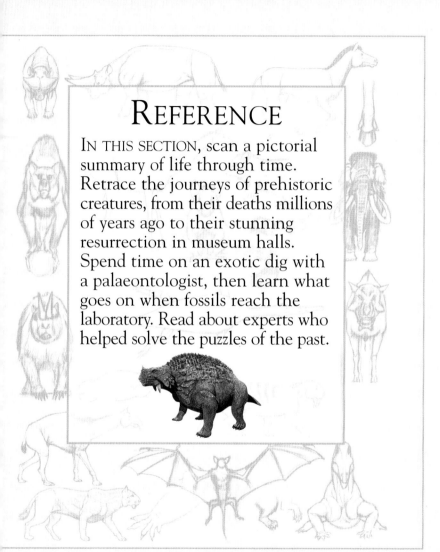

REFERENCE

IN THIS SECTION, scan a pictorial
summary of life through time.
Retrace the journeys of prehistoric
creatures, from their deaths millions
of years ago to their stunning
resurrection in museum halls.
Spend time on an exotic dig with
a palaeontologist, then learn what
goes on when fossils reach the
laboratory. Read about experts who
helped solve the puzzles of the past.

DINOSAUR DISCOVERERS

PEOPLE HAVE been finding dinosaur fossils for thousands of years. But it was not until 1841 that scientists first identified the dinosaur group. There have been many well-known dinosaur hunters, made famous because of the dinosaurs they have discovered.

SIR RICHARD OWEN (1804-92) was a famous British anatomist. He coined the name "dinosaur", which means "terrible lizard".

WHAT HE DISCOVERED
Owen worked at the Natural History Museum in London, where he studied fossils found in Europe. He not only realized that some fossils were reptiles, but were unknown types of giant reptiles. He concluded that they must have belonged to a group of extinct animals, and named this group dinosaurs.

DR. GIDEON MANTELL (1790-1852) was a medical doctor from Sussex in England. He was also a keen fossil hunter. He spent much of his early life collecting fossils in the hills near where he lived. But it was one fossil find that put his name in the history books.

WHAT HE DISCOVERED
In 1820, Gideon Mantell and his wife, Mary Ann, found some large teeth and bones in some gravel near a stone quarry. They belonged to an unknown, iguana-like animal. In 1825, he named it *Iguanodon*, although he did not realize at the time that it was a dinosaur.

DEAN WILLIAM BUCKLAND (1784-1856) was the first professor of geology at Oxford University in England. He was fascinated by fossils from an early age.

WHAT HE DISCOVERED
In 1824, a large jawbone with a giant tooth was found near Oxford. Buckland recognized it as belonging to a previously unknown giant reptile. This reptile was named *Megalosaurus*, which means "big lizard", and was the first dinosaur to be named. Like Mantell, Buckland did not know that *Megalosaurus* was a dinosaur.

JOHN BELL HATCHER (1861-1904) was a fossil collector for Othniel Marsh. Hatcher is recognized as one of the greatest collectors of dinosaurs in the history of American palaeontology.

WHAT HE DISCOVERED
In 1888, Hatcher found part of a huge horned skull beside the Judith River in Montana, USA. It turned out to be a *Triceratops* skull, and was the first fossil of this dinosaur to be discovered. It was also the first of the horned dinosaurs to be found, which introduced a new dinosaur variety to palaeontologists.

EDWARD DRINKER COPE (1840-97) was an American from Philadelphia. He was a scientific genius, and dinosaurs were just one area on which he was an expert.

WHAT HE DISCOVERED
Cope started his scientific career after the American Civil War. He travelled with fellow scientist Othniel Marsh on many of his early trips. They eventually became fierce rivals. Among his many finds, Cope discovered several primitive Triassic dinosaurs from New Mexico.

OTHNIEL MARSH (1831-99) was an American palaeontologist born in New York. Along with E.D. Cope, Marsh was one of the great pioneers of dinosaur fossil hunting in the United States.

WHAT HE DISCOVERED
Marsh discovered many dinosaur fossil sites in the United States. The most famous were Como Bluff in Wyoming and several sites in Colorado. His intense rivalry with Edward Drinker Cope was nicknamed the "Bone Wars".

EBERHARD FRAAS (1862-1915) was a German palaeontologist. He went on long expeditions to Africa in his search for dinosaur fossils.

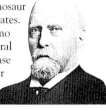

WHAT HE DISCOVERED
In 1907, Fraas was told of some dinosaur bones in a site in Tanzania, Africa. Fraas led an expedition to explore the site and, in 1909-12, the first fine specimens of *Kentrosaurus*, *Elaphrosaurus*, *Barosaurus*, and *Brachiosaurus* were discovered there. The *Brachiosaurus* skeleton Fraas discovered is now in a museum in Berlin, and is the largest mounted skeleton in the world.

GEORGE F. STERNBERG (1883-1969) was an American palaeontologist who started collecting fossils at the age of six. He continued to work on fossils for the next 66 years.

WHAT HE DISCOVERED
Sternberg made his most important dinosaur discovery in 1908: he was the first person to find an impression of dinosaur skin, which belonged to *Anatosaurus*. Sternberg made many other amazing discoveries, including the first fossil of *Edmontosaurus*.

EDWIN COLBERT (1905-2001) was an American palaeontologist and an expert in Triassic dinosaurs. He was the first to find dinosaur fossils in Antarctica. He has written several books about the history of dinosaurs.

WHAT HE DISCOVERED
Colbert found the first complete *Coelophysis* skeletons in New Mexico, USA in 1947. Some skeletons held the bones of young *Coelophysis* in the rib cage. This indicated that *Coelophysis* may have been a cannibal.

ANDREW CARNEGIE (1835-1919) was originally from Scotland. He emigrated with his family to the United States at the age of 11. He made his fortune in the steel industry in Pittsburgh.

WHAT HE DISCOVERED
Carnegie set up the Carnegie Museum in Pittsburgh. He sent fossil hunters on long expeditions to find dinosaurs for his museum. They discovered two complete skeletons of *Diplodocus*. A replica of one of the skeletons stands in the Natural History Museum in London.

ROY CHAPMAN ANDREWS (1884-1960) led the first American expedition to the Gobi Desert in Mongolia in 1922. Andrews went with a team from the American Museum of Natural History (AMNH).

WHAT HE DISCOVERED
Andrews and his team discovered many new dinosaurs in the Gobi Desert. Among them were *Velociraptor* and *Oviraptor*. But the most significant find was some fossilized eggs – the first dinosaur eggs to be discovered.

EARL DOUGLASS (1862-1931) was an American from Utah. He worked at the Carnegie Museum in Pittsburgh. Andrew Carnegie, who founded the museum, wanted to exhibit skeletons of the giant dinosaurs.

WHAT HE DISCOVERED
In 1909, Douglass was sent by Andrew Carnegie to hunt for fossils in Utah. Douglass' discoveries included *Diplodocus* and *Apatosaurus*. The site where these dinosaurs were found was turned into the Dinosaur National Park, which still exists today.

BARNUM BROWN (1873-1963), an American, was hired by the American Museum of Natural History in New York because of his skill in finding dinosaur skeletons.

WHAT HE DISCOVERED
Barnum Brown's expertise in fossil hunting earned him the nickname "Mr. Bones". He found the first *Tyrannosaurus* fossils, and named *Ankylosaurus* and *Corythosaurus*. The AMNH houses the world's greatest display of Cretaceous dinosaurs as a result of Brown's collecting.

JIM JENSEN (1910-1998) was a self-taught palaeontologist. He was the curator of the Vertebrate Palaeontology Research Laboratory at Brigham Young University in Utah, USA.

WHAT HE DISCOVERED
Jensen discovered some of the largest dinosaurs. In 1972, he found a partial skeleton of a sauropod, which he named *Supersaurus*. *Supersaurus*'s height is estimated to be 16.5 m (54 ft). In 1979 he found a partial skeleton of another new sauropod. He named it *Ultrasaurus*, and it is thought to be even bigger than *Supersaurus*.

BILL WALKER (b. 1928) is a British quarry-worker who is also an amateur fossil collector. In 1982, he made an important dinosaur discovery when exploring a muddy clay pit in Surrey, England.

WHAT HE DISCOVERED
Walker found a huge claw, which broke into pieces when he held it. He took it to the British Museum in London, which organized an excavation to recover more of the creature. It turned out to be a new dinosaur, which was named *Baryonyx walkeri*, in honour of Walker.

RECORDS AND MYTHS

AS SCIENCE HAS ADVANCED, so has our understanding of dinosaurs. With almost every new discovery, we learn more about these giant reptiles. The early dinosaur experts had beliefs about dinosaurs which we now know to be incorrect. The largest, smallest, fastest, most intelligent, or the least intelligent dinosaur also changes as our knowledge increases.

DINOSAUR RECORDS

• The smallest dinosaur ever found was called *Mussaurus*. It was only 20 cm (⅔ ft) long, but the single skeleton found may have been a hatchling. The smallest adult dinosaur we know of was *Compsognathus*, which was about the size of a chicken.

• *Dromiceiomimus* may have been the fastest of the dinosaurs, running at speeds of more than 70 km/h (43 mph).

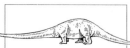

• The sauropod *Mamenchisaurus* had the longest neck of any dinosaur. The length of the neck was around 14 m (46 ft).

• *Giganotosaurus* is the biggest meat-eating dinosaur found so far. It is longer even than the previous record-holder *Tyrannosaurus*. It was about 15 m (50 ft) long and had teeth as long as 18 cm (½ ft).

• The longest dinosaur that we know of was the sauropod *Seismosaurus*. It was about 40 m (131 ft) long and weighed about 51 tonnes.

• The herbivore hadrosaurs had about 960 teeth – more than any other dinosaur. That was about 480 tightly packed teeth in each jaw.

• *Troodon* had the largest brain in proportion to its size of any dinosaur.

• *Stegosaurus* had the smallest brain in proportion to its size.

• *Diplodocus* had the longest tail of all the dinosaurs, at more than 13 m (43 ft) in length.

DINOSAUR MYTHS
- In 1822, Gideon Mantell made a reconstruction of *Iguanodon*, based on the few bones he had found. He had only one thumb spike, which he thought belonged on *Iguanodon's* nose. This was similar to the nose spike of an iguana lizard, after which *Iguanodon* was named. It was not until the discovery of several skeletons in the late 1800s that scientists realized this mistake.
- In China, the word "konglong" means both "dinosaur" and "terrible dragon". The Chinese have been collecting dinosaur fossils for 2,000 years. Since the third century CE, and perhaps before then, the Chinese believed that dinosaur bones were actually the remains of dragons.

- Many films and books portray dinosaurs and humans living at the same time. In fact, dinosaurs became extinct more than 60 million years before the first humans appeared.
- It was once thought that all dinosaurs dragged their tails on the ground, like modern lizards. Some sauropods probably did, but most dinosaurs had stiffened tails, which they held horizontally off the ground.
- *Hypsilophodon* was once thought to have lived in trees. It was believed that their long tails helped them to balance in the branches, and their sharp claws were used for clinging. We now know their fingers and toes were not designed for gripping branches.

- Many people think that dinosaurs were all huge and cumbersome. But the vast majority were only about as big as an elephant, and some were as small as a chicken. Most were very agile, too.

- *Brachiosaurus* was once believed to have lived in water because of the high position of its nostrils. But the great water pressures at depth would not have allowed it to breathe.
- *Iguanodon* was the first dinosaur to be reconstructed. At first it was shown as a slow, sprawling lizard, dragging a fat belly on the ground. We now know that *Iguanodon* was actually bipedal and much slimmer.

DIGGING UP DINOSAURS

BOTH AMATEUR and professional collectors are capable of making important dinosaur discoveries. Once discovered, fossil bones should be removed only by experienced professionals, because they are often fragile. The method of removing the bones generally follows a similar procedure.

1 SITE
Once a dinosaur site has been uncovered, the fossil bones have to be excavated (dug up). This delicate operation is carried out using special tools.

2 EXCAVATION
Hammers, chisels, and picks are used to remove most of the matrix (earth and stone material surrounding the bones).

3 EXPOSING THE BONES
Whenever possible, the matrix is removed close to the bone. This is done with great care so as to not damage the bone. The bones are exposed to reveal their full size so that no fragment will be left behind when removed.

5 JACKET ON OTHER SIDE
Once the exposed part of the bone has been coated, the rest of the bone, including some of the matrix, can be dug out of the ground. It is then covered with a plaster and burlap jacket.

6 REMOVAL FROM SITE
The jacketed bones are sometimes so big and heavy that a crane is needed to lift them onto a truck.

4 PLASTER JACKET
The exposed part of the bones are coated with glue and covered with a jacket of plaster and burlap (a type of canvas). This will protect the bones as they travel from the site to a museum, where they can be studied in more detail.

PREPARING DINOSAURS

SCIENTISTS TRY TO arrange dinosaur skeletons in different poses at museums. The team at the American Museum of Natural History in New York showed a *Barosaurus* skeleton reared up to defend its young against an *Allosaurus*. As the fossil bones of *Barosaurus* were very fragile and too heavy to display, a lightweight replica of the skeleton was made.

MAKING A MOULD
To make a mould of an original bone, liquid rubber is painted on to the surface of the bone and left to set. When the rubber has set, it is removed from the bone in sections. The rubber is then supported by cotton gauze and surrounded with a plastic jacket.

POURING THE MOULD
The inside of the rubber moulds is painted with liquid plastic and strengthened by sheets of fibreglass. The mould sections are then joined together to recreate the bone's shape, and are filled with foam plastic.

Filing away the rough edges of the joins

Pouring the foam plastic into the bone cast

FINISHING TOUCHES
The joins in the cast bones are smoothed by filing. The plastic bones are then painted to match the colours of the original bones.

MOVING THE CAST
The skeleton is completed in sections before being mounted in its final position. As the casts are lightweight, it is quite easy to move the skeleton in large sections, such as the entire ribcage.

PLACING THE NECK
Barosaurus is mounted on a fibreglass replica of a natural landscape. The height of the *Barosaurus* skeleton rearing up is over 15 m (50 ft). The neck has to be lifted by a crane and placed carefully into its final position.

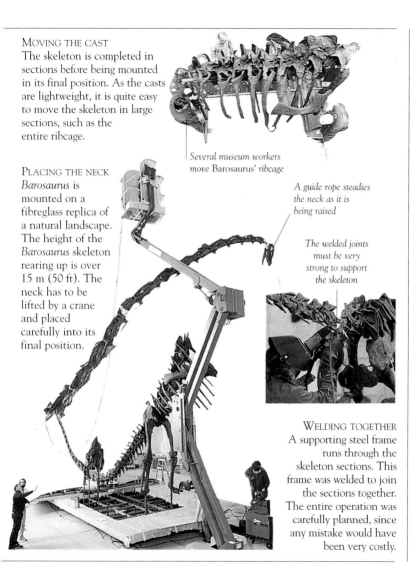

Several museum workers move Barosaurus' *ribcage*

A guide rope steadies the neck as it is being raised

The welded joints must be very strong to support the skeleton

WELDING TOGETHER
A supporting steel frame runs through the skeleton sections. This frame was welded to join the sections together. The entire operation was carefully planned, since any mistake would have been very costly.

STORING FOSSILS
The dinosaur fossils on display in museums are often just a fraction of the fossils the museum possesses. Sometimes thousands of fossils are housed in storerooms.

DINOSAURS ON DISPLAY

THE MOST popular feature of many natural history collections around the world is the dinosaurs on display. Scientists can use museums for storing fossils, and as laboratories for studying dinosaurs and other fossil remains.

LIFE-SIZE SKELETON
Full-size reconstructions of dinosaurs, such as this *Tyrannosaurus* skeleton, give us an impression of how they may have looked.

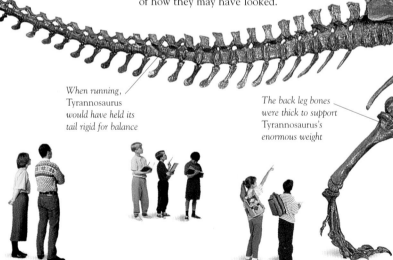

When running, Tyrannosaurus would have held its tail rigid for balance

The back leg bones were thick to support Tyrannosaurus's enormous weight

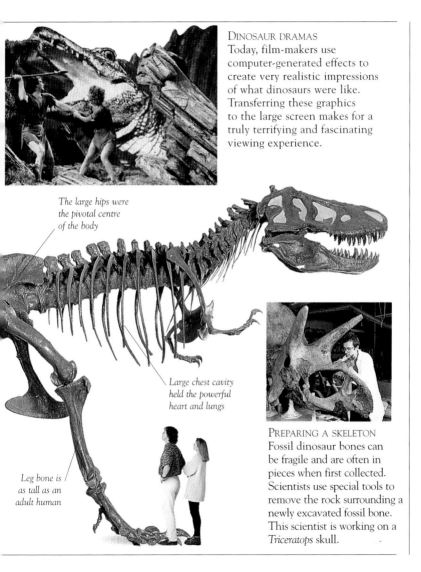

DINOSAUR DRAMAS
Today, film-makers use computer-generated effects to create very realistic impressions of what dinosaurs were like. Transferring these graphics to the large screen makes for a truly terrifying and fascinating viewing experience.

The large hips were the pivotal centre of the body

Large chest cavity held the powerful heart and lungs

Leg bone is as tall as an adult human

PREPARING A SKELETON
Fossil dinosaur bones can be fragile and are often in pieces when first collected. Scientists use special tools to remove the rock surrounding a newly excavated fossil bone. This scientist is working on a *Triceratops* skull.

389

GLOSSARY

Amniotes Tetrapod vertebrates whose young develop within a special protective membrane called the amnion.

Amphibians Cold-blooded tetrapod vertebrates whose young use gills to breathe during the early stages of life.

Amphibious Inhabiting both water and land.

Ancestor An animal or plant from which others have evolved.

Arthropods Invertebrates with segmented bodies and a hard (outer) exoskeleton.

Bipedal Walking on the hindlimbs rather than on all fours.

Brachiopods Marine invertebrates with a two-valved shell.

Carnivores/The Carnivora A group of sharp-toothed, meat-eating mammals, including cats, dogs, bears, and their relatives and ancestors.

Clade A group of organisms (such as dinosaurs) sharing anatomical features derived from the same ancestor.

Cladogram A branching diagram showing the relationships of different clades.

Class In the Linnaean system of classification, a group of organisms containing one or more related orders.

Cold-blooded Depending upon the heat from the sun for body warmth.

Crustaceans A large class of arthropods named after the hard carapace, or "crust", that encases their bodies.

Cycads Palm-like, seed-bearing plants that are topped by a crown of fern-like leaves.

Descendant A living thing that is descended from another.

Diapsids A major group of reptiles, typically with two holes in the skull behind each eye.

Dinosaurs A great group of advanced archosaurs with erect limbs.

Echinoderms Marine invertebrates with a hard, chalky skeleton and a five-rayed symmetry.

Ectotherm A cold-blooded animal.

Eon The longest unit of geological time.

Epoch An interval of geological time that is longer than an age and shorter than a period.

Era A unit of geological time that ranks below an eon.

Erosion The wearing away of the surface of the Earth by natural forces, such as wind and moving ice and water.

Evolution The process by which one species gives rise to another. It occurs when individual organisms pass on changes in genes controlling such things as body size, shape, and colour. Individuals with beneficial mutations pass these on, so their kind multiplies, and new species eventually arise.

Exoskeleton An external skeleton.

Extinction The dying-out of a plant or animal species.

Fossil The remains of a prehistoric organism preserved in Earth's crust.

Gastroliths Stones that are swallowed to help grind up food in the stomach.

Geological Concerning geology, the scientific study of the composition, structure, and origins of Earth's rocks.

Gondwana The vast southern super-continent that included South America, Africa, Antarctica, Australia, and India.

Herbivore Any animal that eats only plants.

Insectivore Any insect-eating organism, including some plants, but especially the group of mammals including moles, shrews, and hedgehogs.

Invertebrates Animals without backbones.

Juvenile A young or immature individual.

Lissamphibians Living amphibians and their closest ancestors.

Mammals Warm-blooded, hairy vertebrates that secrete milk and suckle their young.

Marsupials Mammals that give birth to small, undeveloped young that grow and mature in a skin pouch on the mother's stomach.

Metazoans Many-celled animals (this applies to the vast majority of animals).

Ornithischians – "bird hips". One of the two major dinosaur groups (see also *Saurischians*). The pelvis of ornithischians is similar to the pelvis of birds.

Ornithopods A group of large and small ornithischian dinosaurs: plant-eaters that walked on their long hindlimbs.

Palaeontology The scientific study of fossil plants and animals.

Parareptiles – "near/beside reptiles". Primitive reptiles, including the mesosaurs. Some people have used the

term to include all the reptiles known to anapsids.

Peccary A pig-like type of hoofed mammal native to the Americas.

Perissodactyls – "odd-toed". Hoofed mammals, including horses, rhinoceroses, tapirs, their ancestors, and various extinct forms.

Phalanges (singular: phalanx) Toe and finger bones.

Placoderms A class of jawed fish, protected by armour-like plates. They flourished in Devonian times.

Placodonts Aquatic reptiles of the Triassic. Some "rowed" with paddle-shaped limbs, others swam with webbed digits and by waggling their tails.

Predator Any animal or plant that preys on animals for food.

Primitive At an early stage of evolution or development.

Pubis One of the two lower hipbones of dinosaurs (the other one was the ischium). In some dinosaurs, the pubis anchored the muscle that pulled the hind legs forward.

Quadrupedal Walking on all fours.

Reptiles Lizards, snakes, turtles, crocodiles, dinosaurs, and their extinct and living relatives.

Reptiliomorphs Small, lizard-

like tetrapods that gave rise to true reptiles.

Sacrum Fused vertebrae that are joined to the pelvis.

Scutes Bony plates with a horny covering set in the skin of certain reptiles to protect them from the teeth and claws of enemies.

Species In the classification of living things, the level below a genus.

Synapsids The group of tetrapod vertebrates that includes the extinct pelycosaurs and therapsids, and the therapsids' descendants – mammals.

Temnospondyls – "cut vertebrae". A group of early tetrapods

Trilobites – "three lobed". Palaeozoic marine arthropods with external skeletons divided lengthwise into three lobes.

Ungulates Hoofed mammals.

Vertebrae (singular: vertebra) The linked bones forming the backbones of vertebrate animals.

Vertebrates Animals with an internal bony or cartilaginous skeleton including a skull and a backbone made up of vertebrae.

Warm-blooded Keeping body temperature at a constant level, often above or below that of the surroundings.

INDEX

ACKNOWLEDGMENTS

Picture Credits
The publisher would like to thank the following for their kind permission to reproduce their photographs:

Abbreviations key: t-top, b-bottom, r-right, l-left, c-centre, a-above, f-far

2 DK Images: Bedrock Studios tl, tc, tr, tr, cla, cr, cr, bl, bc, br, cbr, cfr; Gary Ombler clb. 3 DK Images: Bedrock Studios c. 4 DK Images: Colin Keates br. 5 DK Images: Bedrock Studios tcl; Jonathan Hately br; Lynton Gardiner/American Museum of Natural History cfr. 6 DK Images: Tim Ridley cra. 6-7 DK Images: Bedrock Studios. 7 DK Images: Bedrock Studios tr. 10 American Museum Of Natural History: clb. 10 Jean-Loup Charmet/Bridgeman Art Library: cfl. 10 Corbis: Juan Echeverria crb. 11 DK Images: Colin Keates/Natural History Museum, London br; Harry Taylor/Hunterian Museum, University of Glasgow car. 11 Museum National d'Histoire Naturelle: Paleontologie (Paris), D. Serrette bl. 14 Corbis: Roger Garwood & Trish Ainslie clb. 14 DK Images: Colin Keates cr. 15 J & B Sibbick: cr. 16 Corbis: Bettmann tr. 16 DK Images: Christopher and Sally Gable cb; Rob Reichenfeld br. 17 DK Images: Dave King cra, cbl; Harry Taylor/Hunterian Museum University of Glasgow cfl. 21 American Museum Of Natural History: C. Chesek clb. 21 DK Images: Bedrock Studios cla, cfl; Colin Keates crb, bl, br; Colin Keates/Natural History Museum, London clb; Jon Hughes cl; M.McGregor cla; Malcolm McGregor cra. 22 DK Images: Colin Keates clb. 22-23 Corbis: Roger Ressmeyer. 23 DK Images: Colin Keates cra, br. 24 S.Conway Morris: bl. 24 DK Images: Colin Keates cl. 24-25 S.Conway Morris. 25 S.Conway Morris: tc, cra. 26 DK Images: Colin Keates cfr; Colin Keates/Natural History Museum, London tc, bc; 26-27 DK Images: Colin Keates/Natural History Museum. 27 Hunterian Museum: Dr Neil D.L.Clark tl. 28 DK Images: Natural History Museum tc, cb, cbr. 28-29 DK Images: Colin Keates; Colin Keates/Natural History Museum, London. 29 DK Images: Colin Keates tr; Natural History Museum c. 30 DK Images: Harry Taylor/Royal Museum of Scotland, Edinburgh c; University Museum of Zoology, Cambridge tr; Natural History Museum bc. 30-31 American Museum Of Natural History: C.Chesek. 31 DK Images: Colin Keates cra; Harry Taylor/University Museum of Zoology, Cambridge, on loan from the Geological Museum, University of Copenhagen, Denmark tl. 32 American Museum Of Natural History: D.Finnin c. 32 DK Images: Harry Taylor/Royal Museum of Scotland, Edinburgh tr; Natural History Museum tr. 33 DK Images: Colin Keates cfr; Natural History Museum bc. 34 DK Images: Colin Keates c; Colin Keates/Natural History Museum, London tl, tcl; Natural History Museum bcr. 35 DK Images: Natural History Museum cr; Natural History Museum bl. 36-37 Exhibit Museum of Natural History, University of Michigan. 38 DK Images: Colin Keates/Natural History Museum, London br; Natural History Museum c. 38-39 DK Images: Colin Keates/Natural History Museum, London. 39 DK Images: Harry Taylor/Natural History Museum, London tr; Natural History Museum cl, cb. 40 DK Images: Colin Keates/Natural History Museum, London bc; Gary Ombler tc; Natural History Museum cr. 40-41 DK Images: Natural History Museum. 41 DK Images: Colin Keates/Natural History Museum, London tcr; Natural History Museum cr, bl. 42 DK Images: Natural History Museum cra, bc. 42-43 DK Images: Lynton Gardiner. 43 DK Images: Natural History Museum c, cr, bl. 44-45 N.H.P.A.: Daniel Heuclin. 46 DK Images: Hunterian Museum ca; Natural History Museum bcr. 46-47 DK Images: Natural History Museum. 47 DK Images: Natural History Museum bcl. 48 DK Images: Harry Taylor/Natural History Museum, London tcr; Natural History Museum c, br. 48-49 DK Images: Colin Keates/Natural History Museum, London. 49 DK Images: American Museum Of Natural History tr; Natural History Museum cr, bl. 50 DK Images: Natural History Museum tc, cfr. 51 DK Images: Colin Keates/Natural History Museum, London bl, tcl; Natural History Museum cr. 52 DK Images: Eric Robson cr; Natural History Museum tc; Peter Chadwick br. 52-53 DK Images: Colin Keates/Natural History Museum, London. 53 DK Images: Peter Visscher cfr. 54 DK Images: Dave King c; Neil Fletcher and Matthew Ward cfr. 55 DK Images: Andrew McRobb bl; Cyril Laubscher cfr; Dave King tl. 55 Topfoto.co.uk: Press Association tcr. 58 DK Images: Colin Keates bl; 58-59 DK Images: Harry Taylor/Royal Museum of Scotland, Edinburgh. 59 DK Images: Peter Bull tr, cra. 60-61 DK Images: Bedrock Studios. 62 DK Images: Peter Bull bl. 62-63 DK Images: Colin Keates. 63 DK Images: Colin Keates b; Colin Keates/Natural History Museum, London tr; Natural History Museum tr. 64 American Museum Of Natural History: cr; Jim Coxe cr. 64-65 DK Images: Bedrock Studios. 66 DK Images: Bedrock Studios ca; Harry Taylor/Hunterian Museum, University of Glasgow car; Harry Taylor/Royal Museum of Scotland, Edinburgh cra; Peter Bull cb, crb, bc, bcr. 67 DK Images: American Museum of Natural History tl; Geoff Dann/Barleylands Farm Museum and Animal Centre, Billericay tr; Peter Bull c, car, cfl; Peter Visscher cr. 68 DK Images: Natural History Museum bl. 68-69 DK Images: Harry Taylor/Natural History Museum, London. 69 DK Images: Peter Bull ca. 69 Oxford Scientific Films: Norbert Wu tr. 70 American Museum Of Natural History: D. Finnin br. 71 DK Images: Harry Taylor/Royal Museum of Scotland, Edinburgh bc. 72 American Museum Of Natural History: cl; D.Finnin br. 73 DK Images: Bedrock Studios t. 74 DK Images: Colin Keates/Natural History Museum, London cb. 74-75 DK Images: Harry Taylor/Natural History Museum, London. 75 American Museum Of Natural History: tr. 75 DK Images: Natural History Museum cr, cfr. 75 Hunterian Museum: br. 76 DK Images: American Museum of Natural History tr. 77 DK Images: Colin Keates/Natural History Museum, London tr. 78 American Museum Of Natural History: C. Chesek bl. 78 Oxford Scientific Films: Max Gibbs tr. 78-79 DK Images: Bedrock Studios. 79 American Museum Of Natural History: D.Finnin tr. 79 Bruce Coleman Ltd: Hans Reinhard br. 80 American Museum Of Natural History: C. Chesek clb. 80-81 DK Images: Harry Taylor/Hunterian Museum, University of Glasgow. 81 American Museum Of Natural History: Denis Finnin b. 81 DK Images: Natural History Museum tr. 82-83 DK Images: Luis Rey. 83 American Museum Of Natural History: crb 83 DK Images: American Museum of Natural History b. 86 DK Images: Peter Bull crb, bc, br, cbl; Peter Visscher cra, cr, cfr. 87 DK Images: American Museum of Natural History cla; Jerry Young/Zoo Museum tcl; Peter Bull cra, cl, c, cfl; Peter Visscher tr. 88 DK Images: M.McGregor/University Museum Oxford cb; 88-89 DK Images: University Museum, Oxford. 89 DK Images: Harry Taylor/University Museum of Zoology, Cambridge,on loan from the Geological Museum, University of Copenhagen, Denmark br; Zoo Museum tcl. 90 American Museum Of

Natural History: br; C. Chesek clb. 90-91 DK Images: American Museum of Natural History. 91 DK Images: M.McGregor bcl. 92-93 DK Images: Bedrock Studios. 94 DK Images: Tim Brown c. 94 The Natural History Museum, London: bl. 94-95 DK Images: Bedrock Studios. 96-97 American Museum Of Natural History. 96-97 DK Images: M.McGregor. 97 DK Images: John Downes/John Holmes - modelmaker/Natural History Museum, London br. 100 DK Images: Bedrock Studios cfl; Peter Bull bc, br. 101 DK Images: Bedrock Studios tc, tr; Peter Bull c, bl, cfr. 102 American Museum Of Natural History: bc. 102-103 DK Images: Bedrock Studios. 103 DK Images: Harry Taylor/University Museum of Zoology, Cambridge bc. 104 DK Images: Colin Keates/Natural History Museum, London clb. 104-105 DK Images: Bedrock Studios. 105 American Museum Of Natural History: tr. 106 DK Images: AMNH, Denis Finnin, Roderick Mickens and Megan Carlough clb; 106-107 DK Images: Bedrock Studios. 107 DK Images: M.McGregor cb. 107 Royal Tyrrell Museum of Paleontology: Alberta Community Development br. 112 DK Images: Robin Carter clb. 112-113 DK Images: Bedrock Studios. 113 Dr.David Martill: tr. 116 American Museum Of Natural History: Anderson bl. 117 DK Images: Natural History Museum clb. 117 The Natural History Museum, London: tr. 118 DK Images: Michael Benton/ Natural History Museum, University of Bristol b. 118-119 DK Images: Bedrock Studio. 119 DK Images: Natural History Museum cfr; Robin Carter cl. 120 DK Images: Peter Bull bc, br. 120-121 American Museum Of Natural History: J.Beckett/Denis Finnin. 121 American Museum Of Natural History: Bierwert & Bailey bl. 121 DK Images: Peter Bull tr. 122 Oxford Scientific Films: Maurice Tibbles br. 122-123 DK Images: Bedrock Studio. 123 American Museum Of Natural History: cb. 123 DK Images: Peter Visscher tcr. 124 DK Images: Harry Taylor/Natural History Museum, London cfl; Robin Carter cb. 124-125 DK Images: Gary Ombler. 125 American Museum Of Natural History: Denin Finin tc. 126 DK Images: Gary Ombler br. 126-127 DK Images: Gary Ombler. 126-127 N.H.P.A. 127 DK Images: Gary Ombler bc. 132 DK Images: John Woodcock bl. 132-133 DK Images: Andy Crawford. 133 DK Images: Colin Keates br. 134 DK Images: Dave King tr. 134-135 DK Images: Dave King. 136 DK Images: Andy Crawford/ Centaur Studios - modelmakers c; Ray Moller bcl. 139 DK Images: Andy Crawford/Royal Tyrell Museum, Canada br. 140 DK Images: Andy Crawford; Colin Keates tr. 141 DK Images: Dave King br. 142 DK Images: Dave King bl. 144 DK Images: Colin Keates/Natural History Museum, London tl; John Downs/Natural History Museum, London r. 145 DK Images: Royal Tyrrell Museum, Canada tr. 146 DK Images: Andy Crawford/Royal Tyrrell Museum, Canada tl; John Downes/Natural History Museum b. 147 DK Images: Colin Keates/Natural History Museum, London tl, cl, br. 148-149 DK Images: Colin Keates. 150 DK Images: Colin Keates/Natural History Museum, London tl, cl; Jerry Young br. 151 DK Images: Colin Keates/Natural History Museum, London tr; Lynton Gardiner clb, br. 152 DK Images: Colin Keates/Natural History Museum, London bl. 154 DK Images: Andy Crawford/Royal Tyrrell Museum, Canada bcl; Colin Keates/Natural History Museum, London bl; 154-155 DK Images: Jon Hughes. 155 DK Images: Gary Omble/Luis Rey - modelmaker bl. 156-157 DK Images: Andy Crawford/Royal Tyrrell Museum, Canada. 157 DK Images: Colin Keates/Courtesy of the Natural History Museum, London cfl; Dave King br; Lynton Gardiner/ Peabody Museum tr; Natural History Museum tl. 158 DK Images: Dave King l. 159 DK Images: Ann Winterbotham cl. 163 DK Images: Miguel Periera tcr. 163-164 DK Images: Harry Taylor/Royal Museum of Scotland, Edinburg 164 DK Images: Andy Crawford cr. 170 DK Images: Andy Crawford/Roby Braun - modelmaker bcr; Dave King cbl. 172 DK Images: Andy Crawford/ State Museum of Nature bcl. 173 DK Images: Andy Crawford/Royal Tyrrell Museum, Canada t. 174 DK Images: Jon Hughes b. 175 DK Images: Jon Hughes b. 176 Carnegie Museum Of Art, Pittsburgh: cra. 176 DK Images: Andy Crawford/State Museum of Nature cl; Gary Ombler b. 178 DK Images: Smithsonian Institute bl; Jon Hughes br. 179 DK Images: Jon Hughes b. 180 DK Images: Smithsonian Institute bl; Tim Ridley/Roby Braun - modelmaker tr. 181 DK Images: Andy Crawford/State Museum of Nature bl. 182 DK Images: Steve Gorton/Roby Braun - modelmaker c. 183 DK Images: Jon Hughes b. 184 DK Images: Bedrock Studios c; Colin Keates/Courtesy of the Natural History Museum, London bcr. 188 DK Images: Jonathan Hately 189. 190 DK Images: Andy Crawford/Royal Tyrell Museum, Canada t; Andy Crawford/Senkenberg Nature Museum bl. 191 DK Images: M.McGregor cfr. 192 DK Images: Jon Hughes r. 193 DK Images: American Museum of Natural History bl; Andy Crawford cfr. 201 DK Images: Colin Keates c. 206 DK Images: Andy Crawford/Royal Tyrrell Museum, Canada c; Royal Tyrrell Museum, Canada tr. 207 DK Images: Royal Tyrrell Museum, Canada r. 208 DK Images: Colin Keates cra. 208 Getty Images: b. 209 DK Images: Jon Hughes b. 210 DK Images: American Museum of Natural History cra; Bedrock Studios c. 211 DK Images: Luis Rey b. 212 American Museum Of Natural History: r. 213 DK Images: Gary Ombler br. 214 DK Images: Natural History Museum b; Jon Hughes. 215 DK Images: Natural History Museum tl. 216 DK Images: Dr. Eric Buffetaut, Laboratoire de Paleontologie des Vertebres, Paris, France tr; Jon Hughes bl. 217 DK Images: Jon Hughes bl; Senekenberg Nature Museum br. 218-219 DK Images: Andy Crawford/Tubingen Museum. 219 DK Images: Lynton Gardiner cra. 225 DK Images: Peabody Museum of Natural History, Yale University. crb. 227 DK Images: Yorkshire Museum c. 228-229 DK Images: Bedrock Studios. 229 DK Images: Andy Crawford t. 232 DK Images: Jon Hughes b. 233 DK Images: Jon Hughes r. 234 DK Images: Leicestershire Museum b; Natural History Museum cra. 235 DK Images: Yorkshire Museum cb. 236-237 DK Images: Jon Hughes. 237 Carnegie Museum Of Art, Pittsburgh: tl. 237 DK Images: Lynton Gardiner br. 238 DK Images: Colin Keates/Natural History Museum, London c. 239 DK Images: American Museum of Natural History cbr. 240 DK Images: Jon Hughes r. 240 The Institute Of Archaeology, Beijing: cfl. 241 DK Images: Giuliano Fornari cra; Jon Hughes b. 242 DK Images: Colin Keates/Natural History Museum, London bl; 242-243 Corbis: W.Wayne Lockwood, M.D. 242-243 DK Images: Jon Hughes. 246-247 DK Images: Bedrock Studios; Jon Hughes. 247 DK Images: Colin Keates/Natural History Museum, London tcr; Museo Arentino De Cirendas Naterales, Buenos Aires bl. 252 DK Images: Andy Crawford/Royal Tyrell Museum, Canada bl; 252-253 DK Images: Jon Hughes. 253 DK Images: Colin Keates/Natural History Museum, London tr; Smithsonian National Museum of Natural History cb. 254 DK Images: Bedrock Studios b; Colin Keates/Natural History Museum, London cra. 255 DK Images: Kim Sayer/National Museum of Natural History, Smithsonian Institution cb. 256 The Natural History Museum, London: bl. 256-257 DK Images: Andy Crawford/John Holmes - modelmaker. 258-259 Corbis: Charles Mauzy. 258-259 DK Images: Jon Hughes. 259 DK Images: Natural History Museum, London tr, cra. 260 DK Images: Jon Hughes b; Ligabue Study and Research Centre, Venice tr. 262 DK Images: Andy Crawford/Royal Tyrrell Museum, Canada c; Gary Kevin tr. 263 DK Images: Lynton Gardiner b. 264 DK Images: Lynton Gardiner br. 266 DK Images: Natural History Museum tr, cl. 266-267 DK Images: Dave King/Graham High and Centaur Studios – modelmakers. 268 DK Images: Lynton Gardiner/Natural History Museum, London cra. 272-273 DK Images: John Downes/Natural History Museum. 273 DK Images: Colin Keates/Natural History Museum, London tr; Cyril Laubscher cra. 274 DK Images: Lynton Gardiner/Natural History Museum, London b. 275 American Museum Of Natural History: cra. 278 DK Images: Natural

History Museum cfl; Tim Ridley br. 279 American Museum Of Natural History: tr. 279 DK Images: Jon Hughes br. 280-281 DK Images: Jon Hughes. 280-281 Getty Images: Stone. 281 DK Images: Colin Keates/Natural History Museum, London br; Natural History Museum, London tr. 282-283 DK Images: Andy Crawford/Royal Tyrrell Museum, Canada. 283 DK Images: Andy Crawford/Royal Tyrrell Museum, Canada br; Royal Tyrell Museum cal. 284 DK Images: Andy Crawford/Royal Tyrrell Museum, Canada tr; Royal Tyrell Museum, Canada bl. 285 DK Images: Jon Hughes b; Royal Tyrell Museum tr. 289 DK Images: Bedrock Studios c; Colin Keates/Courtesy of the Natural History Museum, London br. 290 DK Images: Andy Crawford/ Senekenberg Nature Museum cl. 291 DK Images: Colin Keates/Natural History Museum, London clb. 292 DK Images: Leicester Museum bl. 294 DK Images: Andy Crawford/Royal Tyrrell Museum, Canada cr, cfr. 294-295 Getty Images. 295 DK Images: Senekenberg Nature Museum tcl. 296 DK Images: Royal Tyrell Museum, Canada tr. 297 DK Images: Andy Crawford/Royal Tyrell Museum, Canada cl. 298 DK Images: Jon Hughes b. 299 DK Images: Bruce Cowell/Queensland Museum b. 301 DK Images: Witmer Lab tl. 302 DK Images: Jon Hughes bl. 303 DK Images: Andy Crawford/Royal Tyrell Museum, Canada cfr; Jon Hughes b. 304-305 DK Images: Andy Crawford/Royal Tyrrell Museum, Canada. 306 DK Images: Natural History Museum, London c. 307 Natural History Museum, London: tl. 308-309 DK Images: Luis Rey. 309 DK Images: Bedrock Studios cb. 310 DK Images: Simone End bl. 310-311 DK Images: Bedrock Studios. 311 American Museum Of Natural History: AMNH Photo Studio c; D. Finnin/C. Chesek tcl. 312 South African Museum Iziko Museums of Cape Town: Photographer Clive Booth, copyright Iziko: museum of Cape Town bcl. 312-313 DK Images: Bedrock Studios. 313 American Museum Of Natural History: AMNH Photo Studio tr. 313 DK Images: crb. 314 American Museum Of Natural History: AMNH Photo Studio clb. 314-315 DK Images: Harry Taylor/Edinburgh City Art Gallery, on loan from The Yorkshire Museum, York. 315 CM Studio: tl. 315 South African Museum Iziko Museums of Cape Town: Photographer Clive Booth, copyright Iziko: Museum Of Cape Town tr. 316 DK Images: Colin Keates/Natural History Museum, London cb. 316-317 DK Images: Bedrock Studios. 317 DK Images: Colin Keates/Courtesy of the Natural History Museum, London bcr; Simone End tc, tr. 318 Carnegie Museum of Natural History: Mark A.Klinger bl. 318-319 DK Images: Bedrock Studios. 319 DK Images: Neil Fletcher/Courtesy of the Booth Museum of Natural History, Brighton tr. 320 DK Images: Kenneth Lilly bl. 320 Dr RT Wells, Flinders University: F.Coffa cfl. 320-321 DK Images: Bedrock Studios. 321 DK Images: Natural History Museum tr. 322 American Museum Of Natural History: bl. 322 DK Images: Malcolm McGregor cfl. 322-323 DK Images: Bedrock Studios. 323 DK Images: Colin Keates/Natural History Museum, London bcl; Malcolm McGregor cra. 324-325 DK Images: Harry Taylor/Natural History Museum, London. 325 American Museum Of Natural History: cfr. 325 DK Images: Harry Taylor/Courtesy of the Natural History Museum, London br. 326-327 DK Images: Denis Finnin, Roderick Mickens and Megan Carlough, American Museum of Natural History; Gary Cross. 327 DK Images: Peter Visscher tr, ca. 328 American Museum Of Natural History: cbl. 328-329 DK Images: Bedrock Studios. 329 DK Images: Natural History Museum tr. 330 American Museum Of Natural History: cfl. 330 DK Images: Colin Keates/Natural History Museum, London bcl. 330-331 DK Images: Bedrock Studios. 331 DK Images: Bedrock Studios tcr; Dave King tr. 332-333 Corbis: Tom Bean. 332-333 DK Images: Bedrock Studios. 333 DK Images: Bedrock Studios cl, cr. 334 American Museum Of Natural History: clb. 334-335 DK Images: Bedrock Studios. 335 American Museum Of Natural History: tl, tr. 336-337 Corbis: Marc Garanger. 336-337 DK Images: Bedrock Studios bl. 338 DK Images: Harry Taylor/Natural History Museum, London clb. 338-339 DK Images: Bedrock Studios. 339 DK Images: Peter Bull cra, crb, cfr. 340 DK Images: Robin Carter bl. 340-341 DK Images: Bedrock Studios. 341 DK Images: Robin Carter crb, tcr. 342 DK Images: AMNH clb; 342-343 DK Images: Bedrock Studios. 343 DK Images: AMNH cfr; Harry Taylor/ Natural History Museum, London tr. 344-345 DK Images: Bedrock Studios. 345 American Museum Of Natural History: br. 345 DK Images: Harry Taylor/Natural History Museum, London tr. 346-347 DK Images: Bedrock Studios. 347 DK Images: Robin Carter tr. 348 American Museum Of Natural History: cra. 348-349 DK Images: Bedrock Studios. 349 American Museum Of Natural History: tr. 349 DK Images: Peter Bull br. 350 DK Images: Peter Bull clb. 350-351 DK Images: Bedrock Studios. 351 American Museum Of Natural History: A.E.Anderson cbr. 352-353 Corbis: Carl & Ann Purcell. 352-353 DK Images: Bedrock Studios. 354 DK Images: Dave King/Natural History Museum, London cra. 354-355 DK Images: Natural History Museum, London. 355 DK Images: Dave King/Natural History Museum, London c, tcl; Harry Taylor/Natural History Museum, London cra. 356-357 Corbis: Wolfgang Kaehler. 356-357 DK Images: Bedrock Studios. 358 American Museum Of Natural History: cl. 358-359 DK Images: Bedrock Studios. 359 American Museum Of Natural History: crb. 360-361 DK Images: Andrew Nelmerm/Royal British Columbia Museum, Victoria, Canada. 361 American Museum Of Natural History: cfr. 361 DK Images: Dave King/National Museum of Wales tc. 362 American Museum Of Natural History: cr, bl. 363 DK Images: Bedrock Studios ca. 364 American Museum Of Natural History: tr, cla, clb, cfl. 364-365 DK Images: Bedrock Studios. 365 DK Images: M.McGregor tr. 366 American Museum Of Natural History: clb. 366-367 DK Images: Bedrock Studios. 367 American Museum Of Natural History: crb. 368 DK Images: M.McGregor cl. 368-369 DK Images: Harry Taylor/Natural History Museum, London. 369 DK Images: Harry Taylor/Natural History Museum, London ca. 370 DK Images: Natural History Museum cfl. 370-371 DK Images: Bedrock Studios. 371 DK Images: Frank Greenaway tr; Harry Taylor/Natural History Museum, London clb. 372-373 DK Images: Bedrock Studios. 373 American Museum Of Natural History: Denis Finnin, Roderick Mickens and Magan Carlough tr; Denis Finnin, Roderick Mickens and Megan Carlough cb. 374 American Museum Of Natural History: bl. 374-375 DK Images: Bedrock Studios. 375 American Museum Of Natural History: bl. 375 Bruce Coleman Ltd: Sarah Cook tcr. 376-377 DK Images: Luis Rey. 377 DK Images: Bedrock Studios cb. 378 DK Images: Colin Keates/Natural History Museum, London crb. 379 DK Images: Dave King/ Graham High and Centaur Studios - modelmakers tr. 380 DK Images: Andy Crawford/State Museum of Nature cfr. 381 DK Images: Andy Crawford/State Museum of Nature crb; Colin Keates tr. 386 DK Images: Lynton Gardiner crb, bcl. 387 DK Images: Lynton Gardiner/The American Museum of Natural History tr, cfr, l. 388 DK Images: Lynton Gardiner tl; 388-389 DK Images: Senekenberg Nature Museum.

All other images © Dorling Kindersley.
For further information see: www.dkimages.com